MISSIONAL

MAP-MAKING

SKILLS FOR LEADING IN TIMES OF TRANSITION

Alan J. Roxburgh

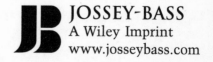
JOSSEY-BASS
A Wiley Imprint
www.josseybass.com

Published by Jossey-Bass
A Wiley Imprint
989 Market Street, San Francisco, CA 94103-1741—www.josseybass.com

Jossey-Bass books and products are available through most bookstores. To contact Jossey-Bass directly call our Customer Care Department within the U.S. at 800-956-7739, outside the U.S. at 317-572-3986, or fax 317-572-4002.

Jossey-Bass also publishes its books in a variety of electronic formats. Some content that appears in print may not be available in electronic books.

Library of Congress Cataloging-in-Publication Data
Roxburgh, Alan J.
    Missional map-making : skills for leading in times of transition / Alan J. Roxburgh.—1st ed.
      p. cm. — (Leadership network)
    Includes bibliographical references and index.
    ISBN 978-0-470-48672-6 (cloth)
      1. Change—Religious aspects—Christianity. 2. Mission of the church. I. Title.
BV4509.5.R69 2010
253—dc22

                                        2009041094

Printed in the United States of America
FIRST EDITION
HB Printing   10 9 8 7 6 5 4 3 2 1

LEADERSHIP NETWORK TITLES

The Blogging Church: Sharing the Story of Your Church Through Blogs, Brian Bailey and Terry Storch

Church Turned Inside Out: A Guide for Designers, Refiners, and Re-Aligners, Linda Bergquist and Allan Karr

Leading from the Second Chair: Serving Your Church, Fulfilling Your Role, and Realizing Your Dreams, Mike Bonem and Roger Patterson

The Way of Jesus: A Journey of Freedom for Pilgrims and Wanderers, Jonathan S. Campbell with Jennifer Campbell

Leading the Team-Based Church: How Pastors and Church Staffs Can Grow Together into a Powerful Fellowship of Leaders, George Cladis

Organic Church: Growing Faith Where Life Happens, Neil Cole

Church 3.0: Upgrades for the Future of the Church, Neil Cole

Off-Road Disciplines: Spiritual Adventures of Missional Leaders, Earl Creps

Reverse Mentoring: How Young Leaders Can Transform the Church and Why We Should Let Them, Earl Creps

Building a Healthy Multi-Ethnic Church: Mandate, Commitments, and Practices of a Diverse Congregation, Mark DeYmaz

Leading Congregational Change Workbook, James H. Furr, Mike Bonem, and Jim Herrington

The Tangible Kingdom: Creating Incarnational Community, Hugh Halter and Matt Smay

Leading Congregational Change: A Practical Guide for the Transformational Journey, Jim Herrington, Mike Bonem, and James H. Furr

The Leader's Journey: Accepting the Call to Personal and Congregational Transformation, Jim Herrington, Robert Creech, and Trisha Taylor

Whole Church: Leading from Fragmentation to Engagement, Mel Lawrenz

Culture Shift: Transforming Your Church from the Inside Out, Robert Lewis and Wayne Cordeiro, with Warren Bird

Church Unique: How Missional Leaders Cast Vision, Capture Culture, and Create Movement, Will Mancini

A New Kind of Christian: A Tale of Two Friends on a Spiritual Journey, Brian D. McLaren

The Story We Find Ourselves In: Further Adventures of a New Kind of Christian, Brian D. McLaren

Missional Renaissance: Changing the Scorecard for the Church, Reggie McNeal

Practicing Greatness: 7 Disciplines of Extraordinary Spiritual Leaders, Reggie McNeal

The Present Future: Six Tough Questions for the Church, Reggie McNeal

A Work of Heart: Understanding How God Shapes Spiritual Leaders, Reggie McNeal

The Millennium Matrix: Reclaiming the Past, Reframing the Future of the Church, M. Rex Miller

Shaped by God's Heart: The Passion and Practices of Missional Churches, Milfred Minatrea

The Missional Leader: Equipping Your Church to Reach a Changing World, Alan J. Roxburgh and Fred Romanuk

Missional Map-Making: Skills for Leading in Times of Transition, Alan J. Roxburgh

Relational Intelligence: How Leaders Can Expand Their Influence Through a New Way of Being Smart, Steve Saccone

Viral Churches: Helping Church Planters Become Movement Makers, Ed Stetzer and Warren Bird

The Externally Focused Quest: Becoming the Best Church for the Community, Eric Swanson and Rick Rusaw

The Ascent of a Leader: How Ordinary Relationships Develop Extraordinary Character and Influence, Bill Thrall, Bruce McNicol, and Ken McElrath

Beyond Megachurch Myths: What We Can Learn from America's Largest Churches, Scott Thumma and Dave Travis

The Elephant in the Boardroom: Speaking the Unspoken About Pastoral Transitions, Carolyn Weese and J. Russell Crabtree

CONTENTS

About Leadership Network　*vii*

Introduction: An Uncertain Journey　*ix*

PART ONE　WHEN MAPS NO LONGER WORK　1

CHAPTER ONE　Maps Shaping Our Imaginations in Modernity　3

CHAPTER TWO　Leading in an In-Between Time　19

CHAPTER THREE　When Common Sense Is No Longer Common　41

CHAPTER FOUR　From Playing Pool to Herding Cats　59

CHAPTER FIVE　Why Strategic Planning Doesn't Work in This New Space and Doesn't Fit God's Purposes　73

CHAPTER SIX　Eight Currents of Change and the Challenge of Making New Maps　87

CHAPTER SEVEN　Lessons from the Formation of the Internet for Leading in This New Space　111

PART TWO　THE MAP-MAKING PROCESS　125

CHAPTER EIGHT　Cultivating a Core Identity in a Changed Environment　127

CHAPTER NINE　Cultivating Parallel Cultures of the Kingdom　143

CHAPTER TEN　Map-Making Partnerships Between a Local Church and Neighborhoods and Communities　163

Notes　*189*

The Author　*196*

Index　*197*

To my parents Alex Roxburgh (1911–1994) and Jessie (Crosby) Roxburgh (1912–2000).
I stand on your shoulders and all those from whom you came—you shaped my life like Blake's finely woven fabric of joy and woe. The demons were real but so was the courage, risk, and crazy humor. I am thankful!

ABOUT LEADERSHIP NETWORK

Since 1984, Leadership Network has fostered church innovation and growth by diligently pursuing its far-reaching mission statement: to identify, connect, and help high-capacity Christian leaders multiply their impact.

Although Leadership Network's techniques adapt and change as the church faces new opportunities and challenges, the organization's work follows a consistent and proven pattern: Leadership Network brings together entrepreneurial leaders who are focused on similar ministry initiatives. The ensuing collaboration—often across denominational lines—creates a strong base from which individual leaders can better analyze and refine their own strategies. Peer-to-peer interaction, dialogue, and sharing inevitably accelerate participants' innovation and ideas. Leadership Network further enhances this process through developing and distributing highly targeted ministry tools and resources, including audio and video programs, special reports, e-publications, and online downloads.

With Leadership Network's assistance, today's Christian leaders are energized, equipped, inspired, and better able to multiply their own dynamic Kingdom-building initiatives.

Launched in 1996 in conjunction with Jossey-Bass (a Wiley imprint), Leadership Network Publications present thoroughly researched and innovative concepts from leading thinkers, practitioners, and pioneering churches. The series collectively draws from a range of disciplines, with individual titles offering perspective on one or more of five primary areas:

1. Enabling effective leadership
2. Encouraging life-changing service
3. Building authentic community
4. Creating Kingdom-centered impact
5. Engaging cultural and demographic realities

For additional information on the mission or activities of Leadership Network, please contact:

Leadership Network
(800) 765-5323
client.care@leadnet.org

INTRODUCTION: AN UNCERTAIN JOURNEY

The summer of 2007 was a confusing time for many in England. On a terrible day in mid-August, Gary Newlove stepped out of his home in Warrington, Cheshire, where youth gangs were harassing people and damaging property in the working-class neighborhood. Within minutes, Newlove lay in a coma; taken to a hospital, the young father died the next day. In London, a young man asked a gang to stop throwing junk at his sister's car. Minutes later, he lay dead on the street. In the Midlands, a young boy was knifed to death because he refused to join a gang. In Liverpool, a young boy, Rhys Jones, was shot and killed while returning home from soccer practice in an upscale part of Liverpool called Toxteth.

I was in the UK during the last two weeks of that August, observing how newspaper columnists, television reporters, and the public tried to make sense of these events. I heard all kinds of recommendations for fixing the problem. Some people demanded more police on the streets and in the communities; others called for raising the drinking age yet again. More money for urban redevelopment, more education, more programs for young people, more social workers, better health care, more parental responsibility—on and on went the list as everyone tried to understand the causes behind these awful events. On the day after Gary Newlove's death, I was watching *The Richard and Judy Show*, a typical morning talk show with the usual expert analysis and proposals. The assumption seemed to be that more money, another set of law-and-order legislation, or another distinguished committee studying the problem would resolve everything. This "expert analysis" rang very hollow. But then a panel member, in his early fifties, asked:

> What has happened to us? How did we get here? When I was growing up as a young boy, we did lots of things that were wrong, but nothing like this. Back then [he's talking about the late fifties and early sixties], we all lived inside a way of knowing what was right and wrong. We all knew the story of Jesus, and there was a Christian background. It didn't mean we went to church, but we all knew the same story. These kids today have nothing like that anymore! There's no common story shaping us. How did that happen?

Silence!

In that moment was the recognition that we're all living in a confusing, sometimes terrible time when it feels as though the maps that once shaped our understanding and practices of how we lived together no longer seem to be reliable. Many of us feel like we're suddenly in unfamiliar land where our internal maps of how things should be no longer match what's going on around us. Just recently, I was sitting inside a very large church in downtown Toronto, built almost a hundred years ago on the model and scale of an English cathedral. It could be mistaken for a cathedral given its size and design. The minister responsible for this church, a man respected across the country and known as a successful leader in his denomination, sat across from me in his office. He told me that inside this building where people expected church services to take place, he knew what to do. Then he waved his arms toward the cityscape of high-rise condos and office towers that filled his large windows and said, "Honestly, when it comes to the world outside there, we don't know what to do anymore! We're making it up as we go because our maps of how church operates in the world don't make sense anymore."

We don't need to be pastors to relate to this experience. In the wake of the economic meltdown, we read daily reports from the automotive and finance sectors of the economy where CEOs and once-trusted experts keep saying we are in uncharted territory and no one knows what kinds of maps we need for traveling in this unfamiliar world. Similarly, in its many forms and traditions across North America, the church finds itself suddenly facing a changed world where many of its established maps no longer make sense.

We are all sharing this struggle to make sense of the world that is emerging around us. Recently, I listened to a good friend struggle to communicate the maps that she thought should be guiding the decisions of her soon-to-be-married thirty-year-old daughter. My friend, in her late fifties, was raised in a Mennonite community and has lived out her Christian convictions all her life. Her daughter is a wonderful and talented individual with all the strengths and gifts of her mom and dad. But the Christian life of her parents has not "stuck." She's marrying an energetic, creative, entrepreneurial young man who isn't interested in God-talk at the wedding ceremony. She tells her mom that she and her husband-to-be are going to be OK because both have parents whose marriages have endured the test of time. Their assumption—that the modeling will stick—isn't a bad one, but it misses some crucial connections. The source of my friend's marriage, the "sticking together" over so many years, is something deeper than mere modeling. It is the Christian story. My friend was trying to communicate to her daughter that the inner story one lives matters because it shapes commitments. It gives us a map for what life is about and how to live it in a particular place and time. My friend's fear is that her daughter is marrying without a story and consequently has no internal maps within (except the implicit and now borrowed examples of her parents) by which to navigate the demands and challenges that make a marriage rich and full. Many of us identify with these stories, but what do we mean by the idea of maps, and why is this so important in understanding the challenges confronting the church and its leadership?

The idea of a map in this book is our internal understanding about how things ought to work and the habits and practices we develop over time based on these inner understandings. A GPS is a helpful illustration. When you purchase a GPS, it comes preloaded with a set of maps. One of the first things you do is download updates from your computer into the GPS. Similarly, we are all born into and shaped by a world in which we develop internal maps about how the world works and how we are to function within it. We don't think about these maps or decide if we want to use them; they become so much a part of our ingrained way of relating to the world in families, churches, and societies that we assume that our internal understanding and practices of how the world works is precisely how the world works. When I get into a car in a new city, for example, I switch on the GPS and simply take it for granted that its internal maps will get me to exactly where I want to go. Because the GPS rarely fails me, I develop a basic trust for its maps and pay little attention to the road signs or geography I am passing through. The same is true of the internal maps of the word into which we were born and formed. We may need to make some adjustments to them as we go along, but these maps have generally worked well, and so we haven't needed to question them.

Recently, I was in Lexington, Kentucky, heading for the airport in Louisville. I switched on the GPS, typed in the airport address, and headed down the road at a relaxed pace to catch my flight to Chicago. As I entered Louisville, I couldn't see signs to the airport, but hey, no problem, my GPS knew the way, so I kept following the nice lady's voice telling me which turns to make. After a few minutes, however, I became concerned because the road I was on just didn't look like it was heading for a large airport. In fact, my GPS was leading me away from the airport. What ensued was a period of mounting confusion, frustration, and anxiety: I didn't know were I was and was afraid of missing the last flight out that day. The GPS's internal maps failed, and in that moment, I was disoriented and confused. In this book, I propose that many of the maps we have internalized about what it means to be the church and how to shape churches in our culture no longer connect with or match the dramatically changing environments in which are living. Because of this, we find ourselves in a situation where have to become map-makers in a new world.

Stories illustrating this reality are everywhere. A bishop sits with friends at a conference telling them how her clergy are anxious about what they are facing in their parishes and struggling to make sense of the new demands people are placing on them. She states forthrightly that most of her clergy were not trained to deal with the world now shaping the communities in which their parishes are located. The parish system assumed that people living inside a given geographical area were, in some sense, a part of that church. The role of clergy was to provide religious services to those in the community who came to the church. Nowadays, people drive out of their neighborhood to a church of their choosing, rather than attending the one in which they might have been baptized as a baby. Most, however, simply stay home on Sunday morning. This bishop's clergy have little sense of what to do when people no longer come to their church because all their training, and the maps inside their imaginations that describe what ministry is about, involves serving people when they come. The conclusion among a growing number of bishops and clergy, therefore, is that the parish system is dead—a huge jump coming from leaders following a map that for hundreds of years has presumed that the parish is the appropriate destination for which leaders were trained. This map, the bishop was saying, no longer makes sense of the contexts in which we live.

In a thriving city in the southeastern part of the United States, I sat for lunch with the pastoral staff of a large and growing evangelical church known throughout the area for its programs. The senior staff acknowledged that they had created a highly attractional church based on a needs-centered ministry, and it was working. They also acknowledged that the back door to the church was as busy as the front, with people leaving to go to other program-driven, attractional churches. What is interesting is that these leaders had concluded that if they believed in their "kingdom of God" vision statement, then a program-driven attractional church missed the point because it shaped a church around meeting people's needs rather than forming them in self-sacrificing disciples of the kingdom. But to use a phrase attributed to Martin Luther, they were like "cows staring at a new gate." It's not a complimentary image, but Luther wasn't known for tact. It describes leaders who know they need a different way of being the church but have few ways of knowing what it would look like.

I was meeting with the executive minister of a denomination on the West Coast as he addressed several hundred of his pastors at a retreat. He was telling them honestly that after being an effective pastor of several churches over two decades, he didn't know how to address the changing cultural context in which he knew these leaders were now working. His reasons for being flummoxed weren't difficult to name. The ways this executive learned to practice church no longer connected with the changed contexts in which his denomination's churches now found themselves. It was as if he had grown up using a trustworthy map of a country that no longer reflected the country's present-day terrain. In interviewing the lay leaders of several churches in the Midwest, one young executive of a large corporation put it this way: "We've tried everything possible to make our church work in this community, but nothing we throw against our decline and loss sticks. We don't know what to do anymore; our maps for how church should work no longer match the world we've tumbled into." These experienced leaders are struggling with contexts where the maps that once served them brilliantly no longer help them make sense of the situations they now encounter.

CHURCH WHEN THE MAPS HAVE CHANGED

The executive I've just mentioned had found a succinct way of stating the issue: "We keep trying lots of things, but nothing seems to stick." A church decides to reach its community by planning a huge street sale. Lots of people come to the Saturday morning event, but none of it translates into new church attenders. The staff of a church is hired to "fill the pulpit" because its fame in the denomination for years has been based on its reputation as a preaching center. But now people don't come to church as they once did; giving and attendance are down, and the board doesn't know what to do. A social scientist on the staff of a large ethnically-based denomination shows a gathering of its key leaders pie charts on PowerPoint slides that reveal that birth rates of denomination members fell below the replacement rates six years ago. The writing is on the wall, he tells them: the denomination grew not because of evangelism but thanks to immigration and the ability of if members to produce babies. Neither of these options is now open, and the denomination is dying. The members of a presbytery (a regional grouping of congregations) gather for a conversation about the growing number of its churches that can no longer afford full-time pastors. They are disoriented, not knowing what to do in a world where pastors might not be an option. A young leader, named as one of the top twenty-five young leaders under the age of thirty-five, sits with a group of other leaders and confesses that he finds himself in a world were he no longer has the answers or knows what to do next. The executive of a judicatory calls up to say that the strategic plans of the last eight years have done nothing to change the downward direction of the churches: the money is running out, and he doesn't know what to do next.

In a recent phone conversation with a ministry student in the Pacific Northwest, I heard a familiar question, one that told me he and I lived in different worlds when it came to our understanding of leadership. He spoke of the business world and its use of *metrics* to assess goals, outcomes, and performance around vision. Acknowledging that the metrics of business may not be the same as those of the church, he wanted to know what kinds of metrics I was using to measure success in missional churches and what measures I had for determining when one has achieved a missional perspective. I paused before responding. What struck me was the confident certainty of the questioner that the objectivity of numbers would provide a metric that would normatively quantify and give assurance of missional life. I reflected on how best to respond, given that the person on the other end of the phone had a vastly different imagination than I did; we were trying to communicate based on differing internal maps. I too had once been certain about the use of metrics to measure and thus shape goals. That way of reading the world had been, for me, upended; I no longer had confidence in this map for making church work. How would I find a way of talking about the differing maps that were predetermining not just how we saw the world outside ourselves but also how we heard one another?

So many of the books on missional life these days are written without much reflection on the maps that shape our understanding of the world. And in my experience, when I challenge people's unspoken assumptions—such as the notion that if we work to make our churches better, people will come as they once did—they often look at me as though I am just some grizzled old person who wants to be negative. The other possibility is that we have crossed a threshold and entered a new space where the maps we've created profoundly misdirect us. This was certainly the case when Alan Greenspan talked about his response to the financial meltdown last year. He told the U.S. Congress that he never saw it coming. As we will discuss later, Greenspan's point was that his inner maps about how the financial world worked never prepared him to see the radical changes that were coming. The urbanologist Richard Florida has called this crossing of a threshold the end of a chapter in American history and, "indeed, the end of a whole way of life."[1] The president of a seminary stood before a meeting of his peers and said, "I have just been elected president of a seminary that trains men and women for a world that no longer exists! What do I do?"

If we have crossed such a threshold into a new space, what are the maps that will enable us to navigate this other world into which we have been brought? What does it look like to form God's people in a place where the maps that once guided us so well no longer help us make sense of the territory in which we find ourselves? Irrespective of age or vocation, we are all starting to discover that our old maps have become less and less reliable guides. The doctor was once a symbol of caring presence and personal attention within a community; medicine was a vocation focused on healing people. Rapid and profound changes in technology and economics are now redefining how medicine is practiced, and the local GP has become an endangered species. A friend, after practicing medicine for thirty years, resigned her position because she could no longer deal with the time constraints insurance groups put on her seeing patients, the mountains of paper work she had to fill out, and the restrictions on diagnostic treatments mandated by HMOs focused on the bottom line. This reframing of the meaning of her vocation created stress and a profound sadness about her role. On the economic front, as noted earlier, Alan Greenspan sat before Congress in late 2008, and this great high priest of the economic system his country has embraced since the Reagan era simply said of the meltdown, *"I never saw it coming!"*

The maps church leaders were given no longer correspond to the realities they face in local churches and the systems that serve them. One leader put it this way:

> When I accepted the call to be the executive pastor of a presbytery in the Presbyterian Church USA, I was excited, enthusiastic, and full of energy for my new challenge! A little over three years into the position, I was discouraged, frustrated, and depressed. I found myself caught in the downward spiral of a regulatory agency that had no tangible rewards. Dealing with rules, regulations, conflicts, and an unending pile of administrative problems made me feel like the church was a vampire sucking the love of ministry out of my system. I didn't know how long I could continue to function in the role I had felt called by God to fill. I did not see any hope for change on the horizon and didn't know if I would ever really be able to make a difference in the lives of our pastors and our congregations. . . . I was trained to lead and minister in a world that no longer exists. I learned methodologies and strategies that don't work in today's culture. I did not understand how to really change the culture of a church system.

JOURNEYING TOWARD ALTERNATIVE MAPS

As church leaders, many of us find ourselves in an extraordinary place that just a decade ago few would have imagined. One does not need to be a prophet with exceptional insight to sense that a genuinely fundamental transformation is under way. We find ourselves in a moment where assumptions we've taken for granted about ourselves and this amazing creation in which we live are being called into question. Just being a good preacher, teacher, or caregiver in a church no longer connects with the people in our communities. We are now faced with a world of multiple religious views, no religious views, and a deep mistrust of the institutions that gave us our identity as nurturers of God's people.

Creating a great seeker-driven program church seems to be getting harder and harder as people scurry about the countryside in their cars to find the church that meets their own personal needs. A group of seminary educators confess that they no longer go to church—it simply doesn't connect with them anymore. They find affinity groups that meet at some coffee shop off a highway. The leader of a young self-proclaimed "emergent" church struggles to know what to do with people once they all get excited about a certain style of gathering and meeting around a certain age and stage group. What to do next? Something is dying, and something different is being born. We find ourselves no longer living in a kindly, well-ordered world where our assumptions make sense and our planning processes bring us the intended ends for which they were designed. We are in a new space—and we do not as yet have the maps for it.

In this book, I suggest a way of understanding how we form our maps and what happens when the landscape changes and requires us to become map-makers. I propose a way of journeying in this new space by addressing how we should be cultivating local communities of witness and mission in a world where metrics no longer provide useful information. I don't offer quick solutions. Across professions and disciplines, we are all pioneers, struggling to discern the nature of leadership in this new space. A quick look at books on leadership in any airport bookstore makes clear the variety of proposals and metaphors presented as guides in a new terrain. We're invited to build the bridge while we cross it, discover "blue ocean" leadership, and distinguish between the spider and the starfish. The proliferation of metaphors and images suggests a search for alternative maps. Again, we're in a world for which few church leaders were prepared. In this book, you will be given tools to become map-makers in local churches, for what such leaders need is to become cartographers of the new terrain.

Twenty-five years ago, as a young pastor in a growing church, I felt that something was terribly wrong with how I was functioning as a leader. I had been trained in three different seminaries and considered myself a well-schooled evangelical Christian. Within eighteen months of my first pastorate among wonderfully generous, patient, and understanding people, I figured out how to make a church grow but intuitively sensed that I was missing the big questions about how the Gospel engaged the generations of men and women who no longer saw the Christian story as having any relevance for their lives. In my denominational system, I found few who were asking similar questions. Most were content to manage their church, look after whoever who came in, and get involved in the committees and politics of the denomination. In those days, I hadn't yet learned to articulate the questions inside me, even for myself, and so my engagements with others in the denomination must have been experienced as attacks and criticisms rather than an eager desire to figure things out.

After eight years, I moved from the first church I led into a dying congregation in downtown Toronto. It was there that I finally connected with a network of pastors struggling with the questions I was trying to address. This network had picked up on the central question raised by a retired missionary named Lesslie Newbigin when he asked, "Can the West be converted?" A question like that rearranges one's maps! The Gospel and Our Culture Network (GOCN), a network of North American Christian missional leaders formed in the early 1990s, was shaped by the discipline of missiology and the work of missiologists like Newbigin and David Bosch. The basis of GOCN was Newbigin's question, stated more precisely on the first page of his book *Foolishness to the Greeks:* "What would be involved in a missionary encounter between the gospel and this whole way of perceiving, thinking, and living that we call 'modern Western culture'?"[2] I had grown up in a world that assumed that the West was already Christian. In North America, people flocked to churches. Even in the late 1970s and early 1980s, a sense of the Christian story still held at the center of the culture. Newbigin's ideas focused the questions with which I was struggling, but I knew that almost all the church leaders I met still lived with a map that assumed that the church remained at the center. For them, the problem was marketing and figuring out how to meet the needs of a new generation of "customers." For Newbigin and the GOCN, the issues lay far deeper, having to do with a radical transformation of Western culture that would soon mean that the maps with which church leaders had been trained would increasingly not accurately reflect the emerging culture.

The GOCN gave me a company of friends and a framework to think about the church in North America. I participated in a writing team seeking to articulate a framework for a North American missional ecclesiology. *Missional Church: A Vision for the Sending of the Church in North America* became the book we wrote together over three years.[3] It invited a dialogue about the church and its mission on this continent. The book's publication popularized the term *missional* as well as assisted me in understanding why the maps of leadership and church life shaping my imagination no longer matched the reality of the world in which I found myself. The process of writing that book took me deeper into a world that would need alternative maps. As I was trying to understand what it meant to be the church in a context (Canada) where most of my peers, and almost everyone younger than myself, had given the Christian story a pass, the missional conversation was a great gift.[4] This understanding of the local church as called to fulfill the mission of God in its particular context shaped my imagination then and now shapes this book.

OUR MAPS SHAPE OUR ACTIONS

The movie *Thirteen Days* addresses the nature of leadership in critical times.[5] It is the story of the Cuban Missile Crisis, a two-week period in 1962 when the United States and the Soviet Union came precipitously close to global nuclear war over the installation of Soviet ballistic missiles in Cuba. The movie tracks events with some accuracy. The Kennedy administration must confront the complexities of this grave situation. From the perspective of Kennedy's advisers, every scenario they evaluate ultimately leads to nuclear war.

The situation is extremely complicated. First, the United States' only contact with Soviet leadership is through back channels. Trying to penetrate the intentions of that leadership is like an enigma wrapped in a cloak of mystery. Second, U.S. military leaders argue forcefully for a full-scale military response at the earliest possible moment; their instincts and experience convince them that no other option exists but to strike fast and hard, even if it inevitably leads to nuclear war. These military leaders are so locked into their assumptions that they work to undermine Kennedy's directives by creating incidents designed to precipitate Soviet responses, thus making war inescapable. Kennedy's challenge is to sift through these complex elements while at the same time dealing with a rapidly closing window for effective response to the missiles in Cuba, which will be operational within a matter of days.

A pivotal scene sets the stage for what unfolds. Talking with his brother, Bobby, and his political adviser, the president describes reading

Barbara Tuchman's book *The Guns of August*, an exhaustive study of the causes of World War I. Tuchman's argument, states Kennedy, is that the generals in both the Allied and Axis powers all assumed they understood the military mind of their enemy and were convinced they could manage a brief war by relying on the assumptions that grew out of the traditions they knew and the experience they'd had in previous wars. Because of these assumptions, the generals were blinded to the fact that the very nature of war had changed. Technology, a new idea at the beginning of the twentieth century, created a situation in which all the rules and commonsense assumptions about the nature of war were blown apart. The most notable innovation was the machine gun, which had been used in the nineteenth and early twentieth centuries to colonize Africa and India, where massive numbers of poorly equipped indigenous peoples were literally mowed down by a few European soldiers sitting behind a few stationery machine guns. But the generals didn't pay attention to this changed reality; they pursued warfare according to standards established before these new technological developments, with the result that the people of Europe were dragged deeper and deeper into a conflict more horrible and intractable than anyone ever imagined. When the Europeans turned their technology against people who lacked it, people who fought with horses and spears, the devastation was immense. But when both sides had access to the same technology and they turned their machine guns against each other, the result was the smashing of Western consciousness in the bloodiest slaughter ever seen in the world to that point.

For Kennedy, the sea change was not the machine gun but nuclear bombs and ballistic missiles. After reading Tuchman, Kennedy seeks an alternative way of engaging a radically new kind of world. He intuitively grasps that the instincts of the generals will lead to disaster: their old maps cannot solve the challenges of the new context.

The Cuban Missile Crisis is an apt metaphor for the North American church over the past half-century. The crisis is the ending of the Christian narrative as the operative, controlling map of North American culture. The emergence of postmodern maps is putting the churches into a radically different situation. Like Tuchman's generals, churches continue to believe they can navigate this new terrain with the maps that got them to this place. It's a dangerous illusion! This book traces some of the ways we've formed our old maps and proposes fresh ways we can become map-makers in the changing landscapes in which we now live.

PART ONE

WHEN MAPS NO LONGER WORK

CHAPTER **ONE**

MAPS SHAPING OUR IMAGINATIONS IN MODERNITY

Several years ago, my wife, Jane, bought the Launch Edition Mini Cooper. It had a number inscribed on the tachometer indicating its special status as one of the few launched. It was one sweet vehicle. In the early days, Jane made it clear that I would have limited driving privileges. So I was delighted when one Saturday morning she said, "Why don't you drive?" Jane was in the passenger seat. She pointed into the distance and said, "Just look at that mess. I've got to fix that right away. Those birds are so messy!" I followed her finger into the distance, looking for birds or evidence of their mischief. "What are you talking about?" I asked. "I can't see any mess!" Jane laughed and pointed again. "Look!" she exclaimed. "Can't you see that? The birds must have done it while we were in the store." This time the finger seemed to be pointing a little lower on the road. I leaned forward to take a closer look. "I can't see a thing!" I reiterated. Then Jane realized what the problem was. "No!" she laughed, "not the road; the windshield! Look at the mess on the windshield. I've got to get it cleaned before it bakes on!" Finally, I "saw"; the mess wasn't "out there" but on the windshield.

When driving, we see *through the windshield* but *not the windshield itself.* Most of the time, we are unaware it is there. Maps work the same way. When navigating the streets of Vancouver where we live, we envision the maps in our heads and just take our directional certitude for granted. We use them to move about easily and freely but hardly ever stop to think about the maps themselves.

We use these inner maps to control and manage our world. In modern, Western societies, we have assumed ways of driving on the road, for example. In the world of church and ministry, despite denominational and other differences, we have a basic inner map of how a pastor should function in a church (notice even the image we use here, where the place of a pastor is *in* a physical location called a church). We have been given internal maps about how to go about raising children; these are often quite different from the ways, for example, children are raised in non-Western cultures. These inner maps of how things are supposed to work have been very effective in enabling us to manage and control our environments. Obviously, many of these inner maps are still just as effective and important for our everyday life in the modern West. Other maps that we have taken for granted, however, are being challenged. The nature of marriage is one current example. Another is the map of our economic life: the way our pensions and retirement were supposed to work no longer matches the financial realities many of us are facing. Within the church, other real and important overarching inner maps are also being challenged, such as the role of church leadership and who should lead. Many of us have shared the strong inner conviction that as church leaders in times of change, we must find ways of regaining control over our increasingly unclear church environments. When we sense that our inner maps of church leadership are becoming less and less effective and the images of leadership in which we were trained are not robust enough to encompass our current reality, another inner map tells us that we have to find a way of taking control in order make things work again. A simple story illustrates the persistence of these inner maps.

I'd had a long week crisscrossing North America in airplanes and was heading home—the interrupted schedules and mechanical breakdowns were far from my mind. When I called home, Jane picked up the phone to tell me she had our granddaughter Madeline in her arms. Maddy was communicating that she wanted down; she didn't want to be held too long in anyone's arms. My joy is holding Maddy, but she isn't someone who wants to be held much, or at least is willing to be held only on her terms. She isn't going to be managed; she has her own sense of what she wants.

I thought of Maddy as I boarded my flight and absorbed my first inklings that this would be a night when plans for getting home at a decent hour would evaporate. The flight was already ninety minutes late. When we were finally on board, the captain's voice crackled in the speakers. A computer wasn't working; a mechanic would need to replace it. I calculated: it would be midnight before we landed. Anticipation of ending the late summer day on our deck had just been thrown out. Life messes with our plans. A woman then called an attendant. She was connecting in Vancouver with a fight to Thailand; she wasn't going to make it and didn't want to overnight in Vancouver. She wanted off the flight. As she walked off, the captain came back on to tell us the ground crew had to reopen the compartments below and remove this passenger's luggage. It would be 1 A.M., four hours later than scheduled, when we would land in Vancouver. So much for best-laid plans.

I thought of Maddy, of the ways I want to hold her and how she is always saying "up" or "down" to tell me she doesn't belong to me. I won't be managing this relationship according to my preferred imagination. Like all important relationships, ours will follow the mysterious and unpredictable unfolding of interconnected lives, not some tidy picture I dream up. The mystery of our differing person-hoods will weave a tapestry neither of us, nor anyone else, will be able to map or control.

Strapped into my seat, I reflected on this powerful inner map that we think lets us plan, predict, measure, and control the directions and outcomes of other people's lives. Where did this delusion come from? Why, after years of experience to the contrary, do we still think we can have a wonderful plan for other people and, moreover, expect their lives to unfold according to that plan? For years, this internal map told me that it was possible, with the right vision and the right plan, for a church to build a roadway along which people would move toward the goals and mission I and other leaders had articulated with such passion and conviction. On the plane home, I wondered why I had been so blind as to actually try to control, manage, and align people in the churches I served. This conviction that leaders need to come up with a plan around which all the church's life is aligned is a deeply embedded map still shaping the actions of many church leaders. We need to understand why we as leaders have so strongly embraced this map because we are now in a space where this kind of map is less and less helpful.

HOW MAPS WORK

We're born into a world with cultures that already have maps. The argument of this chapter is that for us in the West, our primary map has been modernity, and modernity has in many ways profoundly reshaped, and even deformed, the Christian imagination in our culture. From birth, we're formed and shaped by the common understandings of the culture into which we're born to the point where we assume that our culture's map describes the world the way it is. Our cultural map of modernity shapes how we see the world, ourselves, and our relationships. This map "makes sense" to us because we live in the world it depicts.

These cultural maps use metaphors, images, symbols, and stories that enable us to navigate our worlds: even to this day, for example, church steeples dotting the landscape remind us how thoroughly church attendance once ordered our lives as a culture. The maps lie so deep in our imagination and reach so far back to our earliest memories and education that we find it difficult to recognize them as our cultural maps. Instead, we perceive them as the taken-for-granted descriptions of the way the world works, and our culture rewards us for adhering to them (similarly to how some societies drive on the left side of the road and wonder how others could be crazy enough to drive on the other side, the "wrong" side). Another example of culturally ingrained maps would be the ways church leaders, especially in the United States, aspire to *modernist* maps of leadership highly dependent on techniques of church growth and markers of success such as numbers of people in attendance or numbers of decisions made at a meeting or the percentage of the congregation involved in certain midweek programs, but as we move more into a globalized *postmodern* world, these inner maps of success bear little correspondence to the desire of people who seek not to fit into an institution but rather to discover empowerment and liberation. In some parts of the world, married women have few rights and cannot leave the home without permission of the husband, whereas in other cultures, married women are considered equal partners with their spouses. The power of these inner maps is made painfully manifest when people from such cultures move to the West and engage with Western ideas of gender equality. Married women from parts of India, for example, have been beaten or murdered by their husbands when they begin to adopt Western practices of equality. Another instance of these cultural differences are the attitudes toward alcohol. In Muslim countries, the consumption of alcohol is completely frowned on. In America, it is seen as part of a dependency culture, whereas in Europe, it is more a part of a merriment culture. The differences in our inner cultural maps were starkly apparent with the 2003 invasion of Iraq and the Bush administration's accompanying belief that any country would naturally welcome a liberator and adopt some universal sense of democracy even if that meant the end of many of its own traditional institutions. Maps like these are in operation all the time, shaping how we make decisions, see the world, and take action; they are so much a part of our lives that we don't actually notice them. That's why we speak of them existing in our imagination. In this sense, imagination doesn't mean make-believe but suggests an image or picture that represents some object that isn't directly accessible to us. For example, when we encounter the phrase "North America" in this book, the actual landmass or histories of the nations that comprise North America aren't directly before us, but we each have in mind a picture or image of what "North America" embodies. Our imagination *makes accessible what would otherwise be unavailable to us.*[1]

Let's consider an illustration from a different culture to help us see how our own maps shape our imaginations. The Passover Seder is a ceremonial meal that Jewish families have practiced every year for millennia. *Seder* means order; it describes the specific order in which the supper is to be celebrated in terms of prayers, eating, storytelling, and song. It begins with the youngest son asking the father, "Why is this night different from all other nights?" The father's response begins, "On this night we remember we were slaves in Egypt . . . and the Lord . . . delivered us." Whenever the members of a Jewish family participate in this liturgy, they are following a map that forms their identity as few other things ever will. The food they eat that night is filled with symbols that remind them of that other night, thousands of years before, when their ancestors were slaves and God delivered them. This mapping of identity is profound. The table ritual begins with the pronoun *we*—this is more than a memorial. It is memory made present. Those at the table are also the *we*, distinguishing Jews as God's chosen people. The story roots them in memories of slavery and deliverance, the work of death on them as a people, and God's liberation of them as a people. These powerful maps of identity determine present actions. Here is an example of how someone following this map expresses this imagination. The poem, written by a rabbi, is about the killings in Darfur. It goes all the way back to the Passover and its lived imagination.

> We Jews see with ancient eyes and attend with ancient ears.
> We were not born yesterday.
> Not long ago we swore over the cremated bodies of our fathers, mothers and children a solemn oath. From the depths of our souls we cried, "Never Again." That oath carries the past into the present and pledges to do today whatever is in our power to prevent the perverse plots to extinguish the promise of life.
> "Never Again" will we allow the world to dissemble, to pretend that we are voiceless, soundless, without legs or hands.
> Ours is a solemn oath in memory of those who were slaughtered in deathly silence.
> We are pledged to wake the world from the paralysis of will. We are partners with God in protecting His Children. We dare not shut our eyes or our mouths or our ears.
> Who is Darfur to us? And who are they to us?
> They are us.[2]

The maps in our imaginations tell us who we are; they provide for us the geography of our identity as a culture and inform the ways we act. They're part of who we are, but they are also so pervasive in our imaginations that we don't notice them. Anyone who walks into a medieval cathedral will be struck and overwhelmed by the power and beauty of its height drawing us upward, its huge stone pillars and curved arches. On the ground, the overall design of the nave, aisle, and transept (note how the language itself now sounds unfamiliar to us—we sense we know but can't quite attach an image to what each word designates) described a world, mapped an imagination, about the relationship between earth and heaven, humans and God, that we can hardly imagine for ourselves. The stained-glass windows are of immense beauty, but beauty was never the point; rather, these windows mapped the journey of life on earth and described the future after death. The cathedral was a living, physical map of the Christian imagination. It is a way of understanding our place in the world that no longer carries meaning for us. We cannot decipher the meanings written into the brick, mortar, carvings, and glass. These are no longer part of the ways we see or construct the meaning of our lives as modern people. Indeed, this other map we call modernity has come to shape our imagination of how the world is supposed to work. It's crucial for the church and its leadership to grasp the pervasiveness and power of modernity's maps when it comes to the ways we lead and form our churches.

MODERNITY'S MAPS

Modernity is the cultural map that has profoundly shaped the West, dominating the cultural imagination of people in Europe, North America, Australia, and New Zealand. Its roots reach back to the Enlightenment, when the French philosopher René Descartes rejected the traditions of the medieval intellectual map, questioning the scholasticism of his day with its notions that physical actions could be explained in terms of God acting on things and developing a method of approaching the world we now know as rationalism. This was a massive shift in imagination, a revolutionary new way of seeing the world.

Central to the map of modernity are convictions about the sources of truth and knowledge and the method for attaining truth and knowledge. Compared to all previous maps across cultures, in which a divine being was the source of truth and knowledge, modernity places the autonomous individual at the center as the source of truth and knowledge.[3] This autonomous self is radically separate and above everything else, a subject relating to myriad objects. With this shift in imagination came a method by which this rational subject could compel truth and knowledge from the objective world. This form of rationalism came to be known as the scientific method. These two elements combine to create the basic terrain of modernity's map: a fundamental division of all reality between the subjective human self and an objective, external world.

According to this map, we habitually assume that the world is composed of a set of objects divided into separate and distinct parts. With the right techniques, sufficient knowledge, and enough metrics, it is possible to break things down into their simplest, most discrete pieces in order to understand them and then put them back together in ways that give us control and predictability over our environment.

Alasdair MacIntyre, in *After Virtue*, helps us see more nuanced detail in the map of modernity by describing two perceptions—one social and the other philosophical—that control the modern imagination.[4] Sociologically, modernity partitions each human life into a variety of segments, each with its own norms of behavior. Thus the public is divided from the private, the corporate from the personal, fact from value, truth from faith, childhood from old age. These divisions reflect a part of the modern map that assumes that all of reality is made up of separate, distinct parts. This is why, for example, it was possible to see the world as a collection of separate objects (the *atomistic* view of the world) that we could use and manipulate as we chose. What we have in modernity, on one side, is this tendency to "think atomistically about human action and to analyze complex actions and transactions in terms of simple components. In this way the view that particular actions derive their character as parts of larger wholes is a point of view alien to our dominant ways of thinking."[5] A classic illustration of this atomistic thinking is the way individuals claim they can do what they like as individuals because it is their action alone and nobody else is involved. This is why some people can justify getting behind the wheel of a car after drinking: it's their choice, one that doesn't affect anyone else. In modernity, we have built a world that we believe is made up of individual, personal actions that don't have any effect on others. If we stopped to think about this for a moment, we might be appalled at such a notion, but because this is one of the default maps, we keep acting as if it were the case, in spite of evidence to the contrary. The individual is sharply separated and distinguished from the particular roles he or she may play in society, exemplified in the notion that what someone does behind closed doors is nobody else's business. Recent scandals in which well-known North American religious leaders have been "outed" in some form of moral compromise illustrate this aspect of the modern imagination at work.

The self is the center of modernity's imagination. Modernity automatically thinks individualistically, or atomistically, as if human beings are independent, separate entities functioning out of their own self-determined worlds. According to this map, an individual can and should generate his or her own independent meanings.[6] Frank Sinatra's boast that "I did it my way" in the Paul Anka song "My Way" is one expression of this. I was in a store recently returning a printer. While waiting for service, I heard the voice-over on a video advertisement for sales personnel. It went something like this: "The salesperson we're looking for is an independent self-starter looking to develop his or her full potential and express his or her own special self in a forward-looking context of . . . " This script is straight out of modernity's map, but few people in the store would have reflected on that fact.

Reflecting on our maps helps us see the stories and assumptions that shape us. Modernity is only one particular story of how to read and order life. It is not particularly old (three to four hundred years, compared to more than two millennia for the Passover story), but it became our culture's normative way of reading the world. Modern notions of the self and the individual, for example, are still powerfully present in our imagination; any quick reference to advertising or television programs still shows that the self remains at the center of our story. We don't quickly or easily leave behind something that has shaped us so indelibly for such a long period of time.

It is important to remember that maps continue to shape us long after we think they're in the past. I remember when Jane and I were first married. We had come from such different kinds of families that there were a lot of negotiations along the way, some of them quite humorous. I was raised in postwar England when there were huge shortages of basic staples. The refrigerator was an invention for the rich who lived in what seemed another world. In the late fifties, we moved into a rental home with a refrigerator. My mother made it very clear that no child was ever to go near the fridge. By the time I left home, I had developed a high level of skill at sneaking into the kitchen to get food from the fridge. One evening, several months after Jane and I moved into our first apartment, I was studying at my desk and got hungry for a snack. Without thinking about what I was doing, I quietly moved to the kitchen and sneaked into the refrigerator. Just then Jane asked me, "Alan, why are you sneaking around like that?" After an initial response of denial and hurt, I realized that the practices I had learned as a boy were still determining the way I moved about in a home where Jane and I owned the refrigerator. Maps don't disappear just because our reality changes. They stay with us, continuing to shape our habits. The challenge we face as leaders is that we find ourselves in a new space where we keep trying to navigate with maps that represent a reality that no longer exists. I grew up in Liverpool for the first fifteen years of my life, but I can't go back to Liverpool and try to get around with the internal maps I had then—the geography and the space have changed.

THE DEVELOPMENT OF MODERNITY

We live in a time when people find interesting ways of encountering the past. A magazine I was reading recently showed a picture of Manhattan Island, a strange picture. The left side of Manhattan was all green and lush, covered with grass and trees. The right side of the picture showed the cityscape as we experience it today. The point of that picture was to show how much Manhattan has changed since a group of Dutch explorers entered the mouth of the Hudson River several hundred years ago. We human beings construct our spaces and make maps to manage those spaces. Over time, tremendous change occurs. The human story can be imagined as a long, flowing river moving through time with unpredictable and unexpected twists and turns. Sometimes that river flowed in a long, straight line like the Nile in Egypt or the Seine in France. At such times, generations developed predictable habits and practices for managing life along the river and controlling their destinies. These habits and practices become predictable and help us control our worlds. At other times, the waters have turned unexpected corners and churned into great, swirling rivers, such as the Iguaçu in Brazil, a river that can't be managed or controlled. Like the Iguaçu's twists and turns, modernity is one part of the river that has shaped our imagination and maps.

In the distant past, human community shifted from *hunting-and-gathering clans* toward *agrarian civilizations*. Population centers emerged, forming the basis for these agriculture-based civilizations. Such changes took thousands of years. Then, for further thousands of years, the basic character of civilizations settled around an agrarian culture. This was a long, continuous, stable period of human history. Changes occurred as tools and implements developed and crop management and husbandry improved; however, the basic forms of culture remained relatively stable. Even with great disruptions, like the barbarian invasions of Europe in the fourth through sixth centuries, the culture gradually returned to its base as a farming civilization. Over time, people developed myths and stories that formed the narrative explanations into which generation after generation was born. Such stories and myths were essential for continuity and stability. We still carry the memory of these stories in the agrarian practices of the equinoxes, harvest festivals, and the ancient dances around the rites of spring.

In Europe and North America, agrarian culture lasted into the late seventeenth century, when another transformation got under way.

Following the Thirty Years' War, as towns and cities developed into important centers of commerce, the Industrial Revolution began tearing apart a way of life that had lasted for thousands of years. The French Revolution (1789), with its destruction of the Ancien Régime, signaled the emergence of a Europe that would move rapidly away from the primary social formations of an agrarian world. For the first time in thousands of years, the nature of civilization underwent a dramatic transformation. This was the birth of the modern era; the stage on which Western culture played out its life and passed on its narrative stories had been forever changed, the scenery replaced, and the players given radically new scripts.

In the river metaphor, human culture had settled at a point along the bank establishing a particular kind of known world: agrarian civilizations. Suddenly, after thousands of years of living embedded in this location, the river turns a massive corner and careens over a roaring waterfall into a radically different location. These are the white waters of eruptive, discontinuous change that cause massive shifts in civilizations. Few people are prepared for such radical changes. The Industrial Revolution restructured social life in the West and then the whole world. In historical terms, industrial society lasted some three hundred years in the West. While the transition from agrarian to industrial civilization was profoundly destructive of social life and human meaning, it happened over a long enough span of time for new forms of social life to emerge; people gradually settled into a new kind of known world: the industrial world, with its growing cities, new kinds of technology, a new understanding of time and place, and new forms of social organization, such as unions, and classes of people. One of the most profound of these social changes that we take for granted today was the formation of what are called *societies*. These were a radically new kind of organization in which people chose to associate freely with one another in a club or organization. Prior to this point, in the feudal world, people were bound by an age-old system of social organization that marked their place and ranking in the social order. In the new industrial cities, these predetermined orderings of society broke down and practically disappeared. What emerged in these industrial countries were laws and guidelines for how these new kinds of societies were to act in terms of regular meetings and essential bylaws. What's important about this illustration is that these new laws in the industrial countries became the templates for determining how churches and denominations could operate in this new world. Thus the yearly church business meeting according to a church's constitution and bylaws is directly taken from the formation of these societies in the industrial age. What can be easily missed is the profound transformation in our social maps this simple legal procedure brought about. Societies are associational organizations. In other words, they are organizations that individuals freely choose to join and leave. Thus what gets built into Protestant church life in the West, in spite of wonderful theologies about covenant, are church cultures that are fundamentally associational or based on voluntary membership. We take these features of church life for granted with very little awareness that they reflect a social map created at the beginning of the industrial age. We have therefore built all our church systems on the basis of individual rights to associate as and when they choose, and when they meet, they are directed by legal codes and bylaws. This is not an argument for or against this kind of process but an illustration of how changing maps shape the ways we go about being and leading the church.

It was in this period, between the seventeenth century and the early twentieth, that many of the leadership and organizational forms of the church were reshaped. It is instructive, for example, to observe how deeply some denominations, such as the Baptists, are invested in and shaped by *Robert's Rules of Order*, a set of processes designed to enable early industrial age organizations to function as the associational societies I've just described for decision making in the emerging industrial society.[7] Yet since then, the character and pace of civilizational change has picked up dramatically. The *electronic age* made an early appearance at the great Chicago and Paris world fairs at the beginning of the twentieth century. In the final decades of that century, thanks to the introduction of the computer, the electronic age resulted in another radical and rapid transformation, the emergence of the *information age*, which, though connected with the previous period, is also strikingly discontinuous. Each of these innovations—the industrial, electronic, and information ages—represents a developing stage of modernity, when rational technique and the search for control and predictability came to be part of our central ethos. Each age has required us to readjust and change our understanding of work, self-identity, social relationships, and the meaning of place.

The electronic age, for example, gave us electric light and electrified trams and trains, resulting in people staying up a lot later and engaging more in local community activity. New technologies made work less physical for many people and began the emancipation of women in the home. These and other technologies created new kinds of experts and professionals that increased the diversification of work as well as brought people into more face-to-face interactions (as the automobile enabled people to travel to see each other, for example). The information age represented another huge shift in our mapping of social life. One of the best volumes addressing this latest and most conspicuous shift is *The Rise of the Network Society* by Manuel Castells.[8] The information revolution gave birth to the network society (including the Internet), which has revolutionized how we understand the nature of economic systems; it has changed the basic relationships people have with their work (less loyalty to a company or organization and more a feeling that people are empowered as "information workers" to control to the ways they work) and is fundamentally altering the ways people communicate with each other: younger people are more at home carrying on three or four texting conversations with various people at the same time, disembodied from physical space, than sitting across from one person in a conversation; conversation now moves in multiple directions at once, including a diversity of people with a variety of opinions, creating far more open, diffuse sense of authority or the sources of knowledge. These are massive, recent changes in the ways we relate and work in the world.

We once had thousands of years to digest and adjust to seismic cultural shifts that required the drawing of new maps. Eventually, transformations of such magnitude were compressed into centuries and now decades. The various landscapes onto which we are thrust are changing with great rapidity, and known world maps are disrupted at an ever-increasing pace.

MAP-MAKING AND THE EMERGENCE OF MODERNITY

In his novel *A Mapmaker's Dream*, James Cowan tells the tale of a sixteenth-century Venetian monk who tirelessly works to create the most accurate maps of the world.[9] The monk, Fra Mauro, was born in the twilight of a medieval, premodern time. He had his ways of making sense of that world shaped by his time. But he could sense something shifting; the world was in flux, and the habits and imagination of his time were beginning to change. It was a period of anxiety and creativity. Great journeys of exploration were under way. An awakened

Europe faced dazzling stories of exploration, new worlds, and strange peoples. Fra Mauro came to dream of a new map that would describe the emerging world unfolding before him as he listened to the stories of travelers and saw the sketches they made of places no one in Venice had seen before. He did not so much extrapolate from known maps that for hundreds of years had defined the shape of the world as listen to the stories of travelers who had stepped off the paths of known maps to encounter places and peoples that could not be correlated with established maps. Like other men of that time, he struggled to "give form to something that was not of this world."[10]

This "stepping off the page" created dissonance about the known maps and led to a redrawing of the world. In so doing, the monk draws new maps by which travelers might navigate around the strange, emerging world of the sixteenth century. The stage on which European life had been shaped for hundreds of years underwent massive change.

THE CALL FOR MAP-MAKERS

Fra Mauro was one of those risk takers who dared become a map-maker rather than a copier of maps. He sensed that the maps he had received from his forbears were no longer sufficient to capture the stories he was hearing. Like Fra Mauro, we live in a time when the maps of modernity, with their promises of management, control, and predictability, are no longer sufficient to describe the places where we find ourselves. The rapidity and extent of these changes create disequilibrium, anxiety, confusion, and disorientation among people in North American culture, and this means that our maps need to be reimagined. We are required to become map-makers. The maps we have inherited no longer adequately describe the realities we face. Like Fra Mauro, we must relinquish the desire to copy our inherited maps and learn to listen to the stories of pioneers so that we can make new maps. In this way, we can reshape the imagination of God's people.

For some, this is an exhilarating adventure, for others, it is a disconcerting process taking them ever further from the familiar world of modernity they've known. Some try to live according to the familiar scripts modernity gave them but find that the stage keeps changing such that the scripts no longer work. Others quickly adopt scripts for the new stage. Most struggle, however, trying to make the scripts they were given work again.

Not everyone has been shaped by all parts of our North American cultural maps. Within the church, for example, some groups have steadfastly resisted the frameworks of modernity, seeking to describe themselves as a contrast society (Mennonites, for example), while the great bulk of Protestant churches have drunk deeply of modernity with its emphases on techniques of control and predictability (programs that guarantee growth and "health," such as Natural Church Development or Forty Days of Purpose) and focus on the individual ("needs-centered" and "seeker-centered" churches). Others, especially from African American, Native Indian, Hispanic, and other recent immigrant cultures, have resisted aspects of modernity. Native American Christians, for example, are much more at home doing decision making in a circle together rather than having some strong leader provide a vision statement with a plan.

Some more recent groups cluster themselves under amorphous titles like "emergent" or "postmodern" and believe they are in a vanguard that is moving beyond things modern and writing their own maps. These are signs of people experimenting, stretching into new territories to discover on the journey other forms of leadership and church life. It is important to note that the overall cultural map of the last three hundred years was shaped by a shifting modernity, and it may be that this modernity still shapes these groups in one form or another. The power of modernity's maps continues to shape much of the church. It is not easily thrown off. The Spirit of God, however, is hovering among all these groups and types of churches, just as the Spirit hovered in the creation story. The voice of God is being spoken over the church in all its diverse and contradictory forms. The next chapter invites us to follow this voice.

CHAPTER TWO

LEADING IN AN IN-BETWEEN TIME

Each painting of Picasso, each symphony of Mahler, even every one of those epic Freudian interviews—all of them were like beautiful, fluent reports sent in from a distant field station. . . . These artists and scientists, with their deeper instinct for the vibrations of history and culture, were making maps of a new psychological country without quite knowing what they were doing. It was to be called the twentieth century.

But if a few people could label this new world precisely, most of the continent's great figures were oblivious. They were stuck—as many of our leaders are now—with old ideas.[1]

The media in 2008 and 2009 were filled with information and advice about how to survive the economic meltdown. China's economic miracle that everyone was talking about in the first part of 2008 had turned into a huge unemployment crisis, its government increasingly fearful of riots among the urban poor, who were compelled return to their rural homes, where their prospects were even bleaker. The *New York Times Winter 2009 Fashion Magazine* offered its high-end merchandise in the form of "a stimulus package" in an effort to kindle spending on the same old formula of convincing people they would feel important by purchasing Louis Vuitton or Fendi. Some are trying to fix the system, others tell us it has to be remade,[2] and there is no going back to business as usual. A growing number of those who think a lot about the multiple levels of change moving through our world are saying that the certainties and established maps of our time are no longer workable.[3] We are in a new place where the maps of that have shaped us for the last hundred or so years have lost their relevance.

I visited Ellis Island in New York Harbor for the first time a few years ago. The ferry took us out past the Statue of Liberty to this famous island, now a treasured national museum, that witnessed the stories of so many immigrants from all over the world who came to these shores in the late nineteenth and early twentieth centuries. Most came with nothing. The pictures on the walls of the old buildings depict men, women, children, and families in various poses, dressed in the clothes of differing homelands, looking gaunt and confused. What must it have been like to leave the place you were born, the land and language that shaped you, to come to an unknown place in full awareness that you would never see your homeland or friends again?

In a conference I led, I asked a group of lay and pastoral leaders to reflect on their feelings about what is happening to their churches. In order to shape their reflection, we spent time together reading Psalm 137, a psalm of lament and loss after the citizens of Jerusalem were taken captive to Babylon. The captives from Jerusalem sit and weep beside the waters because they don't know how to sing God's songs in a strange land. The leaders at the conference wrote their own contemporary Psalm 137. What they wrote was amazing. Here's an example:

137 FOR 2010

In the midst of this crazy world I look around and wonder what has happened.
How do I talk to a kid with a ring in his nose?
Does "The Old Rugged Cross" mean anything to him?
He asks me to sing a song about "my Jesus."
From what I can tell he is from another planet, or am I the stranger here?
I think it's time to sell the Wurlitzer.
So how do I tell Martians about Jesus,
when the only language I speak is 1955?
How do I write a headline for them
that doesn't screw up the Good News?
I kind of wish it were the way it was,

but it's not. So I need to figure out
how to sing the old lyrics
with a whole new tune.

This leader is expressing his Ellis Island experience. He is confounded
by the fact that the map he understands (modernity) no longer seems
to fit the challenges he faces in today's world. He's not alone! Honest
church leaders share their struggle; they realize that the church is in
an "in-between" place where modernity's maps are inadequate but
new maps have yet to be created.

NOTHING NEW FOR THE CHURCH

Coming to such a realization can generate great frustration and anxiety. But none of this is new for God's people. The Spirit has continually disrupted the church throughout its history, taking it to places
where once accurate maps no longer applied. This is not a time for
fear or dire predictions of the church's demise. G. K. Chesterton
noted that many commentators through the ages have predicted that
the church was going to the dogs with no hope for any new life. But,
said Chesterton, it is the dogs that have gone and the church is still
here.[4] This is because the church, in all its forms, is the creation and
work of the Spirit. That being said, today's church requires a transformation of imagination, organization, practice, and leadership.
In the young church in Jerusalem, for example, this transformation
of imagination was wrought by a geographical shift of its center from
Jerusalem to Antioch. Jerusalem represented the assumption that the
ways of religious life that had worked for centuries, the sense of a
continuous, developmental process from all that God had promised
in the Old Testament to its fulfillment in Jesus and the birth of the
church, would be a seamless development of this past. This church,
as Acts 11 makes clear, was almost totally Jewish in composition. The
overarching assumption in Jerusalem was that Jesus' death and resurrection fulfilled all the expectations of Jewish hope, and the young,
Jewish church was its fulfillment. The early church was and would
remain Jewish in form and nature because Judaism was the young
church's map. The Jerusalem church was rooted in Jewish practices,
rhythms, and leadership forms. Jerusalem represented continuity and
equilibrium; it was the central metaphor for all that God was doing.
Within the young church's imagination were assumptions about what

it meant to be the people of God as well as God's relationship to the rest of the world and the future of the community formed by Jesus. But this map would undergo a radical transformation that shifted the young church out of one world and into another.

In an amazingly brief period of time, the center of Christian life and energy shifted from a Jerusalem-, Jewish-, temple-centered map to a Greco-Roman world symbolized by Antioch. No one saw this coming; it was a massive, unexpected, and disorienting shift that caused a collision of perspectives and imagination about what God was doing in the world. This very young Christian movement was forced into an in-between place that was outside the experience of what the Gospel was supposed to be about. It disrupted the church from purely Jewish categories into the powerful Greco-Roman world of the time. Suddenly, in Antioch, the church became a predomi-nantly Gentile movement that forced leaders, such as Paul and Peter, to wrestle with the implications of Jesus' death and resurrection and the nature of Christian practices for communities of new believers who didn't grow out of Judaism. (For example, should Christians con-tinue to keep Jewish festivals? Should they follow the dietary laws set down in the Jewish Scriptures? What should happen to spouses who were pagan and not willing to convert? How should they teach men and women who knew nothing of the Jewish Scriptures about God's wondrous actions with his people?)

Another example of this type of shift in maps comes from the sev-enteenth century, a time of major transition. In the aftermath of the Reformation and the devastations of the Thirty Years' War, plagues decimated Europe. People felt as if the foundations of the world were being shaken to the ground, that everything solid was melting. Thinkers, artists, and inventors communicated a shared sense that the maps of their world were being torn up. Galileo wrote his *Dialogue on the Two Great World Systems* arguing that the earth, rotating on its axis, moved about the sun. Milton wrote his story of the human journey in *Paradise Lost,* signifying the disorientation and loss people were experiencing. Descartes wrote the *Discourse on Method* to pro-vide a new foundation on which the human knowledge could firmly stand in the midst of all the massive, swirling change.

Into this world spoke John Bunyan, who was struggling to cre-ate new maps. His *Pilgrim's Progress* was a metaphor for the arduous spiritual odyssey this moment in history called forth. It is the story of one person's journey through strange, unknown lands and difficult places. Bunyan sought to create a new spiritual map to guide pilgrims on their journey through a radically changing seventeenth-century world. Descartes created a new intellectual map as a guide for the perplexed. Galileo redrew the cosmological map and redefined our place in the universe. Each struggled to give meaning and shape to a new situation. In retrospect, while their various intellectual, literary, and cosmological maps made sense in the context of their time, they also contained profound misconceptions that continue to affect our imagination. One of the clearest is Descartes' division of all reality into the knowing subject and the known object. This subject-object split continues to shape the way we construct our world even as discoveries in science and literature have revealed it to be an utterly wrong framing of the world.

That period has parallels with our own. Just as in the seventeenth century, we're trying to make sense of huge discontinuities and uncertainties; this is a journey where we can look back and see, just behind us, the slowly sinking horizon of modernity and, with it, a Christian culture that shaped our imaginations, actions, and expectations so profoundly. At the same time, we feel ourselves in a new space where it is difficult to know how to draw those new maps.

To use a different metaphor, this shifting and changing of our time feels as if we have rehearsed all our lives for a well-known play, Shakespeare's *Macbeth*, for example, on an Elizabethan stage. We have memorized all our lines, worked hard at identifying precisely where we should stand on stage in each scene, and grown comfortable with our character and its relationship to other characters in the play. Then we stop for a lunch break, and when we come back, the stage has changed; it is a completely different theater with sets we haven't seen before and scripts we don't recognize. There's no time to adjust; the curtain goes up, and we have to start the play. The church, like other long-standing institutions, is in this space. Even though the church has been a central character for longer than anyone can remember, in this new play, it has been given a different role without negotiation— an old, tired character whose time is past, sitting in a corner. The cast on the stage has changed; old, familiar props have disappeared; the backdrop is redesigned; and it's hard to figure out what's going on. We feel caught between a role we know we can act well and this other role that doesn't fit our perception of what we ought to be doing.

WHY THE IN-BETWEEN?

Why must there be such a state called "in-between"? Why can't we just enter into the next world and "get on with being the church"? To be quite honest, there are many in today's church world who do not recognize this in-between state. In the midst of transition, as people feel the awkwardness and confusion of the in-between, leaders feel pressure to provide clear maps that give clear direction. This is why they look for programs offering answers in a confusing time, promising success and quick results. Programs containing the language of "health" or "purpose" are attractive because people feel they're living without maps. And in desperation, some feel that a new map is better even if it is wrong. Then when the novelty of one program wears off, they place their hope in the next program. One denominational executive stated that over the past thirty years, he had seen new programs turn up every three to four years that the denomination presented as the way to reenergize its churches' life.

Leaders and church systems now turn to the language of the *missional* movement as the new solution to the disequilibrium. One group of denomination leaders decided it would rename all its executive ministers "missional leaders." One executive then wrote a series of position and organizational papers on how to go about creating this new missional organizational structure. These leaders completely missed the point, but their story illustrates their hunger for solutions. Becoming missional in this new space has little to do with writing position papers (which usually try to explain or provide a map for people) or reorganizing roles and structures (as we will see, these practices actually change very little when we are in an in-between place).

This longing for absolute clarity reveals just how much the church has been shaped by modernity. Modernity is all about control, clarity, and certainty. In this in-between place, it's natural to keep looking to old, familiar maps for guidance, even if we know they no longer describe the places where we now find ourselves. Hannah Arendt put it this way: "The actors and witnesses, the living themselves, become aware of an interval in time which is altogether determined by things that are no longer and by things that are not yet. In history, these intervals have shown more than once that they may contain the moment of truth."[5] The Passover story illustrates this. When the Israelites were delivered from Egypt, they found themselves in an in-between place (the desert) where their actions kept being determined by the ways they'd lived in Egypt (notice the ways they kept comparing the desert to their sojourn in Egypt. For example, they wanted, and expected, that all their food needs would be taken care of as they had been in Egypt; they expected security to be provided without risk because this had become the norm in Egypt), even though that world didn't exist for them any longer. They knew where they'd been and how to act in that place but had no sense of what the new land would look like. As Arendt points out, while this is a difficult place, it is also one of real opportunity and gift.

The maps of modernity discussed in Chapter One are less and less able to help us navigate our new context as they once did. This is why some use the language of *postmodernism*. It expresses the experience of our in-between time. In describing in-between times, Arendt uses the word *tradition* rather than *maps:* "The end of a tradition does not necessarily mean that traditional concepts have lost their power over the minds of men. On the contrary, it sometimes seems that this power of well-worn notions and categories becomes more tyrannical as the tradition loses its living force as the memory of its beginning recedes."6 She is saying that in all the shifting and changing, because we don't have new maps yet, we give more power and authority to the maps we have known. Even as we lose our sense of where these old maps came from, we cling to them more tightly. North Americans' response to the climate change crisis is a good illustration: in the face of growing evidence about massive climate change and its roots in the use of fossil fuels, and in spite of the upward-spiraling costs of these fuels, a lot of North Americans bought gas-guzzling vehicles like SUVs. Why? The power of the map of a single individual having the right to drive whatever he or she pleases within the dream of limitless land and limitless resources remains deep in the imagination even as the evidence piles up that this map is the cause of the problems. Maps (traditions, habits) don't simply disappear; they remain in our minds, determining our actions and how we see the world. If we don't recognize this, we will be misdirected in trying to navigate our current context.

WHAT'S WRONG WITH MODERNITY?

I received this e-mail from a pastor joining a leadership cohort I coteach at Fuller Seminary:

> I've just finished reading *The Sky Is Falling* and have to say you have described my parish perfectly . . . faithful people who find themselves on unknown territory. Desperately wanting to go back to the early

'60s and the chock-full Sunday schools, confirmation classes, and days of privilege for the [church] . . . . [My people want] to be accepting and tolerant, and yet [they are] feeling lost and unsure how to navigate in this multifaith, relativistic, increasingly secular society. Many of our older members are completely mystified as to why their kids and grandkids have seemingly abandoned the very faith they learned in those "glory day" Sunday schools . . . .

I also saw myself in your book . . . realizing right after starting pastoral ministry that my seminary education (as good as it was) had prepared me largely for a context that no longer existed. Then there was the frantic "trying to find stuff that worked" phase. And of course, the guilt at not being able to suddenly turn things around. After all, don't great leaders have a "compelling vision" and "get the right people on board"?

This pastor's feelings express her church's struggle over the loss of the map of modernity. But what's wrong with modernity? Why has this map failed us? Modernity disempowered tradition, giving individuals the illusion that they could determine who and what they wanted to be independent of outside influences.

In his book *After Virtue,* Alasdair MacIntyre attacks this foundational assumption of modernity. He writes, "We are never more (and some times less) than the co-authors of our own narratives. Only in fantasy do we live what story we please. In life . . . we are always under certain constraints." He then uses the metaphor of the stage to explain what he means. We are born and "enter upon a stage we did not design and we find ourselves part of an action that was not of our making."[7] This metaphor gives us a fresh perspective on what it means to be human beings born into a contingent world of particular histories. The stage is already set when we arrive on the scene—there is a large backdrop that frames the action, a series of scenes and drops that contextualize various actions and events played out on the stage. Without this larger background, the players would be hard pressed to communicate the meaning of their actions. There are props—objects like chairs or office furniture already infused with meaning that communicate a context for the actions of the players on the stage. The actors are performing (not necessarily in any kind of mechanical or deterministic manner) and interpreting a script that communicates to those watching the actions. All of this, taken together, represents a story or narrative that has meaning for those shaped by the world represented by the stage.

Continuing the stage metaphor, MacIntyre compares the self to a player. "The characters never start literally *ab initio*; they plunge *in media res*, the beginnings of their story already made for them by what and who has gone before."[8] This metaphor does not imply some blind determinism controlling one's life. It establishes that we are not self-creating individuals in the Cartesian sense but human beings who, by necessity, are deeply embedded in the contingencies of our histories. This is how we know and are able to engage the world. We cannot begin where we please or simply jump over or ignore our own historical contexts in reaching for some pure idea, principle, or abstraction. We are constrained in our view of the world by our time and place, by the actions of others, and by the social settings of our lives. But as MacIntyre points out, "It is crucial that at any given point in an enacted dramatic narrative we do not know what will happen next . . . . Unpredictability . . . is required by the narrative of human life."[9] This genuine open-endedness of life invites human beings into a creative and emergent future rather than simply a script actors play out mechanically on a stage—which actors never really do in the first place.

For MacIntyre, a human being enters a society already filled with its stock of stories and narratives, which, like the stage, give that society its meaning and suggest its directions and ends (its teleologies). Through these stories and narratives our lives are formed—this is how children are shaped within communities that tell the stories of the community and the myths of how and why their particular community (family, clan or tribe, specific group, church, or culture) came to be and the reasons it exists and behaves in the ways it does. "There is no way to give us an understanding of any society, including our own, except through the stock of stories which constitute its initial dramatic resources."[10]

Modernity tried to eliminate the stage of the narrative that would guide imaginations. By questioning the source of truth and knowledge, as well as developing a method of attaining truth and knowledge, it tried to free individuals to have their own independent imaginations. The modern experiment has revealed such a goal as pointless, as modernity itself became the stage. We were born the children of modernity; its maps continue to shape us even though they do not reflect reality but determine our primary way to interpret reality.

AN IN-BETWEEN TIME

The maps of modernity have been challenged and come up short. We don't need philosophers like MacIntyre to tell us that the maps don't fit. This sense that our maps no longer describe the in-between place were we find ourselves is described by some as a shift to a post-modern world. The language of postmodernity helps some make sense of their experience of in-between, uncertainty, the venture into the unknown. If we are attentive, we can see indications of how new maps might be shaped.

The changes in physics during the twentieth century represent an early indicator. For scientists in the eighteenth century, the atom, an image at once as old as the Greeks and as recent as the invention of the telescope, formed their basic understanding of how the physical world operated. This picture undergirded Newton's laws, forming our primary map of the universe until the beginning of the twentieth century. Most people born in the first three-quarters of the last century were born onto a stage that understood atoms to be the basic explanatory framework for reality. The explanations of atoms were given in terms of distinct, separate "objects" interacting with one another. This idea of independent, separate objects was one of the key inner maps of the modern period. We built almost all of our understanding of life around this model. Human beings were separate and independent individuals interacting with one another; organizations and institutions were perceived in the same way. What we always saw, therefore, were these independent objects. This meant we were always looking for way to define, manage, and control independent objects in order to get the outcomes we wanted. There was little sense that this map was actually omitting a huge amount of information by paying little attention to the interconnections and networks that shaped our world, which were considered "background noise" that had to be cleared out of the way in order to see the "real" object. We were so programmed to see the world as objects that we missed the point: instead of a world of manageable objects, there is a world of interconnections and dynamic networks always interacting in so many different and diverse ways that we can never really be in control. At the beginning of the last century, the map of modernity was being transformed by developments in relativity and quantum mechanics.[11] The following comments, capture the experience of a young Werner Heisenberg near the beginning of the twentieth century, are a striking illustration of what happens when the maps of one's known world are torn up:

> Exploration of the atomic and subatomic world brought scientists in contact with a strange and unexpected reality that shattered the foundations of their world and forced them to think in entirely new ways .... In the twentieth century ... physicists faced, for the first time, a serious challenge to their ability to understand the universe.... In their struggle to grasp this new reality, scientist became painfully aware that their basic concepts, their language, and their whole way of thinking were inadequate to describe the new phenomenon. Their problem was not only intellectual but involved intense emotional and existential experience, as vividly described by Werner Heisenberg: "I remember discussions with Bohr which went through many hours till very late at night and ended almost in despair; and when at the end of the discussion I went for a walk in the neighboring park I repeated to myself again and again the question: Can nature possibly be so absurd as it seemed to us in these atomic experiments?"[12]

Note the language describing this experience. A change in our map of the world is much more than an intellectual shift. It involves a deep emotional struggle, not just a conscious, intellectual conflict; some of the most strongly held convictions in our lives are challenged and deconstructed. Like a ship foundered by the submerged 90 percent of an iceberg, we figuratively hit all the submerged levels of assumed beliefs and frameworks that have guided our lives for so long. Even people with the brilliance of Bohr and Heisenberg go through this disorienting process. Their worlds are torn up. They refuse, at first, to believe what confronts them. They are compelled to say, "The world can't look like this; it's too different from how I have come to experience it!" Who could have imagined, for example, just a short while ago a world shaped by muons, neutrinos, quarks, and gluons?[13] Who could have imagined melting ice caps, or ten- and fifteen-year droughts in the mid-twentieth century in places that were lush and fertile, like the northeastern grasslands of Australia? Who would have expected SARS or AIDS or al-Qaeda? When U.S. soldiers invaded Afghanistan and then Iraq, it looked like the "shock and awe" power of high technology was still shaping the world. Then small bands of nearly invisible insurgents strung together a bunch of disparate artifacts (like parts of a cell phone, a watch, and the simple action of text messaging) to produce what is now euphemistically called an IED (improvised explosive device), and the heavily strategized shock and awe seemed powerless before this made-up menace designed by nearly invisible networks of highly committed radicals. The old banners of "mission accomplished" were suddenly twisting in confusion before this new reality. The world of atoms and objects was a world of predictability and control where plans could be made and outcomes described, but this new in-between world is one in which the most important elements of change are not clear and distinct objects that can be located and defined: they are networks and intersections of people who cannot be located; they are on the move and innovating in order to thrive in a new world. These are networks and innovations (like IEDs) that cannot be predicted with any accuracy, but what they are doing is transforming the landscape of our reality. In this landscape, the established benchmarks for success (the primary objects we defined as a significant, such as armies, guns, and airplanes) are displaced by radically different kinds of indicators. This is the new world we have entered.

The massive changes to our maps make reality far stranger than the commonsense pictures modernity gave us. Who could have believed the reality of cloning or stem cell research? These discoveries offer potential cures for diseases while creating ethical dilemmas hardly imagined a decade earlier. Who could have predicted the capacity to create human life in a laboratory from one cell of a human being without any of the expected norms of reproduction? One of the often missed points in all this radical shifting of our world is that most of this emerging world is not formed by inadvertent discoveries that usually can't be predicted or named ahead of time through the use of some clear, well-defined method. We have entered a world, to restate Hannah Arendt's observations, where the so-called objective indicators of success may in fact have little to nothing to do with how things actually change. For example, there is still a conviction among church leaders that the way to create healthy churches in this new space is to list the standard indicators of church life (worship, discipleship, evangelism, preaching, passionate spirituality, and so on) and measure how they are doing in a local church. Armed with these measurements, the conviction goes, it is possible to isolate the indicators that need the most work, and the church will then become effective by improving the objective performance of the flagging indicators. But what happens if these weak indicators simply aren't the reasons why churches are getting into more and more trouble? What if modernity's "objective" indicators are actually missing what is happening in this new space by a million miles? What if our way of assessing the health of our churches comes from a modernity that has made us believe there is a "right" way of being the church (and by extension, "right" indicators for measuring our progress), but in fact we are discovering in this time of massive transformation that the world actually *doesn't* operate according to such "objective" indictors? If this is the case, then analyzing these established indicators is actually a dangerous and misguided approach to being the church in a new space. What if the most helpful indictors of how to be the church are to be found in radically different places (which we will discuss later in this book)? What if a church's effectiveness has more to do with what the people in our churches are doing in their conversations across the fence or in coffee shops and almost nothing to do with whether worship or evangelism or discipleship happens in certain kinds of ways? If this is the case, then we are indeed in a revolutionary place as a church; we will need to reimagine a huge amount of what it means to be in leadership, and we will have to come to the uncomfortable recognition that most of the ways we are trying to make the church "healthy" in this new space grow out of the old "shock and awe" tactics rather than an awareness of the new kinds of networks and interactions that characterize our reality. These are the themes that will be addressed in later chapters. These shifts in the locus of our attention and energy as church leaders can still feel so counterintuitive based on our existing maps that to navigate in this new territory, we have to remain alert as to how our old maps continue to shape us.

DIALOGUE WITH MODERN MAPS

In this in-between place, we're moving back and forth across a social and intellectual landscape that is both familiar and alien. We look back to see the shape of the world we knew sinking below the horizon. We've left a shore, but its ways still shape us. The path forward will require that we learn to do things that will feel odd and even counterintuitive to the leadership habits and skills bequeathed to us by modernity. Rather than grand schemes (vision and mission statements) or attention to the usual objective indicators of success, we will need to become comfortable with living in a world were we don't have answers but build communities of dialogue, both inside and outside the church, in which ordinary men and women discover that the imagination for thriving in this new space is among them in their everyday lives. The maps of modernity cause us to place high value on getting enough data and information about an object that we can diagnose and then predict outcomes. In the new terrain, we will need other kinds of skills and habits.

As a teenager, I left my home in the inner city of Liverpool, England, and immigrated to Canada. I'll never forget walking the gangplank onto the boat. Despite my sense of entering a new adventure, I was crying hard but not wanting anyone to know how difficult it was to leave the place that had formed my imagination. As the boat sailed out into the River Mersey and the Irish Sea, I stood on deck, refusing to move, watching my world disappear on the horizon. Darkness came as I watched the last light of the sun reflect off the lowering coast, and then all that was left was endless ocean. My life would be transformed. Within me resided all the maps of being a poor, working-class boy from Liverpool, all the street smarts of survival among gangs. I had no idea that most of those maps could not help me navigate the new world I was about to enter. I had no idea I was entering an in-between world that would lead me to compare and contrast the world I knew with the world that was staring me in the face.

Certain maps have dominated our imagination of what it means to be the church in North America—the maps of certainty and control, the maps that told us that with the right amount of data we could create our preferred futures, the maps that said the church would remain at the center of our culture. At the same time, other movements and themes in modernity (such as the rights of the individual and the dominant belief that faith was personal and had little to do with the world of hard facts and truth) tended to marginalize the churches into ghettos of personal faith and private experiences. Modernity has never been a single thing, a straight line, as it were, that was easy to map and clear to describe in relationship to the church. Through the modern period in America, for example, it has been assumed that the church played a central role in society (this is far less so in the UK and simply not the case in Europe, where there are multiple expressions of modernity, what we call *multiple modernities*). In Europe prior to the seventeenth century, a congruence existed between the overarching values and frameworks of Western culture and the church. Modernity fundamentally changed that congruence. In Europe, this change was radical; in America, it was far less radical but just as significant, as the church was sidelined to the personal and private spheres of the individual's life. Modernity is formed around beliefs about the autonomy of human reason, the self as the center of being, the rational self as the generator of meaning, and the power of the new empirical sciences. As modernity became the map of the Western world, within America emerged a functional Christianity that still saw itself as an essential part of the culture but was increasingly functioning only in the private, personal side of people's lives. So effective was this transition that few people even to this day see the problem of churches focused only on personal, private life with a few forays into what is called social action or mission trips. The church in America has continued to operate successfully within the American cultural expression of modernity. We are in the midst of a process of leaving this comfortable world for something quite different.

What does the uncertainty of this in-between place this mean for us? Catholic theologian and philosopher Louis Dupré helps us understand how we should respond to the current shift by describing the emergence of modernity:

> Cultural changes such as the one that gave birth to the modern age have a definitive and irreversible impact that transforms the very essence of reality. . . . Those who in a particular epoch impose a new pattern of meaning on the life and thought of their time do more than apply a different film of thought on an indifferent reality. They transform the nature of reality itself. . . . Cultural changes leave a different reality in their wake.[14]

When a major cultural transformation occurs, people's basic understanding of reality changes. New patterns of thinking and acting emerge. As a result, cultures begin to act, organize, lead, and think differently. The question for church leaders is how to translate Christian belief and practice into an emerging context where we still don't know what the church might look like and cannot predict its shape because we are in an uncertain space that keeps taking different and at times unthinkably contradictory forms. The end of the medieval period illustrates this challenge, when the transition from a medieval Catholic to a post-Reformation, modern world affected organizational and ecclesiastical forms of church life. Leadership frameworks of the medieval period—the ecclesiastical forms of leadership, structures of power and authority, relationships between clergy and laity, church and state, and organizational forms of church life—did not simply disappear; instead, they all confronted an emerging modernity. Leading out of the habits and perceptions of the medieval mind-set and into the emerging modernity was no easy transition. The Thirty Years' War, the Counter-Reformation, the Radical Reformation, and the ensuing political formations of nation-states were all elements of this difficult and complex transition. Dupre's point is applicable here: significant cultural upheavals change how we come to see reality. Such large-scale changes challenge commonsense views and undermine habits and practices we've taken for granted. We are shifting from one epoch to another.[15] If the church in the West is to engage this new space, its leaders must understand what is going on in this transition from modernity to something else in order to embrace the discontinuity of the in-between. The future does not emerge out of nothing. The opportunity of this in-between time is to reenter our traditions and the biblical narratives to imagine new ways of being the church. Scripture and tradition are filled with stories and examples of how, in these in-between places, the Spirit gives God's people new imagination—the shift in the church's epicenter from Jerusalem to Antioch being one example. We are living in such a moment.

WHAT THIS IN-BETWEEN SPACE MEANS FOR CHURCH LEADERS

In the TV series *Survivor,* high-functioning individuals who do well in the equilibrium of their known worlds are relocated to places where most of their success skills aren't applicable. The challenges they face each week extend their levels of disequilibrium. The group must discover skills and competencies, new ways of working together, in a radically alternative context so that they can survive. The experience of church leaders reflects the *Survivor* world more than the pastoral leadership models taught in seminary.

Lesslie Newbigin speaks to those of us trying to survive in the in-between by describing how modernity shaped the self-understanding of the church and took the Gospel captive.[16] Newbigin's critique of the Western church is that the Gospel was absorbed into and neutralized by the thought forms of modernity. As a contrast, he holds up the way the early church fathers became map-makers. Theirs was a massive intellectual undertaking that engaged the biblical narrative with classical thought through the medium of the Greek language. For the apologists of the early church (for example, people like Justinian or the Cappadocians), the heart of the Christian message was a radically new fact: God had acted. Newbigin writes:

> God had acted in a way that, if believed, must henceforth determine all our ways of thinking. It could not merely fit into existing ways of understanding the world without fundamentally changing them. According to Athanasius, it provided a new *arche,* a new starting point for all human understanding of the world. It could not form part of any worldview except one of which it was the basis, but at the same time it could only be communicated to the world of classical thought by using the language of classical thought.[17]

From the New Testament time forward, believers struggled to communicate Christianity's "new and revolutionary fact in ways that could be grasped in the thought forms of classical culture and [at the same time] prevent the biblical message from being absorbed and neutralized by [classical culture]."[18]

The radical implications of the Incarnation needed time to be grasped; the intellectual struggle lasted several centuries. Without this engagement of believers with their changing cultures, "Christianity would have gradually disappeared, absorbed into the general mix of pagan religiosity in which we are free to construct our own images of God."[19] The Incarnation required a radically new way of thinking about God, one that challenged and overcame the dualisms of its time. The Incarnation made it clear that the Christian story could not be fit into or judged by the assumptions that controlled classical thought. It was from this starting point that the church was compelled to confess the Trinitarian nature of God the Creator and Sustainer and Father of Jesus Christ.[20]

Newbigin's insights about the Incarnation provide some guidance for map-making in the in-between state. First, we can't develop new maps without an appreciation of the maps that have shaped Christian life in the past; hence the importance of understanding modernity. Too many people today are jumping forward into the so-called postmodern church experience without a clear picture of how modernity has actually shaped the church to this point. As a result, much of what is labeled "postmodern" or "emergent" is little more than the modern church repackaged. Without this robust wrestling, we will skip over the in-between state on the assumption that we know what it means to be the church in this new era.

Second, new maps must emerge through an engagement with the biblical narrative. When a world that has shaped us comes to an end, we neither suddenly nor automatically find ourselves transported into some new "promised land" flowing with milk and honey. The Spirit of God invites us to enter again the biblical stories in order to reshape our imagination and thereby our future. In this process, we become participants in the story. Our situation, for example, is similar to that of the church in Antioch. The mission of the church in the Roman, Gentile world came out of this young church. But it also came out of confusion, conflict, and disequilibrium (for example, what did it mean to be a follower of Jesus and a Gentile? What sort of control and power did Jerusalem have over the Gentile Christians? What were the rules for living in this new church made up of Gentiles?). We are in an awkward place that is like Israel's desert after the flight from Egypt, wandering and chaotic. Once the euphoria of freedom ended, the hard part of the change journey began. In this in-between location, the skills of the old, known world don't work the way they once did. At the same time, it is unclear what skills are needed.

The story of the apostle Paul is especially insightful. His encounter with Jesus Christ shifted him away from the equilibrium of being at the center of Judaism and pushed him into confusion and chaos. The result was an exhilarating, liberating, difficult, anxious, and troublesome process, not a smooth change from one reality to another. He had to redraw the maps of his theological imagination and his understanding of what God was up to in the world. The shift of the church's center from Jerusalem to Antioch meant that early Christians had to be converted from some fundamental assumptions of their collective imagination. Leaders—Peter, for example—were taken through encounters where their imaginations were transformed and their most basic maps challenged. One can only guess what it must have done to the imaginative world of Jewish Christians, filled as they were with their scriptural promises of a new creation that had Jerusalem as its center, to face the reality that the Spirit of God was shifting the center away from Jerusalem to Antioch. Many would not have been able to assign such meaning to the events. To them, the shift would have signaled disaster and terrible loss.

This transformation must have caused incredible disequilibrium for the leadership of the young church. Paul's ongoing wrestling with the question of his own people and their place in God's drama of salvation, evident in the book of Romans, illustrates this flux and transition. The young church quickly entered a transition in its adherents' way of thinking and being. The New Testament is witness to the difficulty of that transition. We are in an equally ambiguous situation where confusion, anger, and disequilibrium become our everyday experiences.

From honest engagement with both the Scriptures and the demise of modernity, Old Testament theologian Walter Brueggemann provides helpful descriptions:

> Let me remind readers that I intend this judgment to be descriptive. It is not a recommendation, or a proposal, or a celebration. . . . It is simply, I propose, the great social reality of our time and place. We are unable to detect fully why this long-established imaginative construal should now, at this particular juncture, be exhausted. It may be exhausted simply because it has had a long run, a longer run that any to which it was entitled. . . . It may be that it is God's own spirit that is causing its demise and collapse, for this is indeed a God "who brings to naught the things that exist" (1 Corinthians 1:28). . . . This much I know. . . . The loss of that world is enormously frightening and disturbing to us all. . . . Our culture is one in which the old imagined world is lost, but still powerfully cherished, and in which there is bewilderment and fear, because there is no clear way on how to order our shared imagination differently or better.[21]

Transition is not a zone to move through quickly. It is the place where the imagination for God's future can be born or, in the words of Hannah Arendt, the place that contains the moment of truth. It's the place where we reengage the narratives of Scripture so that they challenge us afresh. In Scripture, the place of transition is where fresh theological imagination is formed. In a culture that tosses tradition onto the dust heap of an irrelevant past and has become strange and alien to the Gospel, entering into this transition is the way we develop new maps.

These two principles from Newbigin, the mutual importance of understanding modernity and understanding Scripture as we move ahead to construct our maps, lead me to a third: the new maps are made on the journey; they can't be drawn ahead of time (by some form of strategic planning or organizational change to create a "missional" system). On this journey, we'll need to let go of some common-sense convictions and address anxieties about not being in control. An illustration from the world of biology might explain what appears at first glance to be a counterintuitive idea and offer important insights into our discussion of how a missional future emerges in the North American church. The massive revolution occurring in enzymes, genetics, and biotechnology is having unimagined impacts on our daily lives, and the emerging world of biomedical technology seems more like science fiction than common sense. Arthur Kornberg, professor emeritus at Stanford University's school of medicine, received the Nobel Prize for his work in the study of enzymes. In an address delivered at an awards ceremony in October 2000, he described how scientists do their work of discovering concrete, practical solutions to human disease. First, he uses the rather unusual metaphor of hunters and gatherers to describe the work of scientists. This is not the refined image we would expect. Hunters and gathers are more suggestive of premodern people scurrying about in search of food. How do hunter-gatherer researchers go about their work? What is the "plan" they use to discover the revolutionary solutions that are emerging in the drugs and therapies we could not have even conceived of a decade ago? How did they map their way to these discoveries? His response is as astounding and nonsensical as the revolution itself.

> With regard to medical research, the best plan over many decades has been no plan at all. The breakthrough of recombinant DNA and genetic engineering, based on the discoveries of enzymes that make and break and seal DNA, were made in academic laboratories. . . . For thirty years, my research on the biosynthesis of the building blocks of nucleic acids, their assembly in DNA replication and the training of more than one hundred young scientists was funded . . . without any promise or expectation that this research would lead to marketable products or procedures. . . . We carried out these studies to satisfy a need to understand the basic processes in cellular fusion. Yet to my great pleasure, such studies of the replication, repair and rearrangements of DNA have had many practical benefits. . . . It may seem unreasonable and impractical, call it counterintuitive, that we can solve urgent problems such as a disease by pursuing apparently unrelated questions in basic biology, chemistry or physics. Yet the pursuit of understanding the basic facts of nature has proven throughout the history of medical science to be the most practical, the most cost-effective route to successful drugs and devices. . . . Investigations that seemed irrelevant to any practical objective have yielded most

of the major discoveries in medicine: X-rays, MRI, penicillin, polio vaccine.[22]

The nature of the creative process that births a new future, with all its revolutionary practical solutions, is not always what common sense dictates. Kornberg suggests that the way to "discover" solutions is, first, by investing one's energies and skills in engaging the most fundamental questions of the system; second, by being shaped by the long tradition within which one has lived; third, by investing oneself in raising up a new generation who are able to do this foundational reflection within the tradition; and fourth, by recognizing that one is not in control of predicting what these practical, revolutionary solutions are going to look like. These are the nutrients of the soil in which a revolutionary future emerges.

The implications for mapping a future in churches and denominations are massive. We cannot predict the shape of our new maps from where we are right now. But if we dare reenter Scripture from the perspective of the edges, of liminality, to read our own traditions from this perspective without the need to create solutions and control outcomes, the maps will emerge.

CHAPTER THREE

WHEN COMMON SENSE IS NO LONGER COMMON

In his book *Beyond the Post-Modern Mind*, Huston Smith observes:

> Quietly, irrevocably, something enormous has happened to Western man. His outlook on life and the world has changed so radically that in the perspective of history the twentieth century is likely to rank— with the fourth century, which witnessed the triumph of Christianity, and the seventeenth, which signaled the dawn of modern science— as one of the very few that have instigated genuinely new epochs in human thought. In this change, which is still in process, we of the current generation are playing a crucial but as yet not widely recognized part.[1]

Smith's words give those of us living in this in-between world language to describe what we are going through. We live in a time when the old perspective is passing and the new has yet to emerge. We are "playing a crucial but as yet not widely recognized part" of being map-makers.

Good map-makers do more than logically describe what is going on. They *enter into the experience of the in-between*, engaging the emotions that come with realizing that common sense is no longer common. The changes identified in the first two chapters are so huge that when we see what is happening, we find ourselves lost and without clear direction. Canadian journalist Alanna Mitchell is one of those people who learned for herself what it means to discover that the commonsense understanding of the world no longer applies to the huge, unthinkable changes we are all moving through. Her book *Sea Sick* tells the story of what is happening right now in our oceans, and it's neither what we expected nor how we tend to think about global warming.[2] We tend to think that the problem in the oceans has to do with things like overfishing and the collapse of fish stocks or the warming of currents. But beneath the obvious is the unthinkable, and it is a crisis beyond imagination. The oceans, writes Mitchell, do two critical things for the planet. First, they produce a huge amount of our oxygen, and second, they clean carbon dioxide. The primary source of these two critical processes is tiny, unnoticed, and hardly considered creatures called *plankton*. These humble one-celled organisms, rather than the spectacular rain forests, are the true lungs of the planet. A third, more obvious role of plankton is that it's the primary food base for some of the largest mammals, such as whales.

Traveling with a group of scientists studying the effects of global warming on the oceans, Mitchell describes their stunning realization that the plankton are dying off at an alarming rate. The earth is being given the equivalent of a diagnosis that its lungs are seriously ill and may no longer be able to sustain life. In Mitchell's words, when one of the scientists looking at the data saw what it was telling her, she ran to the bathroom to vomit. That's how startling and jolting the new, in-between space was for her. We find ourselves at an unthinkable new place on so many levels. Only those who feel and experience the depth of this transition and change we are in will be able to become map-makers for a new world and a different church. The reasons for this are not difficult to explain. If we don't feel the depths of our own crisis like the scientist did in her field, we won't be compelled to think beyond our existing maps. Without this deep, visceral sense that something unimaginable is taking place in our world, we will remain committed to our established certainties and try to make them work again; we will stay inside our established categories, believing that they only need to be touched up or reworked.

This refusal to acknowledge the sea change all around us is precisely what is still happening in our churches and among our leaders when we assume that our crisis can be fixed by working harder at things like improved worship, better preaching, more effective discipleship, and more passionate spirituality. The lessons we are learning from the in-between space is that these standard categories are not the real effects, nor are they primary drivers of the change. We are learning that like the plankton in the oceans or the IEDs described in the Chapter Two, the real drivers of all this change are the unexpected, the things we don't see and can't predict. We are all like Alan Greenspan, the expert who managed the financial economy until it all came crashing down when he finally confessed, "I never saw it coming." The cold, chilling effects of our new reality awaken the pioneers of this in-between space to the recognition that the standard categories and the established maps can be reworked forever, but they will never allow us to navigate the world emerging in front of us.

Without new categories to describe what is happening, we can only describe our existing habits and practices, but we will never be able to face the deeply disorienting experience of being in a new space where we are no longer in control, no longer the experts. To make new maps, we need a language that helps us understand the emotional experience of living and leading in this in-between state. Mitchell's book is an example of how people in the field of ocean science are learning that language and, in so doing, recognizing that their established categories are missing the true picture of what is happening under the seas. Only by allowing ourselves to enter this kind of experience and learn a new language will we navigate the uncertainty and the troubling emotions that are part of the process of mapping a new reality.

OUR CULTURE PREDETERMINES OUR CATEGORIES

Fundamental to the language of the in-between is an understanding of how the culture we live in predetermines the categories we use to read our world. American poet e. e. cummings said that if you have something to hide, hide it in the sun. In other words, the things we assume and take for granted are the very things we can lose the ability to see. This is why relationships fall apart if couples take each other for granted. I travel a great deal and am away from home a lot. What keeps me sane in the midst of all the traveling is the awareness that everything at home stays the pretty much the same. Once in a while,

Jane rearranges the furniture while I'm away or buys something new. Because I'm so used to the way things are around the house, days might go by before I notice the new additions or see that the house has changed. What we take for granted we usually don't see. Our well-worn maps are like that. Imagine trying to teach a goldfish the meaning of water, which would be almost impossible to do. When something lives inside an environment as pervasive as water, it loses the capacity to see its presence. The very thing that gives life becomes invisible; it's not seen because it's everywhere.

This is how culture works.[3] Culture is to humans what water is to fish. Most of the time, we don't think about our culture; it's just the conventional, "commonsense" way of living. Just as a fish would never think about the water as long as the delicate balance it requires to live remains unchanged, so we tend not to think about how culture shapes our lives. When there is a high degree of consensus within a group about the symbols, images, stories, roles, habits, and practices that give meaning, people experience their culture as working well; the consensus validates the map that makes sense of their world.

The way churches and leaders behave, believe, and act is very much like the way a fish operates in water: the culture is not seen, yet it shapes how they organize their lives, interact with their environment, and understand themselves. Local churches and denominations, for example, are organizational systems with a life and dynamic of their own that gives them shape and meaning. In this sense, they are like a living organism. In fact, the biological metaphor of an organism is a helpful way to understand the organizational culture of churches and denominational systems. The stated purpose, structures, and roles of a church, for example, are a function of its formation in a larger story over a significant length of time. In Western societies, for example, there was a long period of time in the medieval and early modern periods in which churches lived in a dynamic equilibrium with the culture. We have come to call this period Christendom and know it well from all the critiques that have been voiced about the church and its captivity to Christendom. At bottom, these critiques stemmed from the conviction that the church became too much like, or synonymous with, the people groups, nations, habits, and outlooks where it was located. For example, up to the latter part of the twentieth century, a relatively high level of integration and equilibrium existed between the story and culture of most churches and the primary cultural stories of North America and Europe. These churches were just like any other organism. Churches and their leaders, functioning in dynamic equilibrium with their cultures, assumed that theirs was simply the normal and appropriate way of "being the church." We need to understand something of this concept of equilibrium in order to see how the church and its leadership have been shaped by the culture of modernity. A way to do that is by looking at how the notion is used in the field of biology.

In biology, equilibrium describes a symbiotic relationship between an organism and its environment. *Equilibrium* is a simple concept with huge implications. It is the zone of balance where the elements an organism requires for life are in sync with its environment. In dynamic equilibrium, it's as if the organism is on autopilot, thriving in its roles and perceptions of reality. This principle of equilibrium is behind every organism's search for balance and harmony within its environment. A water droplet, for example, resting on a solid, flat surface obeys certain laws of physics as it draws its mass together into a spheroid shape that exemplifies its stable, resting state—an equilibrium that holds several conflicting forces together in balance.

When an organism or organization operates in an extended period of equilibrium, as the church did in twentieth-century America or a young child in a secure home throughout the growing-up years, the world makes sense because things function around a coherent unity of taken-for-granted symbols and meaning that give shape and direction to accepted actions and relationships. A humorous story illustrates this sense of coherence and equilibrium we all take for granted when our world works as we expect. For many years, Jane was the principal of a small, private school in downtown Toronto. Our three children, Paul, Sara Jane, and Aaron, were students there and so went with their mom every day to school. It was a wonderful period of equilibrium, and our children all have fond memories of their days at "Toronto Central." One day, Jane and I were talking with friends around the kitchen table about work and vocation. Our three children almost always joined us at the table when friends came for meals. On this occasion, Aaron was still a young boy listening in on the adult situation as he sat on my lap. In the midst of this talk about work, he looked at his mom and said, "But you don't have a job, do you, Mom?" His world was so integrated and in equilibrium that for all intents and purposes, his mom didn't go to work!

THE ENDING OF EQUILIBRIUMS

I remember one Christmas at the church I led as a young pastor in Newmarket, Ontario. This sleepy town of about nineteen thousand people was just entering a period of explosive growth; over the next twenty-five years, it was transformed into a bedroom community of some sixty thousand people. But in the mid-1970s, it still had the feel of an old market town even as new, young families moved into recently built subdivisions. This Christmas, a church member wanted a huge tree cut from his front lawn. A group of friends and I volunteered to cut it down and use is as the Christmas tree inside our beautiful old church. Ten of us dragged it across Main Street, up the steps, and into the church. Stood up, it was over thirty feet tall and reached halfway to the ceiling. Once decorated with lights, it was beautiful, giving our candlelight service a special sense of place. Outside, snow covered the earth, and inside, the tree, the choir, the readings, friends, and the carols all gave a sense of wonderful connection to a long past. Those members whose roots went far back into the town's history were thrilled with how the "young, new" pastor was leading the congregation. They had a sense of returning to and recovering the wonderful days gone by when the church not only stood at the center of the town as a building but also as the main locus of community for those who lived there. As I led that candlelight service, I sensed their joy and expectation. But something else was happening inside me: I sensed that this wonderful moment was little more than a symbol of a time now gone that could only be recovered fleetingly. Huge changes were afoot in the town and among the new people moving into its expanding subdivisions. The equilibrium of these people and their church was going to be stretched to the breaking point. I looked over the full building that evening while leading a joyful event and wondered what was going to happen. Where was I to find the resources to engage the messy, complex changes about to rock our long-standing balance?

The symbols, stories, habits, and methods we develop to cultivate equilibrium explain why everything seems to work so well that we hardly question or challenge our ways of doing things. But like an organism, sooner or later a culture is challenged by a changing environment and must adapt. As wonderful as the Toronto school was for our children, there came a day when Mom was no longer the principal and we no longer drove as a family downtown to school. The world that had been so secure and generative for our three children shifted on its axis, and our way of living as a family was transformed as we moved not just to new schools but to a new city and new roles. When our environments change, we must learn new ways of living and develop ways of engaging the world we are entering. Without adaptation, individuals and organizations lose the ability to thrive. Like organisms, they can shrivel and die.

When the environment changes, the people and organizations in that culture enter a period of discontinuous change where the habits and practices they developed no longer seem to work. The discontinuity parallels the confusion and frustration people feel because they keep calling on their established ways of doing things, but those practices, habits, and skills, along with the conventional wisdom they took for granted, have ceased to help them in the new environment. Without some form of adaptation, people, groups, and organizations become disoriented, confused, reactive, and ultimately dysfunctional. Leaders encounter this when working within denominational systems in the midst of disruptive change. The fact that the culture of their church systems has changed is clear. They can point to declining membership across churches, and they see the dwindling of resources and income, but at the same time, they are confused and disoriented because the skills, habits, roles, and attitudes that used to help them succeed no longer do. In a period of discontinuous change, organizational structures, leadership styles, habits, and attitudes that once functioned well become prisons. The former equilibrium that gave organizations the ability to thrive becomes instead a source of confusion, frustration, and loss. Some illustrations of this shift taken from history, nature, and contemporary life will help make this point.

History

In her wonderful biography of Galileo, *Galileo's Daughter,* Dava Sobel describes Galileo's conflict with the church over the question of whether the earth was the center of the universe or rotated on its axis as it traveled about the sun.[4] Such questions would not concern us. Our commonsense understanding is that the earth does rotate around its sun. In Galileo's day, common sense required a radically different understanding. Since Aristotle, in the fourth century B.C., and Ptolemy, in the second century A.D., common sense placed the earth at the center of the universe. It was believed that Scripture, the central source of truth, confirmed this as fact. This long-established, conventional wisdom permeated seventeenth-century Europe. Astronomers built models and designed maps that explained the movements of the heavens based on the conviction that the earth was the center of the universe. The model wasn't "broken" nor was it questioned; indeed, it was used to navigate the globe. Equilibrium existed between this understanding of the universe and the travels of explorers; their maps worked for them.

This belief in a stationary earth at the center of the universe had been the conventional wisdom for over a thousand years and was deeply embedded in people's imagination. Sobel captures its power when describing the arguments church leaders made against Galileo. She states that his writing about the earth rotating on an axis about the sun was "the most stunning reversal of perception ever to have jarred intelligent thought: We are not the center of the universe. The immobility of our world is an illusion. We spin. We speed through space. We circle the sun. We live on a wandering star." She shows the power of the conventional wisdom that had worked so well and resulted in such an extensive sense of equilibrium for so long:

> The apparent steadiness of the Earth lulls the mind into a false stability. The body's footing feels so secure that the mind naturally interprets the daily bobbing up and down of the Sun, the Moon, the planets, and the stars as motions entirely external to the Earth. . . . This incontrovertible perception of earthly rest gains support on every hand. . . . If the earth really turned toward the east at a high velocity, falling leaves would all scatter to the west of the trees. Wouldn't they? Wouldn't a cannon fired to the west carry further than a salvo to the east?[5]

While this is no longer our world, we can imagine how deeply embedded this way of perceiving and reading the world must have been before Galileo turned his primitive telescope toward the sun and noticed the revolution of sunspots across its sphere. His observations birthed a revolution that changed the world.

Nature

The authors of *Surfing the Edge of Chaos* recount the story of the dodo, a bird whose habitat was in the South Pacific.[6] Prior to European colonization, the dodo had lived for a long period in equilibrium with its environment. With few predators, this large bird had lost the capacity for flight. When Europeans arrived with firearms, the dodo's world was disastrously transformed into massive disequilibrium in a very brief period of time. The bird had no adaptive defenses and was soon extinct. The dodo is not the only example of a disruption to equilibrium that wipes out a species. "In Hawaii, prolonged isolation gave rise to species of plants and bird life that lacked defenses found in more diverse environments. There was no real threat from indigenous browsing animals, so plants bore no toxins or thorns. Many species of birds found it more convenient to nest on the ground. After the introduction of rats, pigs, goats, and mongooses, 88 percent of Hawaii's native birds and 10 percent of its plants disappeared."[7]

Contemporary Life

In *The Lexus and the Olive Tree,* Thomas Friedman describes how his world of understanding as a *New York Times* reporter was thrown into chaos by, symbolically, the fall of the Berlin Wall at the end of the 1980s. The wall symbolized a Cold War world of dynamic equilibrium that had existed for much of the twentieth century—since before Friedman was even born. Three generations had known nothing but the geopolitical world formed in the first third of the last century with the establishment of the Union of Soviet Socialist Republics under Lenin. That world came to be shaped around some simple, basic stories and myths that formed a culture defined by terrifying political, social, economic, and military dichotomies. The cultural story of this period and its ways of framing reality for generations of men and women in the twentieth century can be illustrated in Table 3.1.

The list could be extended, but the point is made. Within this bipolar world, nations were identified by their relationship to this basic reading of the world. They were labeled as either aligned or nonaligned countries—sides had to be taken; there was little room

East	West
Communism	Democracy
Totalitarianism	Free World
State Socialism	Capitalism
Soviet Union	United States
Dark Empire	One Nation Under God

Table 3.1.   Cultural Equilibrium of the Twentieth-Century World

for neutrality in the Cold War era. Military strategy on both sides of the Iron Curtain was designed to thwart the other, even to the point of having huge arsenals of ballistic missiles aimed at each other's countries in a defense strategy known as MAD, for *mutually assured destruction.*

This world, Friedman points out, was not difficult to understand even if there were many complexities in its details. It was a world of alignments and simple rules. It was a world governed by signs and symbols—the Hammer and Sickle versus the Stars and Stripes, the Berlin Wall versus open freeways and automobiles, collectives versus individuals, Ronald Reagan versus Mikhail Gorbachev. Everyone understood the rules and knew how to take a side. This was an awesome cultural standoff, a world in dynamic equilibrium, where the balance of images, stories, and habits formed a culture in which people (and countries) know how to live in mutual coexistence whether they liked it or not.[8]

In the final decade of the twentieth century, this Cold War world fell apart. A new era of uncertainly emerged, filled with a confusion of values and purposes. The name given to this new space is *globalization.* It is neither a return to equilibrium nor the end of history. In this globalizing world, amazing contradictions exist side by side. Older fundamentalisms have reemerged in forms that scare many (the drive of Islamic fundamentalism in places like Pakistan or its reactions to difference in a place like the Netherlands, where a movie-maker was gunned down for making a video about Islam). At the same time, new ethnic nationalisms (such as Hizballah in Lebanon) function with high-tech cell phones and fight wars with established armies using IEDs. The communications revolution of the Internet and cell phones draws some people closer together while it also becomes the means for terrorism to thrive in small cells in many unknown locations from Birmingham to Beirut.

From within this in-between place, leaders of nations seek to engage a changed environment with the habits and values of the world that has so recently passed from sight. As Joshua Cooper Ramo states, "Some of the best minds of our era are still in the thrall to an older way of seeing and thinking."[9] Some leaders try to restore equilibrium by reasserting a millennial vision of making all the world's governments into democracies through force of arms; others seek to restore religious theocracy through force of arms. Driving them all is the recognition that somehow ours is a time of great transitions where the stories, habits, myths, symbols, and images that once explained our world cannot hold us together any longer. Our maps have become threadbare and no longer explain the land through which we travel with such anxiety and foreboding.

Our problem is that the categories we've learned and absorbed, that shape and lead our worlds (our churches and denominations), remain so deeply embedded within us that we still believe that the way to fix our situation is by reworking these categories. Ramo provides a startling illustration of this in his book. In the early part of the last century, a mathematical equation was developed that claimed to enable us to measure the amount of fish in a lake and give us the formula for how many fish could be harvested without overfishing. It resulted in the development of a model called *maximum sustainable yield* (MSY). The idea was brilliantly simple. By making a careful survey of the current situation in a lake using a precise set of indicators (nutrients in the water, breeding levels of the fish, water levels, and so on), it was possible to calculate how many fish could be taken without affecting the replacement rate. It seemed like a brilliant formula for guaranteeing the "natural" health of the fish in a lake as well as a simple method for indicating what to do to increase the number of fish. Throughout the 1950s and 1960s, this method was preached and practiced all over North America. It was the "natural system" answer to growth and sustainability. It became the basis for international meetings on fisheries and the establishment of new rules for fishing.

Then something completely unlikely and unexpected happened. While their environments were following the rules of the natural MSY approach, fish started to die off in massive numbers. The system looked perfect on paper; people in the know believed in its veracity, but for inexplicable reasons, fish started to die off in huge numbers. What had happened? The problem was the MSY model and its assumption that there was only a certain set of variables, or categories, that needed to be measured. Get these measurements right, and all the rest would fall into place. Those variables, however, had been chosen by a group of people who looked at the world in a certain way, and these were the established, taken-for-granted categories that had always been used. No one, therefore, could imagine that forces totally outside these established categories were powerfully reshaping lake ecology. These forces were what we would call *nonlinear;* that is, they didn't fit the established logic, the taken-for-granted maps on which the "experts" depended. What the scientists did at this point was also highly predictable. As Ramo states, "The scientists went back over their models; they fine-tuned the inputs, recalibrated data, and got, in the end, yet more extinctions." What were they missing? In systems (like churches and denominational systems) in the midst of cultures and societies going through massive change, the real drivers of that change are the unexpected. Focusing on the long-established categories and measurables in disequilibrium becomes less and less important relative to what is actually happening. When there isn't a lot of change going on, it's fine to focus on established measurables. But where change is rapid and discontinuous, such measurements are "worse than useless," Ramos writes. " ... What you can measure in these systems matters much less than what you cannot: How strong are the relationships between different parts of the lake ecosystem? How fast can it adjust to shocks? How far can you bend the food chain in the lake before it breaks?"[10] It is when leaders are faced with the reality that the established categories no longer describe the world unfolding before them that they enter this in-between state of confusion and loss. This parallels the liminal situation of churches and leaders in North America.

EQUILIBRIUM, RESISTANCE, AND LIMINALITY

I have used the concept of liminality to help explain our experience in this in-between space. Liminality describes the transition experience of a group as it is shifted into a place where its status and way of working in a given context are radically changed to the point where the group loses its sense of how to function in this new situation.[11]

Equilibrium isn't always a good thing. While providing solid, predictable environments, it also leads to a loss of awareness, vitality, and ingenuity and may even lead to death. When equilibrium is upset, it's difficult for people to let go of the habits, categories, attitudes, and values that have shaped them. Convention is a powerful default, especially when there has never been reason to question it. I speak to forums of church leaders who express confusion about their roles in this new time. They're struggling to understand who they are as leaders—questions of identity come with the recognition that default systems aren't working. Increasingly, leaders sense that measuring the standard categories of worship, evangelism, discipleship, and the like may get people energized for a while and may even prove that their church is "healthier" than someone else's. But they are also recognizing that their habit of defaulting to known categories isn't producing any change and that something far different is required; they just don't know what it might be. And it is so difficult to break out of the deeply embedded defaults of modernity. Therefore, what these leaders are searching for, in the words of one of them, is a clear, compelling vision of what to do and how to lead. I wish it were so easy! The challenge is getting leaders to see and acknowledge the default systems out of which they're still operating. When I have pointed out why these default maps (improve worship, reshape evangelism, and so on) are no longer sustainable, many times their resistance grows, and they accuse me of criticizing the church or just being negative without offering positive alternatives. They have many reasons for their resistance to these new ideas, but primary among them is that they want me to come up with a new set of measurables, a new set of categories they can use to organize their world, with objectives to manage or master. But in complex change, a new set of objectives is not going to help. It's the little things that make the huge changes; the complexities of the way relationships work are a more potent source of answers than purportedly objective measurables. Leading well in an environment of complex change depends on leading from a different place than management and control. It's tough to break away from default maps. These commonsense conventions operate almost automatically, like the immune system, to protect against foreign substances that threaten equilibrium. The conventional, commonsense wisdom about leadership and church organizations, formed in the stability of modernity, are acting like an immune system blocking contrary ideas from disrupting the equilibrium. It's a lot more reassuring to have a program that promises that you can improve the health of your church if you identify a certain set of measurables than to face the counterintuitive idea that the imagination for a new future lies among the ordinary people of a church and in the relational networks that exist among them and in the community. These kinds of networks can't be measured or quantified. They are like the Spirit and like the wind: we can't turn them into objects and objective measurables. Something radically different in required. How do we enter this other space?

"HOW WE KNOW" SHAPES WHAT WE BECOME

One reason the loss of equilibrium and the resulting experience of the in-between creates such emotional turmoil is that it causes us to question some of our most basic, taken-for-granted assumptions about how we know things and about how we define the world and reality for ourselves. The educator Parker Palmer helps us understand why this happens. For Palmer, what a teacher believes about the way the world works it is a powerful factor in how the lives of his or her students get shaped. What he means by belief is what philosophers call *epistemology*.

Epistemology is a big mouthful of a word that tries to get at our basic ways of knowing by addressing questions such as these:

Why do we believe that this is truth and something else isn't?
How do we come to know that something is true?
What distinguishes true knowledge from false knowledge, and how do we arrive at these distinctions?

Epistemology is about the frameworks that shape *how* we know—the maps we use to interpret the world. Palmer offers helpful ways to understand the challenges leaders face in church systems. What he wants to do is

> try to reach into the underlying nature of our knowledge itself. I want to reach for the relation of community to the very mode of knowing dominant in the academy.
>
> To put it in philosophical terms, I want to try to connect concepts of community to questions of epistemology, which I believe are the central questions for any institution engaged in a mission of knowing, teaching, and learning. How do we know? How do we learn? Under what conditions and with what validity?
>
> I believe that it is here at the epistemological core of our knowledge and our processes of knowing that our powers for forming or deforming human consciousness are to be found. I believe that it is here, in our modes of knowing, that we shape souls by the shape of our knowledge. It is here that the idea of community must ultimately take root and have impact if it is to reshape the doing of higher education.
>
> *My thesis is a very simple one:* I do not believe that epistemology is a bloodless abstraction; the way we know has powerful implications for the way we live. I argue that every epistemology tends to become an ethic and that every way of knowing tends to become a way of living.[12]

Palmer exhorts us to examine the default maps we use to interpret the world to others. The maps inside us are not abstractions but have powerful implications for the way we live and how we communicate. These maps become an ethic (a way of acting toward others); they are a deeply cherished way of living and being that resides at the core of our identity. We resist anyone who questions their veracity. The Bush administration, for example, in the days after the terrorist attacks of September 11, 2001, had already decided that Iraq had weapons of mass destruction and systematically filtered out any contrary reading of the situation. *Leading is about how we know (epistemology) as much as about actions or strategies.* It is as much about the maps within us as getting some bold new vision. Without being aware of the ways we know, our bold new visions will all be for naught because they will be extensions or repetitions of our established categories and convictions. How and what we know profoundly affects how we act. We can't just discard our epistemologies or maps and pick up new ones on a whim. It's far more complex than that.

THE MEANING OF IT ALL

Under normal circumstances, if I were to ask someone, "What are the ways we know the world?" I'd get a puzzled look instead of a response. Normally, we don't consider such *abstract* questions because we assume some broad agreement about what we know and how we know it. It's one of those fish-and-water relationships. We see why the question is important only by distancing ourselves from our own group or time. Imagine that you could step back into twelfth- or thirteenth-century Europe and ask someone, "Why does a specific type of tree grow the leaves it does?" The person would likely respond that it was because the spirit, or soul, of that type of tree caused it to grow in that way. If we pressed a little more and asked how he or she knew that was why the tree grew that kind of leaf, the person would, with a bemused smile, tell us quite simply that Aristotle or Scripture or tradition taught such truths and everyone knew that was the authority by which truth was revealed. If we then went to the late twentieth century and asked the same questions in a high school classroom, we would get a very different set of responses. We would be given a brief statement on species diversification, habitat adaptation, and genetic determination. When asked how they knew this was the case, the students would respond in terms of observation, studies in empirical research using sophisticated tools for dissection, and longitudinal studies in different environments together with data from other species-specific trees in other parts of the world. These strikingly different answers reflect different kinds of knowing. The epistemologies aren't the same.

Different epistemologies create different ways of acting. In the twelfth century, the knowledge that trees had spirits, or souls, shaped the ways people acted toward them. Certain woodlands, for example, were deemed places of sacred energy and needed to be treated as such. But more to the point, people did not see a tree as an object to be used in whatever way they pleased. A tree was animated with spirits who needed to be recognized. If a tree was to be cut down, for example, there might need to be an elaborate ritual to placate the spirit of that tree. By the twentieth century, trees had become inanimate objects, things to be used. This understanding creates a different set of actions—we simply assess utility and cost and then make a decision about how we will deal with the tree. These examples suggest that different ways of knowing result in different *commonsense* ways of behaving. Common sense may not be that obvious after all.

Our epistemology *(how we know) determines our* ethics *(how we act).* This is why Palmer makes the powerful statement that "we shape souls by the shape of our knowledge." What and how we know determines what we deem important and valuable and therefore guides our actions, values, and ethics. Yet in terms of the metaphor of the fish and water, most of the time we're unaware of how we know, of what is shaping our actions.

Our maps are not neutral; they reflect our epistemologies. So to imagine and make new maps, wise travelers will make sure they're aware of the maps that have been guiding them. Leaders tend to believe that their maps of church and leadership are based primarily on theological convictions based in Scripture. Look, for example, at all the books on church structure and leadership that begin with the claim that the author's perspective is the one that is biblical. At a basic level, this is how different denominations justify their organizational structures and their various ecclesiologies; each makes the claim that its type of church form is drawn directly from Scripture.[13] Like fish in water, we often fail to see the extent to which our metaphors, images, and beliefs are determined by the cultural maps of our time rather than some set of pure ideas from the Bible.

How do we recognize our epistemologies—these images and metaphors that shape us? How does a fish see the water in which it is swimming? Newbigin is a helpful teacher here. His ability to describe the maps shaping the church in the West near the end of the twentieth century came from the fact that he had spent the better part of his life outside his own culture as a British missionary serving in India. This cross-cultural experience equipped him to see his own culture through the lenses of another. Returning from India, he understood how deeply he'd been conditioned by his British background. At the same time, by living among and internalizing the peoples of India and learning how their worldviews accounted for the world (their epistemologies), he was able to understand more clearly the epistemologies informing his own European culture. He described this process of becoming aware:

> Initially I am not aware of this as a myth [the worldviews that shape Western culture]. As long as I retain the innocence of a thoroughly western man, unshaken by the serious involvement in another culture, I am not aware of this myth. It is simply "how things are." . . . No myth is seen as a myth by those who inhabit it: it is simply the way things are.[14]

Few of us have had Newbigin's opportunity to thoroughly know cultures by living inside them and juxtaposing our experience in each. But we do live in a period of tremendous transition that can provide a context for seeing our own culture with a degree of outsider's vision. A giant earthquake has shaken the foundations of Western culture, opening up its fault lines and the structures on which it has been constructed. We have a unique opportunity to be like cross-cultural missionaries in our own context, gaining insight into the maps guiding us as congregations, denominations, and leaders. In the next chapter, we will examine these maps, these epistemologies that shape how we act as church leaders in this culture.

CHAPTER **FOUR**

FROM PLAYING POOL TO HERDING CATS

In the mid-1990s, I was offered a position in an organization serving the church at large. This led to a decision to resign from my pastoral role in the church I was serving. I stood to tell the people of my decision. After describing the way my life was being shaped in terms of training, teaching, and writing and explaining that I was not leaving them to go to another church, I couldn't resist saying that leading them had been like trying to herd cats, which are impossible to "lead." They laughed, but some understood that I was scolding them for not following my plans. At the time, I thought myself insightful and correct. There it was; I had defined the problem, and the problem was my congregation: they were "cats."

I now understand that my declaration at that moment was not about assigning a pejorative label but about the reality of what it means to work with people in this land of in-between. This "herding cats" experience sent me on a reflective journey where I began to understand my maps and how they caused me to misread the landscape. In this process, I began to see how some key maps of modernity, such as the conviction that with enough data and measurement one could name and control preferred outcomes, had shaped the church and my leadership. Map-makers in this new space will need to heed Lesslie Newbigin's challenge to understand the maps that have shaped our imagination over the last three centuries.

SEEING SOME OF OUR KEY MAPS

Because our preexisting mental maps are the common way we understand reality, we don't even think about them, and it requires a lot of work and reflection to learn to "see" them. For a long time after leaving that congregation, I struggled with the meaning of leadership, and it took a lot of effort for me to see my maps and figure out how to read them. Something I could neither name nor describe was trying to be born within me. For months, I scribbled notes and started to write about what was trying to find expression, but I couldn't find the right words. Then one day, sitting in a coffee shop struggling with my discovery about cats, it all began to tumble out onto paper. I realized that some of my maps of leadership were misleading me and that they were connected with my perception of how the world worked. These internal maps caused me to determine that people who didn't follow my well-worked-out plan were nothing more than cats. By putting them into this category, I had fitted them into a world that explained their actions and left my carefully designed conception of how leadership ought to work (mission statements and strategies with outcomes, goals, and preferred futures) firmly in place. In that coffee shop, I began to see that my maps of leadership and of how the world worked no longer reflected how I understood the ways of God in the world or how we are called to form people. I also recognized that the maps I had been following were not unique to me; they were ways of leading and seeing the world given to me by the cultural and intellectual world that emerged out of modernity.

Sir Isaac Newton (1643–1727), one of the shapers of the map of modernity, became the Moses of the modern world. His equations became the "laws of nature" that never failed in predicting the tides, the orbits of planets, or the movement of any object that could be seen or felt. Output was exactly proportional to input; every action begat a reaction; and under his influence, Western culture came to see the world as a vast input-and-output machine. Get enough data and information about the inputs, and we will be able to predict and manage the outputs. This measure-predict-manage methodology became the framework for leadership, based on the conviction that we had the capacity and the method (science) to name all the parts and then control those parts to produce our desired ends. Everything was equal to the sum of its parts. The entire universe was seen as a huge clock that could be understood, managed, and controlled by analyzing its individual components. Newton's mechanics seemed so universal in application that they became the organizing principle of postfeudal society; "the best model of government," one authority said in the 1720s, was based on these principles. The principles of mechanics inspired Frederick the Great to structure the Prussian army as an assemblage of standardized parts, equipment, and command language.

> The very equations of economics, including those in use today, were built explicitly on the principles of mechanics and thermodynamics, right down to the terms and symbols. The economy was said to have "momentum," or was "gaining steam." A successful company ran like a "well-oiled" or "fine-tuned" machine; a poorly performing company was "off track" or "stuck in low gear." . . . The Newtonian worldview was appropriate for a time . . . [but] upon closer inspection the science turned out to be—well—wrong, or at best correct only within the tolerances of Newton's instruments.[1]

Newton's brilliant discoveries and elucidation of laws defining the operation of the universe created a new set of metaphors that have shaped our maps for the past three hundred years. In my reflections, I began to see how these metaphors extended far beyond the world of science and technology and into my world of the church and leadership. One of the central elements of Newton's worldview was the law of universal gravitation, in which he argued that gravity was a "force" that caused all phenomena in the universe to operate through predictable, mechanical laws with mathematical regularity. (This image was later translated into Adam Smith's "invisible hand" theory of economics, which still shapes economic imagination today.) By inventing calculus, Newton defined and predicted the actual and possible motions of bodies in space in terms of exact equations, which Einstein described as one of the greatest advances in thought that a single individual was ever privileged to make. Newton introduced a new epistemology to the Western mind, new conceptions about what we know and how we know it. Let's look at three aspects of this Newtonian map and their impact on the church.

The Machine as Dominant Map

A new vision of the world emerged from Newton's description of these universal laws: a great mechanical clock driven by predictable, deterministic laws. This machine map quickly became the way of knowing reality. In 1504, Peter Henlein invented the first portable time-piece in Nuremberg, and the first reported person to wear a watch on the wrist was Blaise Pascal (1623–1662). In the seventeenth century, the clock dominated the imagination of the emerging culture, and the idea of the machine, a mechanical, predictable, controllable human invention, enters the imagination of the West as the primary metaphor for knowing what the world outside of us is about. Descartes declared:

> We see clocks, artificial fountains, mills and other similar machines which, though merely man-made, have nonetheless the power to move by themselves in several different ways. . . . I do not recognize any difference between the machines made by craftsman and the various bodies that nature alone composes.[2]

He makes the connection clear: the map of the world is understood to be about machines. The computer is the parallel example in our time. With its invention, the human mind started to be described as a complex computer. The language of the computer and the Internet is now another map, a way of knowing, that replaces the clock. Parker Palmer's observation from Chapter Three is critical: the way we know becomes the way we live. Marshall McLuhan's famous aphorism is applicable here as well: first we shape our tools and thereafter our tools shape us![3]

How we practice leadership is a concretized expression of our maps. Like water to fish, these epistemologies shape how we lead and organize. When our specific ways of knowing and acting are embedded in our imagination, over a long period of time they become *just the way the world is,* the "common sense" of the culture. If we look closely, we can see how modernity's map underlies the variety of ways churches go about their planning. Church growth models, for example, are mechanistic. The church, a community, and a series of programs are all treated as a set of working parts that, when arranged in the right order with the right functions, bring about success in the form of numerical growth. Witness the proliferation of guide-books that show the precise principles for breaking through specific growth barriers. Look at the ways we assume it possible to name the explicit categories and variables that determine how a church is actually being shaped (measure inputs—data about worship, evangelism, discipleship, membership patters, and so on—and then one can design outputs, such as strategies for growth and health). The map shaping this church imagination is mechanical and modern—it uncritically assumes that the right information (data) and the right pieces in the right places will yield success. The basic conviction is that we can see all the real variables shaping a people in a specific place and time, that power allows us to create our preferred futures. The modern map offers little awareness of how impossible it is to manage and control all the networks of variables shaping even something as small as a local church of fifty to a hundred people, let alone larger communities. It neglects the reality that the real shaping of a community of people comes from the thousands and millions of small, supposedly insignificant interactions we can never see or incorporate into our data and plans.

Reality Is About Things or Objects

Epistemologies answer the question of *how* we know but also determine *what* we know. They answer the question of how we put the world together. The map of modernity depicts the world as a huge and complex machine, an *object* made without any subjective identity. To objectify everything outside the knowing subject is to remove from the rest of the creation any meaning or purpose except whatever we impose on it. This is why having a method of management and control where we can predict outcomes and use metrics to measure results has been so important in our culture. This is the modern imagination's way of being a creator: by controlling the machine, we work our will on the world.

Descartes' map divided reality into two distinct parts. On one side is *res cogitans*, the thinking mind, the center of the independent human self. On the other side is all the rest of reality, described as *res extensa*; the material objects existing outside the self in the physical world. Note how this map predetermines how we look at the world: the world is divided into self and other, and it is only through the rational categories of the thinking mind that we know and define what exists outside ourselves. We therefore "see" the world in terms of objects outside the thinking, rational self. Immanuel Kant applied a similar principle in the area of ethics. For him, the way we know how to act is through objective, universal categories for moral life that are, in effect, abstract moral laws applying to all people, at all time, in all places (for example, keeping the Golden Rule).

In this map of the world, laws and definitions determine actions and define relationships. Imagine a pool table on which a series of billiard balls are set. With enough skill and practice, it's possible to define how and when a ball will strike another, bounce off a specific point on the table, and sink into the predetermined pocket. *In a world mapped by modernity, with the right skills, we can have a high level of control, manageability, and certainty.* This map has persisted for most of the last three hundred years. It led us to believe that we could identify unvarying and predictable laws regulating the operation of all objects. The world would be forced to reveal its secrets, where-upon we would control and direct it. Control therefore became the key image, the primary map, for leadership. This is why leaders get asked for a "compelling vision." What is actually being requested are the keys to getting control and management of the world in order to predict the outcomes. A good deal of strategic planning in churches is shaped by this element of modernity, this belief that with the right alignment of all the pieces, it is possible not only to choose a prefer-able future (mission statement) but manage the parts (the plan) to get to that future.

Laws Provide Predictability and Control over Things

In a world of objects, there are rational laws we discover "out there" in the physical world that give us the power to predict what is going to happen and therefore control outcomes. The method involves reduc-ing things to their simplest components (each billiard ball on the table or each single unit and movement of work in a time-management design or strategic plan). By understanding each discrete element, it's possible to understand and in turn predict and control the whole.

There are important outcomes of this map:

The world outside the self, including other people, is perceived as separate, independent elements to be managed and controlled.
With the right amount of knowledge and skill, it's possible to manip-ulate and manage objects, or persons, to achieve predetermined goals and outcomes (note the use of language such as *alignment* in many planning processes that refers not only to things like build-ings and programs but the people themselves who are supposed to align themselves around a program or vision for the church—this

is the language of objectification; it is a language that turns people into things in order to make everything function around a predetermined set of outcomes, which are the mission statement and purposes of the church. The strange thing is that when this way of leading is pointed out, there are those who furrow their brows in bewilderment and wonder why this method is a problem).

Knowledge breaks apart into separate and distinct areas, or disciplines, as if what we know about the world exists in silos that have little relationship with one another. The ways in which most pastors were taught in seminaries illustrate this understanding of knowledge, where the New Testament is separated from, for example, systematic theology, which is separated from practical theology, and rarely is there any crossing over of these "disciplines" or silos.

Disciplines and skills are fragmented into distinct and separate professions, which are the domain of experts. All those outside the particular profession are laypeople with little or no knowledge or skill in the specific area. This understanding forms societies of experts who have the knowledge of how to act or lead.

The relationships of human beings to one another and the world is one of control and power through expertise and knowledge.

This map led to the conviction that with sufficient information and expertise, we could predict outcomes and control the future direction of organizations to achieve predetermined goals. Like the balls on a pool table, if we could analyze all the potential combinations of ways the separate balls interact with one another, we could "align" the balls to achieve a predetermined goal. This generally accepted "commonsense" map has deeply affected the imagination of the church in terms of its organizational planning and leadership structures. Strategic planning, a methodology used by many church organizations (and assumed to be value-neutral), illustrates the powerful presence of this map within the church and among its leaders. This map reflects a world of linear thinking. It assumes that planning and actions occur in a straightforward, unidirectional manner, as shown in this equation:

$$A + B + C + D \ldots = \text{Preferred Future/Success/Control}$$

It assumes that by identifying the distinct elements of a problem and placing them in an ordered sequence, it's possible to predict solutions that result in successful outcomes (we see this map at work in evangelism programs that plot people's spiritual state along a line that goes from "totally against the Gospel" at one end to "fully devoted followers" at the other).

The equation expresses how this map of linear thinking functions within the process of church strategy. The language of preferred futures is used: developing a "preferred" future for a congregation assumes the ability to determine reality. With the right information or the correct program, we can produce the right solutions. This is why programs that have proved effective elsewhere are deemed successful.

I received a phone call from the pastor of a large mainline church who wanted to shape his church around a missional paradigm. He was called to the church after demonstrating success in a prior congregation. The present congregation had a history of long, stable pastorates (more than twelve years, on average); prior pastors had been essentially chaplains to the congregation. In our conversation, the new pastor described how he arrived three years earlier with a strong mandate from the congregation for change. His reading of missional theology committed him to the creation of a missional church. The board of the church bought his vision without much understanding of what it might mean in terms of the emotional cost as people saw programs change, worship take on alternative forms, staff increase, and buildings be redesigned.

Three years later, the pastor, staff, and board were deep into a strategic planning process purchased from a church information company. They had worked hard as a leadership team to establish their strategic plan for mission based on this program. It had a series of phased-in stages built around a vision for growth. These stages involved staffing for the vision, developing facilities for the vision, and finally, programming for the vision. Each phase was intended to align the congregation and its resources with the vision for growth. This new vision for the church—reaching the young families living in the surrounding neighborhood—and the detailed plan for achieving this goal were continually articulated through biblical preaching, Bible study, and congregational votes. The pastor was describing to me a classical strategic plan, backed by books whose assumptions were borrowed from specific business models and applied to the church.

The reason that this pastor called me was that a lot of the "cats" had left the building. He could describe what was happening, but he was not able to see what was really at work—these elements of modernity's map as I have described them. At one level, everything he shared with his board and the church about the new future they were going to create matched their own internal maps of how the church should work. But when he began the processes of change, assuming the full support of the church, *he was unaware that the Newtonian maps he was using sought to align people around a plan, turning people into objects directed toward achieving the new vision.* It was at that point that the cats got restless.

DECONSTRUCTING MY MAPS

As I started to become aware of my own maps and how they shaped my world of church and leadership, I needed to dig deeper to understand how they were constructed. Lesslie Newbigin proved helpful to me in this endeavor. He saw the maps of modernity rooted in the dichotomy between a public world of "facts" and a private world of "values," an "inner" world of intellect and an "outer" world of objects. In *Foolishness to the Greeks,* he reflects, as a retired missionary to India, on the maps shaping the West. He looked at the water in which the "fish" of English culture swam, describing its basic map in terms of a dichotomy between the public and the private. Table 4.1 illustrates his map.

The left column represents the public world of everyday life—the practical, functional world of our activities and organizations. Truth is normally conceived as whatever functionally and operationally explains the causes of things. It is a world open to empirical verification. The right column describes the private, personal world that functions as a separate realm from the public. This is the world of personal belief, private faith, values, and church life. Here faith predominates in a context that cannot and does not require empirical verification.

PUBLIC	PRIVATE
Truth	Belief
Fact	Faith
Science	Religion
Outer	Inner
	Teleology

Table 4.1.   Operative Frameworks

This dichotomized construction of reality separates the ends from the means. Causes, ends, and means are limited to verifiable, measurable explanations from the left column. Notions of final causes (what theology would call *teleology* and the biblical world *eschatology*) have no meaningful place.

This is why numerical growth has been the primary measure of success in the church. Growth is measurable and controllable; it's about rational goals and appropriate ends (the left column). Congregations and their leaders separate the purposes of God from their short-term goals and strategic plans. Teleology, which is about the purpose of things and addresses the question of what God is up to in the world, is split off from planning, vision statements, and actions. In Table 4.1, teleology is placed on the right side as part of values and beliefs, not facts and truth. As a result, "God questions" have little impact on the planning activities of leaders or the organization of church systems. It is the social sciences that are considered the important element in organizational planning and leadership development. Elements of the right-hand side, such as biblical themes or data, are introduced as *supporting texts* for the decisions made on the left-hand side. What appears to be the innocent and neutral use of demographic data is an illustration of this process. Too often churches simply take these data and enfold them in a series of Bible studies about the nature and purpose of the church, as if the data will tell the church what it ought to do to reach this community. The plans are really shaped by the data; the Bible themes are used to back up and reinforce the plan.

One of modernity's maps in operation here views reality divided into a series of polarities or opposites. One of these, for example, is the separation between what one believes in one's private life and how one acts in public life. We have all heard people make such statements as "This is business, and that is about my private life." Behind such statements is the perception that one's personal faith, what one does in the privacy of one's church or home, does not affect the decisions one has to make in a globalized world of balance sheets, human resources, or purchasing policies. Many also imagine a similar kind of separation between one's politics and one's faith. These dichotomies explain why leaders readily accept models and programs from areas such as business and use them in the church context without any critical reflection on their relationship to or implications for the biblical narrative of God's action in the world or the tradition in which these leaders have been formed. Theological and biblical reflection around the narratives of God's future (teleology) are subject to and placed within the planning and organizational design developed on the left side of the table.

The left column is a world of facts. A Christian understanding of purpose (in the sense of the ends of God in the world) is removed as the primary source of explanation for our decisions and actions in favor of the so-called facts generated on the left-hand side.

This dichotomy accounts for the profound sense of disconnection and loss of a larger purpose people experience in this culture. When means and ends are detached from a larger meaning, their teleology, the result is the creation of a social life in which people become means and ends, commodities to be used or not used in a larger system (as when church leaders develop vision statements and strategic plans that align their people). In this reductionistic world, people are useful to the extent that they fit into a program or plan, and in fact we turn people into the means for attaining our visions and plans. Hence the palpable sense of isolation and loneliness in the North American spirit, evidenced by people turning in on themselves, seeking in their own emotional fulfillment a way of discovering a meaning greater than commodification. Maps are never neutral. They invariably guide a way of being that expresses itself in how we behave toward one another and live with one another.

All this talk of modernism and dichotomy may sound abstract and theoretical at one level; however, it describes how I needed to sort out the implications of the maps that were shaping me at a certain moment in time. I needed to dig deeper into the reasons I had been frustrated as a leader when people weren't aligning with my plans. As I read Newbigin and worked with people like Parker Palmer, I began to see that these dichotomies were essential parts of my maps, and so while I dreamed and talked about a mission-shaped church, I was still functioning like the pastor discussed earlier. I had a plan and was focused on creating a preferred future. My growing awareness of these maps pushed me to explore what the alternatives might involve, which was the beginning of a long journey for me.

RETHINKING CATS

These experiences as a pastor helped me rethink my cat-herding analogy. Rather than regarding my former catlike congregation as an anomaly, I recognized that leading in the church is more akin to herding cats than to operationalizing a strategic plan. Cats are highly resistant to alignment, especially when there are few incentives! Churches do not pay salaries to their members; the notion of a voluntary society that shapes the church makes it unlikely that any form of alignment can be made to work for long.[4]

While my theological imagination was moving deeply into a missional ecclesiology, I functioned as a leader in a "commonsense" world that had taught me how to lead by developing plans and futures for the congregations I pastored. I operated in a dichotomized world. My practical, commonsense side continued to function out of leadership models in which I saw myself as primarily responsible (albeit with others and involving inclusive conversations) for creating a "grand plan" for the future of the congregation that would result in a preferred missional future. I viewed the cat metaphor negatively. The cats were the problem that needed to be fixed. If only I could find a way of getting the congregation to align itself with the plan and commit to actually engaging in the program, all would be well. But that is not how things work in real life.

A year later, I came to a radically different conclusion as my understanding of leadership was turned upside down. I was finally connecting my missional ecclesiology with the question of how to lead the church. My maps were fading and being replaced by ones reflecting a different cartographic imagination. God's people are like cats in many ways. I realized that behaving like a cat in the presence of someone else's plan for my life is a healthy response. Instead of being critical of congregations when they didn't "line up" with the plan, I needed to apologize for my arrogance.

This new awareness helped me bring into focus something I had felt and known for a long time. So much of what happens in our lives and among a congregation is nonlinear; it's neither predictable nor controllable. The smallest, unexpected element creates massive impacts and rearranges our worlds. One small, unforeseen event changes everything. As a young teenager, how could I ever have created a vision and strategic plan that would take into account that my father, at the age of fifty (when I was fifteen), would decide to uproot the family and emigrate across the Atlantic? Everything changed! I now see that unpredictable change is far more the norm than the exception. I see many church leaders who begin with high levels of energy as they are called to a church or judicatory that wants to go through a process of "transformation." The new leader comes in with or develops a plan that is expected to give a new direction over the next five years. How often have I sat with these leaders as they honestly confess that the plan isn't working and they face their own discouragement. So many things happen in the midst of the plan. Key associates leave; time gets taken up managing the demands of people in crisis; the support team that was so with you at the beginning has moved on to other passions and you feel abandoned and alone; people lose interest in keeping the plan going over a long period; it goes on and on.

From a theoretical perspective, I knew all about the way things change. I could describe the experiments of Edward Lorenz, the meteorologist who stumbled into chaos theory. He originally assumed that a very small decimal number in an equation would have no effect on the weather models he was generating, but he discovered that the smallest of changes and perturbations resulted in massive, unpredictable changes in weather patterns. This theoretical framework was not new to my thinking. I understood nonlinearity in an intellectual way. But I still functioned using two radically different frameworks—my theological and intellectual imaginations were not congruent in the ways I actually planned and led. I was being taken from a billiard-ball, linear, manage-and-control world and placed on an entirely different path where I no longer understood leadership as a pool table but as a network of dynamic, noncontrollable interrelationships among ordinary people in local contexts where the wondrously creative Spirit was at work.

It all seems so obvious and clear as I sit at my desk and describe it at this moment, but having come to this rather startling conversion while sitting in a coffee shop on the West Coast, I found myself catapulted into a new imagination about leadership and what God may be about in these strange attractors we call congregations. Before me opened a world for which I was not prepared, a world formed around a question: How does one lead if in fact reality is more like the actions of cats than billiard balls aligned on a table to be managed by strategic plans and preferred futures? When I explained to people what I was wrestling with, when I talked about not needing to be in control or have a great plan for the church and its people, they asked me, "But what do you do then? How do you avoid chaos? Do you just tell people that we do nothing? "Are you just going to become a chaplain to people's needs?" I didn't know how to respond. I hadn't yet learned why you don't avoid chaos! I didn't know why, but I sensed that this chaos was not all bad, that it was in fact a gift I needed to embrace at that moment.

Initially, these questions and my new learning filled me with anxiety and fear. What was happening to me? Had I lost my mind and become a "nonleader leader"? Was I going soft and opting for some "chaplaincy" image of simply "caring" for people but never guiding them toward engagement, growth, and mission? These questions scared me! What would happen to my vision for the church if leadership were not about creating plans that take everyone into the promised land of my (or a congregationally agreed) vision as a leader? These may seem like strange questions, but even though I was very good at denial, these questions churned about inside me and stuck under my skin like an irritant that rubbed and rubbed so that I could never really ignore them.

I filtered my growing discomfort through my theological frameworks, my understanding of God, of creation, of what it means to be a human being, of how I understood the ways in which God calls and shapes us as human beings. I wrestled with biblical frameworks of God's reign, election, and eschatology. And in this process of gestation, I kept going back to my own experiences as a pastor and church leader. Had I always known at some level that my strategic planning had never really been what created the life and vitality, the mission and transformation in the congregations I had served? But still, in this transition from one world to another, I struggled to let go of leadership habits deeply ingrained in my psyche. The glasses I had worn for so many years to read my world were difficult to take off. I knew they no longer brought into view an accurate map of what was happening in the world of cats, but when I took them off for a moment, all I could see was a scary, disorienting blur.

My world was coalescing around other kinds of maps. The scary part was that I didn't know how to function in this new place. I needed to wrestle a little more with why maps of control, management, and predictability could no longer be trusted.

CHAPTER **FIVE**

WHY STRATEGIC PLANNING DOESN'T WORK IN THIS NEW SPACE AND DOESN'T FIT GOD'S PURPOSES

Whenever the frameworks outlined in Chapter Four are presented to groups of church leaders, there is usually a high degree of assent. Each year, I teach a program in missional leadership at a seminary on the West Coast. We recently began a new class of more than twenty pastors and denominational leaders from the United States, Canada, Australia, and Japan. I shared the ideas presented in the preceding chapters of this book. The responses were positive; people appreciated the new language they were given to make sense of their experiences. However, when we looked at the practical implications their unacknowledged maps have had on the ways they led churches, these leaders pushed back with a series of "yes, buts." Leaders are comfortable talking about the maps of modernity but resist examining the implications of those maps on their leadership practices.

Never is this more evident than when I suggest that the process of strategic planning in the church is structured by modernity's map and argue that the ways it is practiced actually undermine what God is about in the world. These are provocative claims.

When I share my experiences after resigning my church position in the late 1990s, most leaders usually follow me. But when I flesh out the practical implications of what I was learning and challenge the role of strategic planning in the church, many cannot go with me any further. As a result, I feel it's important to address the implications of strategic planning and why its practice as a primary form of leadership and innovation in the church leads us astray.

This chapter looks at the implications of modernity's maps for church systems and its leaders through a discussion of the sources and effects of strategic planning. What follows is a critique of strategic planning; it attempts to provide a theological read of why this critique is important as we move ahead and imagine new leadership maps. The final section of this chapter will look at some ways of addressing what you can do if this kind of strategic planning has been a key focus of your leadership to this point.

WHAT I AM *NOT* SAYING

One reason leaders struggle with my description of strategic planning is that they make faulty assumptions about what I'm saying. I do not critique strategic planning for the sake of argument but rather to show that as a function of modernity's maps, it makes assumptions that contradict some basic Christian convictions about what it means to be human and about how human communities engage in transformation. I am not writing off planning as a whole. I am arguing something specific about the kind of planning that developed from modernity's maps and how it cannot be generalized to human communities without importing a great many attitudes, values, and practices that I believe are contrary to human thriving. Before discuss strategic planning directly, I want to clarify several issues that are continually raised about leadership and planning.

First, I am not saying that planning is unimportant. It is a crucial part of leadership. No organization is shaped without goals, structures, and processes for navigating its contexts. Leaders must think about the future and make plans for that future. The issue here is that if we are in a new space where we have never been before, the forms and methods of planning that worked in the old space, the maps of modernity that shaped us, cannot guide us in this new space—that's why we have to become map-makers, and becoming map-makers influences how we go about planning. Commenting on their book *Metavista: Bible, Church and Mission in an Age of Imagination,* Colin Greene and Martin Robinson put it this way:

> Metavista means a "new space." It's a word we invented to describe something genuinely new that's happening—which is rather like the present global financial crisis, which defies all the rules and regulations of global capitalism. What is absolutely new is that financiers, bankers and politicians find themselves in a new space in terms of how to regulate and control how markets and institutions actually work.[1]

The question is not whether the financiers, bankers, and politicians *should* plan; it's *how* they should plan when they know that most of the methods that got us to this place can't take us forward.

Second, I am not saying that there is no place for strategic planning whatsoever. In fact, I will argue that there is an important place for this kind of planning in the church; but leaders need to question where this planning occurs and the purposes it's intended to serve. Let me briefly make some general comments about the uses of strategic planning in the church and the appropriate place for its application. Strategic planning may be one of the wonderful gifts modernity has bequeathed to us, but it needs to be understood in context rather than used as if it were a neutral tool for achieving certain ends. In Chapter Four, I noted that a key narrative of modernity is management, control, and predictability in order to achieve predetermined goals and outcomes. At many levels of our lives, this is a wonderful map with which to operate. Let me illustrate. Almost every week, I fly somewhere on an airplane. Several years ago, I sat in the window seat of a large jet looking out over the wing before take-off. I was surprised to see that every joint, every rivet, and every piece of the wing had a small number on it. Everything on that wing was numbered. Someone was being very careful about what went where. I am sure that behind this work was a team of engineers who had developed an overarching strategic plan to design an aircraft that would take off and land thousands of times without a hitch. Every time I get on a plane, I give thanks for engineers and this form of strategic planning. Here modernity is a wonderful gift to us all. Whether it is in the planning for building aircraft, designing roadways, constructing huge skyscrapers, or designing a drug that kills cancer cells, in a thousand ways we take for granted, strategic planning models are a gift to us.

That said, some important caveats need to be made about the place and role of strategic planning in the church. My illustrations describe the application of such planning to the design of objects using resource materials that are put together to achieve a specific goal and end. In this process, human beings with varying levels of skills and from a variety of professions are paid for their contributions in creating the object. From start to finish, this is a process of clearly negotiated subject-object relationships among people involving the use of raw materials that will be turned into some predetermined object. Strategic planning can be (but often is not) a brilliant process for ordering human and natural resources in ways that align a lot of diverse pieces to achieve some goal. Already, the language ("natural," "resources") provides clues about the problem with strategic planning when it is imported into human, social communities like the church as the primary method for developing and achieving mission and vision goals.

In brief, when we universalize a method and apply it across all levels of systems (which is another one of modernity's implicit maps, this universalizing principle that asserts that what works well in one area of life must work well in all areas of life), the chances of uncritically importing values and practices that are contrary to one level of life are very high. When we universalize a method like strategic planning, a method of achieving preset goals and objectives, we essentially turn every variable in the process, including human beings, into objects to be used in the achievement of a goal. There is no way around this. *Strategic planning uses objectification to achieve ends.* To repeat, when applied to the building of airplanes or the development of life-saving drugs, this method of controlling outcomes can be brilliant. At the same time, there can never be a justification for turning any human being into an object of someone else's goals and vision in the social community formed by the Spirit of God. Once this line is crossed, strategic planning is not a gift but a curse; it is not a means of achieving something for the kingdom of God but a means of denying the kingdom of God because once we turn another person (the "other" or the "stranger" in the biblical narratives) into an object of ends where we want to align people or have them fit into our predetermined plans, we are contradicting some of the most basic ways in which God's kingdom is to be made tangible on earth. The kingdom of God is, at least in part, about releasing people from this kind of objectification: the idea of human freedom and human thriving are written into our constitutions because the Christian story was such a powerful vision of what God intends for us as human beings. This theological conviction involves the ways God is revealed to us in Jesus Christ. In Jesus, and then in the giving of the Spirit, we see God as a dynamic social community. As Jesus points out in his discourses and prayers in John 15:1–7, the church is called into being as the social community whose life reflects the nature of God as dynamic, interacting love and creativity, free of coercion or objectification. When strategic planning is the primary means for shaping and developing the life and character of a church's or a denomination's mission and vision, it will turn human beings into objects of ends, even if those ends are filled with good intentions.

Third, I am not suggesting a leadership method that simply waits on God to drop plans out of heaven. I believe that God works through people by the Spirit, and this involves the best uses of our minds, organizational skills, and leadership imaginations. Arguing that strategic planning cannot be a primary means of shaping communities of the kingdom does not imply adopting some kind of Gnostic spiritualism that assumes that God "works in mysterious ways." The task for leaders is more about how we cultivate environments that call forth and release the mission-shaped imagination of the people of God in a specific place and time. If cultivation of environments and facilitating the work of God's people is the vocation of mission-shaped leaders, then strategic planning is not simply an ill-fitting tool; it will never assist us in forming such people.

Fourth, I am not saying that church leadership is simply about shepherding a flock—that is, just performing the traditional roles of pastoral care, marrying and burying people, administering the sacraments, and preaching the Word. As important as these skills may be, I don't believe that mission-shaped leadership is simply about caring for the people without any concern for cultivating environments and imaginations of mission-shaped life. The leadership required in local churches today calls for the kind of creative thinking that moves beyond these traditional duties.

Finally, I am not arguing for some "backseat," hands-off kind of leadership where everyone does what seems good at the time. I will never forget being part of a church where the pastoral leadership assumed that the priesthood of all believers meant that anyone could sign on to do and be a part of whatever one wanted to in the life of the church and its mission. I can't count the times I wanted to walk out on a Sunday morning because of the awful ways people led worship, these goodhearted people with absolutely no gifts for inviting others into a public journey of worship. One Christmas Eve, my wife and I invited our two sons and their spouses to join us for a worship service. It was unplanned and led by people who should never have been allowed to lead. At the end of that evening, our sons told us never to invite us to that church again. It was a low moment for both of us.

In summary, the question for church leaders isn't *whether* to lead and plan but rather *what kind* of leadership and planning they should do. For God's people, choosing the right kind of leadership and planning must involve asking questions about the nature of the God who has encountered us in Jesus Christ and the implications of this encounter for our planning methods. We must ask theological questions of our planning methods just as much as we ask them about our views of salvation, the Lord's Table, or our practice of sexuality. If we ask theological questions about what God is up to in the world, then as leaders, we will be compelled to acknowledging that anything—any method of planning, no matter how well intentioned and prayed over—that turns others into an object of our ends, no matter how committed we are to them, is not of God or the Gospel of Jesus Christ. The kind of planning processes used in an organization will indicate its most basic convictions about who God is and what it means to be human. Modernity answered those questions, in large part, with methods that objectify human beings along with the rest of God's creation. Once we apply these maps of modernity to the ways we lead, we are automatically objectifying people in the name of some end goal (often given in the form of a vision and a mission statement). In describing the implications of modernity's maps for leadership in this way, I am challenging the dominant planning models used by church leaders these days. Even the great students involved in the seminary program I mentioned earlier, wanting to be formed as mission-shaped leaders, live inside the dichotomized set of frameworks outlined in Chapter Four. They acknowledged that modernity's frameworks presented significant problems for us as leaders. They were not, however, ready to concede that strategic planning came straight out of those maps and was therefore problematic in terms of Christian leadership. Like many other leaders, they wanted to defend this method because it was all they knew. Planning is necessary, but I am convinced that strategic planning cannot form mission-shaped communities. To understand this, we need to examine how strategic planning works in most church systems.

ASSUMPTIONS BEHIND STRATEGIC PLANNING

Thomas Petzinger states that until recently, "people saw their worlds through the Industrial Age metaphor of the machine and built their organizations accordingly."[2] While this world was crumbling as a mental model throughout the second half of the twentieth century, it continued to define the understanding of organizational life and leadership in the church. Petzinger's description applies to most churches and denominations.

> Even as it was toppled from unassailability in science, Newtonian mechanics remained firmly lodged as the mental model of management, from the first stirrings of the industrial revolution right through the advent of modern-day M.B.A. studies. Jobs were divided ever more narrowly, turning workers into so many tiny objects performing mindless, repetitive tasks; the whole, after all, was always equal to the sum of its parts. Management remained an act of calibration and control: input equals output, action equals reaction.... Command and control leadership prevailed to the end of the century. Government policy rested safely in the hands of the "best and the brightest." Leaders skilled at control became leaders of modernity.... Management's job was assembling the right pieces, pointing them toward the optimum, then making sure the system never wavered.... Into the moral void came numbers, only numbers. Optimization demanded measurement; all measurements could be abstractly converted to dollars [read: growing churches]; and profit thus became the principal ethos of business ...[3]

This "commonsense" map, with its logic of analyzing, seeking out experts, and developing planning solutions, shapes the imagination of leaders. It is a map that implies that preferred futures are possible with the right amount of skill, detail, demographics, planning, and management. Many church leaders continue to rely on a map shaped by the conviction that with enough information, analysis, and expertise, they can create a plan that will control and direct the future of their organizations. The fact is that more than three out of four senior leaders in the corporate world report that their strategic-change plans *do not* lead to the designed or promised results. That is equally true—if not more so—in the church world. Margaret Wheatley describes the power of the Newtonian imagination on the world of organization and leadership in this way:

> The machine image of the cosmos was translated into organizations. . . . Responsibilities have been organized into functions. People have been organized into roles. Page after page of organizational charts depict the workings of the machine: the number of pieces, what fits where, who the most important pieces are. . . . In organizations, we focused attention on structure and organizational design. . . . We really believed we could study the parts, no matter how many of them there were, to arrive at knowledge of the whole. We have reduced and described and separated things into cause and effect, and drawn the world in lines and boxes. . . . A world based on machine images is a world described by boundaries. In a machine, every piece knows its place. Likewise, in Newtonian organizations, we've drawn boundaries everywhere. We've created roles and accountabilities, specifying lines of authority and limits to responsibility. We have drawn boundaries around the flow of experience, fragmenting whole networks of interaction into discrete steps. . . . We have even come to think of power—an elusive, energetic force if ever there was one—as a bounded resource, defined as "my share of the pie."[4]

Many church leaders do not believe that these descriptions characterize themselves or their organizations. Yet these maps continue to shape and frame how leaders function in developing vision, mission, and programs. While pastoring a large church on the West Coast, I invited our elders away for a weekend retreat focusing on our small-group plans. We reserved a large room with wall space for all the sheets of newsprint that would record our plans. We'd prepared for this weekend, praying for God's leading in our time together. We worshiped, prayed, and set aside time for play in the midst of an ambitious planning process. We wanted to draft a vision for the church around small groups and develop a strategic plan to achieve these ends. We began by identifying the challenges to be addressed: we wanted to become a small-group-based church rather than a church with small groups, but we didn't have a sufficient percentage of people in groups at that point. (Note that even before we began our retreat, we were inside a narrative about what we thought the church needed and how everyone coming into the church ought to belong.) We needed a way of recruiting and training more leaders in anticipation of getting a higher percentage of people into small groups. We then mapped out a solution on the newsprint, ably designing the strategies for approaching the goals necessary to achieve our vision for the church. We named people who could be small-group leaders and then brainstormed ways to get them to sign on. Our excitement grew as the framework came together; we followed up with a detailed plan for how we would work to achieve this solution. The plan was based around a series of steps or stages involving initial communication, one-on-one conversations, developing training manuals, recruitment, training, and getting more people into ever more small groups. By the end of our retreat, the walls were covered with our well-crafted plans.

You might ask, What's the problem here? It looks like a common, ordinary, everyday way of going about planning. Isn't this the way it's supposed to be?

That's how maps work. They shape how we see our world so that we assume that it is just the way things are when in fact we are working within a framework of assumptions that we don't question. This mechanistic, objectives-and-outcomes planning framework shapes the imagination of many leaders even while they desire to form mission-shaped communities. Its mental map assumes that (1) if we define a problem clearly enough through analysis (usually meaning breaking the problem down into a series of parts), then (2) we can define a preferred solution, which (3) results in a strategic plan to operationalize the solution and achieve our stated goals (usually in the form of a mission statement).

What is not immediately seen in this process is how it's shaped by the public-private dichotomy Lesslie Newbigin described as a core of modernity. The public (truth, fact, social science method) is the primary reality because it assumes that leadership is about the kind of effectiveness that can be empirically measured and evaluated, hence the preoccupation with demographics that has pervaded church planning for the past decade. The private is limited to the personal beliefs, faith, confessions, and doctrines one chooses to believe. For all practical purposes, strategic planning processes have little room for this private world because faith and science (the public world of facts and data and method) do not commingle.

The public realm of the social sciences and business management have become the default maps shaping assumptions about planning and leadership. We see this in any sampling of books on church organization and leadership; the findings of business management are simply baptized into a Christian perspective through the attachment of Bible verses. Strategic planning models assume that all reality, including human beings in their social communities, is based on a nexus of cause and effect. They assume that leaders can predict then control factors in such a way as to achieve intended outcomes. In my story of a planning retreat, we assumed that if we recruited the right people, trained them in the right ways, and set them up with the correct support systems, we would meet our goals for small-group growth and assimilation of church members through groups. Things did not turn out as we planned. People did not line up with the plan. Some key leaders stepped down from leadership due to circumstances beyond their control. The couple with the most potential to lead rejected our invitation to participate in the vision (oh, those shortsighted people who couldn't get the big picture or wouldn't understand how great our plan was for their life). Another pair decided that they did not fit the direction we were going and left the church. A year later, we had the same number of groups as we had when we laid out our strategic plan. What went wrong? The strategic plan we developed during our retreat looked good on paper. The problem was not in the quality of the plan but in our assumption that we could predict the actions of others, align them with our goals, and control their actions. We also assumed that we were functioning in a world of continuous, gradual, incremental change, and by extension, we believed that the world was predictable and we could therefore manage the future because it looked like the past.

THE STAGES OF STRATEGIC PLANNING

Planning methods followed in the church are usually based on a traditional strategic planning process outlined in this chapter. In a recent set of meetings with two major denominations numbers of the regional and association executives spoke, off the record, confirming that their regions and associations had recently gone through the process outlined in this chapter, acknowledging that after several years of working at such plans there were aware it did not result in the changes or preferred outcomes that had been planned.

Stage I: Internal and External Audits

Strategic planning usually begins with what is called an internal audit, which gathers data and information about the organization and its members. The normal result is a report assessing where the organization currently finds itself. Following the internal audit is an external audit that gathers a similar set of data about the organization's context, such as the neighborhood around the church or a profile of the people who live within a three- to five-square-mile radius of the church, covering demographics and lifestyles. The purpose is to gather information on the beliefs, values, habits, and convictions of various groups in the designated target area. The two audits produce an overall picture of the church and its ministry context.

Stage II: Mission Description

The second stage involves establishing a mission statement based on the information gathered in the two audits and cast in terms of God's purposes. People might engage in Bible study or reflection on key documents within the church's own theological world, such as *Great Ends of the Church* in the first section of the PC-USA's *Book of Order*. In a congregation, a team may be formed to discern God's goals for the church. The process may involve many meetings across the membership. At the end, what emerges is a written description of the congregation's mission that defines its core convictions and values.

Stage III: Vision Statement

The next step is to create a vision statement, based on information gleaned in the first two stages, that is a clear, compelling picture of the preferred future the congregation or denominational organization wants to achieve given its mission statement (the decision to plant a certain number of churches, or revitalizing a specific number of congregations). The vision can include descriptions of what the church wants to achieve in such areas as evangelism, growth, leadership, and worship. It is normally stated in terms of preferred outcomes three to five years into the future. It assumes a linear world of continuous change in which there is a simple cause-and-effect relationship between the present and the future.

Stage IV: Alignment

The congregation next develops a plan that features a series of concrete, measurable actions plotted along a timeline toward achieving its vision. This stage is often called alignment because the plan is intended to bring all programs, resources, ministries, and people in the congregation into alignment with the vision plan through a series of action stages. Today, many of these strategic planning models attempt to deal with the reality that we are no longer functioning in a world of regular, predictable, continuous change by creating what are called *feedback loops.* This means that the plan creates points in its progress where, on the basis of new information and feedback from inside and outside the church, adjustments are made from time to time to fine-tune progress of reaching the goal of the vision.

DISCOVERY OF ANOTHER WAY

In my own wrestling with the implications of the missional theology being developed by people like Lesslie Newbigin and David Bosch, I knew that the strategic planning model I was trained in no longer fit. I was coming to understand that the intellectual frameworks of modernity, based on a billiard ball world of cause and effect, were at odds with this emerging missional way forming in my imagination. I knew my planning model needed to change but had no other maps to help me find alternatives.

Once, after I had presented the themes of this chapter in a meeting, the pastor of a multistaff team stood up and said, "I have just spent a year and sixty thousand dollars working with a group to develop the kind of strategic plan you've just described. I'm already experiencing kickback from staff and members of the church; what do I do now?" What do you do as a leader if you've developed strategic planning processes and are now aware of the issues raised in this chapter? First, it's important not to shift gears suddenly and move in a completely different direction. In the short term, it is better to stay on course. In most congregations, people know that strategic planning is largely a top-down process that is more about meeting the needs of the leaders than innovating a process of real discernment among the people. As a result, most people in the church typically lose interest and focus after several months. Most people's lives are just too busy and too complex to pay much sustained attention to a strategic plan launched by the leadership of a church. Fundamentally, most of us don't have a sustained interest in things we don't own or weren't a part of creating. We are passionate about those things that catch our imaginations, things that speak to us. This doesn't mean good leadership is just about meeting people's needs. It's about facilitating, nurturing, and naming (what I described as *calling forth*) what God is up to in the lives of the people of a local church. In short, don't be overly anxious, and don't make sudden swerves in direction. One of the most basic rules of good leadership is to do what cultivates trust in your leadership. Trust is critical for innovating a culture of missional transformation. Further, as you become aware of the problems inherent in strategic planning, give time to deepening your understanding, working on some of the theological assumptions described in this chapter; take time to understand what the alternatives to strategic planning involve. As an initial step, develop a reading list to help you reframe your own understanding so that you can change your maps, freeing yourself from the old maps of strategic planning that dictated how you saw reality and understood people and the nature of change. Time is required to understand and dwell in an alternative map. The following works might be a good place to start.

Reading for Map-Makers

Peter Block, *Community: The Structure of Belonging* (San Francisco: Berrett-Koehler, 2008)

Joseph Jaworski, *Synchronicity: The Inner Path of Leadership* (San Francisco: Berrett-Koehler, 1998)

Chris Lowney, *Heroic Leadership: Best Practices from a 450-Year-Old Company That Changed the World* (Chicago: Loyola Press, 2003)

Peter Senge, C. Otto Scharmer, Joseph Jaworski, and Betty Sue Flowers, *Presence: An Exploration of Profound Change in People, Organizations, and Society* (New York: Doubleday, 2005)

Nassim Nicholas Taleb, *The Black Swan: The Impact of the Highly Improbable* (New York: Random House, 2007)

Francis Westley, Brenda Zimmerman, and Michael Q. Patton, *Getting to Maybe: How the World Is Changed* (Toronto: Vintage, 2007)

Margaret Wheatley, *Leadership and the New Science* (San Francisco: Berrett-Koehler, 1999)

CHAPTER SIX

EIGHT CURRENTS OF CHANGE AND THE CHALLENGE OF MAKING NEW MAPS

O n the border of Brazil and Argentina, the Iguaçu River cuts through a huge expanse of rain forest. When viewed from a plane, the great, winding river seems tranquil as it meanders through the forest. Then, suddenly, the river turns a bend and explodes down the length of the Iguaçu Falls. Hundreds of waterfalls converge with an overwhelming beauty that makes navigation and travel impossible.

There's no longer a need to convince anyone that we find ourselves tumbling in the turbulent white waters of change. I was speaking with a friend who had just returned from a conference for leaders of large churches where the missional conversation was front and center. None of these leaders needed to be convinced that missional ideas were needed in the face of overwhelming change. Then recently, I spoke with an executive of Procter & Gamble, who was describing to me the state of his church. He didn't need to be convinced that our world is going through huge change. He spoke about his denominational leadership at the regional and national levels, describing them as competent, skilled men and women with a great deal of expertise, energy, and creativity. He listed the programs they've implemented and talked about the "service" culture they have created. But, he said, the denomination is in steady decline, and no matter what programs or plans are thrown at the problem, the decline hasn't stopped. From within the churning waters, the majority of church leaders are well aware of the scale of change. What they are often not seeing or grasping are the multiple, complex forces of change that have come together and propelled them into a new place of uncertainty where they don't know how to navigate their way forward. Without understanding the ways these forces of change have come to together, it is difficult to understand why we need new maps for leading and planning. This chapter and the next provide the bridge between the critique of modernity's maps as seen in strategic planning and the proposal for how to lead in this new place.

WHY MAKING NEW MAPS IS HARD

Have you ever made a resolution to lose weight? Have you stood on the treadmill determined to work hard and change your eating habits only to discover, weeks later, how hard it is to change habits? If journeying in a new space were as easy as knowing that things have changed and that we have to act differently, change would be easy. But change is not easy because things don't work that way—not for you personally, not for your local church, and not for a denominational system. Most of us are wired to resist change—just ask the Israelites as they headed out into the desert. Our inborn resistance to change partly explains why we see intelligent, skilled people reading information about a changed world and still living as if nothing had really changed. The North American auto companies aren't unique in this. When we marvel at how a company as big and filled with bright people as General Motors could be pushed to bankruptcy because of its inability to respond differently in the face of a new reality, we scratch our heads in disbelief. In actuality, GM behaved the same way most of us behave most of the time. When confronted with new information, when convinced that the world has changed and we are in a new space (take, for example, the information and data we have about the environment and the melting of the ice caps), we agree that there is a need to change, but we keep acting in all the ways that got us to where we are. Why? Because the habits, skills, and experiences have served us well in the past (or at least haven't seemed to hurt us), we're comfortable with them, and we want to hang onto them because we really don't want to go through the pain of learning how to behave differently. That is why good, well-meaning leaders can provide endless information on how the world has changed and still come up with programs and answers that are just more of the same.

We learn to function at high levels of performance using our preexisting maps; we know the rules and have become good at being successful within those rules. Our ingrained habits give us not just success but identity because they have provided us with a place in an organization or community. Therefore, we can agree that the world has changed and then just work harder to follow those preexisting maps. This is just the way we function as human beings in social communities. Continuing to do what has worked for us in the past is what makes for stability, and as humans, we value stability. But when the world has really shifted, doing the same old things won't preserve the steady, predictable environment we are used to. As the Proctor & Gamble executive said to me, we keep coming up to the plate and swinging but nothing alters the fact that we keep declining. An executive I met recently expressed it well. About three years ago, he was brought into a denominational system that was in serious decline and embroiled in conflict, with the mandate to turn around the decline and overcome the conflict that had caused previous executives to resign in frustration. Everyone in the denomination agreed that something had to change or there would be no future for the churches of that denomination in that city. Three years in, the executive is bruised and beaten by all the resistance to almost everything he has proposed.

It is one thing to agree that some kind of change is needed in churches and denominations, but if we don't also see the complex forces that have propelled us into a new place of uncertainty, we will try to navigate our way forward on the basis of our existing maps. Without understanding these forces of change, it will be difficult to see why we need new maps for navigating in this new place. What are some of these forces of change?

FORCES OF CHANGE

While we face a long list of challenges, this chapter focuses on eight that are radically changing our world right now. The purpose in highlighting these eight is not to explore them in depth but to show how the combination of these forces of change coming together at this point in time are tumbling us over a waterfall and into the kind of white waters where it is no longer possible to plan and predict using the methods and maps that have guided us to this point. We are, to use Joshua Cooper Ramo's phrase, in an *age of the unthinkable* but trying to address this new space with all the maps of a time when we assumed it possible to identify our challenges and develop plans to create the preferred futures we wanted.

Globalization

Just a short time ago, we lived in a bipolar world where nations aligned according to the categories of East versus West. Economies were carefully managed and determined by the polities of nation-states. Twenty-five years ago, this East-West alignment and the power of national economies were considered the long-established norm for political and economic life. Since the demise of the Soviet bloc, symbolized by the demolition of the Berlin Wall, that world has been swept away. *Globalization* has become the alternative vision of social and economic life. It has become the single most powerful narrative reshaping the economies of the world, national identities, and social relationships between peoples. Around the world, practically no one is immune from the effects of globalization. Poor peasant farmers in rural India have the prices of their rice crops determined by unknown people in Kansas working with mathematical formulas on computers and e-mailing their decisions around the world in an instant. United Auto Workers in Detroit suddenly find themselves without jobs or facing huge pay cuts because of the workers in China who affect the price of oil or car manufacturers in Japan and Korea building cars. New technologies spawned in the latter half of the twentieth century now connect the economic life of the world in a global economy so vast that few can grasp it.

Although globalization seems very new, it represents a resurgence of eighteenth-century laissez-faire free-market capitalism, with its concept of the invisible hand and notion of a natural law inherent in economics that, freed from government control, would result in economic blessing for all.[1] The invisible hand requires that global markets and local economies be free of government regulation.[2] This is a secular theology with its own vision of salvation and eschaton, where an unfettered market creates a new utopia that renews the whole world.

The power of this conception of how the world should work is in its capacity to captivate the imaginations of large numbers of people in North America who buy the marketed message that we are on the cusp of an ever upward economic movement that will carry everyone with it. While there has recently been some loss of faith in this ideology, with incredible rapidity we have accepted the free-market implications of globalization as an *inevitability*. Globalization has become a primary concept overarching all the rest of our lives.

Churches and their leaders are largely silent in the face of the fact that in this massive globalization of economies, work, and production, the definition of what it means to be human is being transformed into *Homo economicus*. What is happening to a culture where the first and most important advice that came from President George Bush after the September 11 tragedy was a call not to pray but to spend? In the midst of the global financial crisis that started in 2008, the dominant concern remains one of getting people to spend again, to buy the goods and services brought in from all over the world. It is no small matter that human beings become commodified. One of the effects of globalization is that workers at all levels of our society feel that they must now take lower wages and work longer hours just to try to keep their jobs and pay their bills. At the same time, companies and governments at all levels cut taxes to attract globally competitive business. To compensate for losses in tax revenues, social benefits are being cut; companies compete with cheaper overseas competitors by cutting pension plans or switching from full-time workers to contract labor, thereby reducing costs. One result is that more and more people feel more and more insecure; they find themselves working longer hours as if they are strapped to a massive rocket of economic inevitability that is beyond their control.

There are huge costs to the current practice of economic globalization. People are being overwhelmed by the reality that the downsizings, offshoring, and clawing back of work security affect some of the most basic relationships that make us human. People no longer have time for life. The new economic realities of globalization require families to spend almost no time together. Parents work longer and longer hours, with children in expensive day care (if they can afford it). When the weekends come, family time is consumed by all the practical elements of family life that couldn't be done in the week (cleaning, shopping, and so on), and Sunday becomes practically the only day when people can find a small moment to relax and do as they please. With the zeal of a religious vision, globalization promises to remake the world through a universal free market. In this evangelistic movement, the local and the particular are encumbrances. All peoples and places are to be homogenized into a single McVillage.

Increasing numbers of people working harder and longer and yet becoming less able to make ends meet in the midst of communities that have been their world? What is happening when young couples with professional jobs and young families have nothing left at the end of month and can't see their way to purchasing even the smallest of homes? Why is it that when we have greater means of communications with everyone, everywhere, there is less and less time for the connections that make life worthwhile? Why do we feel like we've been afloat in a sea of myriad choice that keeps us disconnected in terms of belonging and identity? Have we made a Faustian bargain of terrible proportions? How is it possible for churches to talk about anything and everything except the very forces that pull the most basic human relationships apart?

The pastor of large, successful church described a meeting of his board one evening recently. One member is a heart surgeon working in a busy practice, another is a senior executive of a large company, and a third is the president of a small company. That evening, the agenda was their lives. The surgeon was in distress; he shed tears about the lives in his hands each day and those who died because of their heart disease. The pressures on the hospital's ability to function under massive cutbacks and with reduced resources (the consequence of the reengineering of economic life so that the country can compete more effectively in the global market), along with the reduction of supporting personnel such as nurses, respiratory therapists, and social workers, who performed essential activities, mean that his life as a doctor is increasingly driven by the invisible hand of free-market economics and global competition to the point where he has begun to feel like a soul disembedded from his most basic places of life and meaning. He has little time to be with his family, and his staff are angry because they are all working under the huge pressures of diminished resources and increased demands. He feels a million miles from the vocation he entered, in what feels like another universe. The senior executive nodded as she spoke of a similar experience of life. Living in the new global world that promised a utopia for all is more akin to being chained to a massive rocket of change where people are uprooted from those relationships and social institutions that give life its cohesion.

These themes are ever more familiar in the lives of the busy men and women who turn to churches for rooting and meaning. What they get, however, are courses on how to live "balanced" lives (who can imagine this possibility today?) or plans for more growth in the church or suggestions for committees on which to serve. Globalization represents a great transformation in the form of an uprooting from social relationships that give life; it is the emergence of a social experience of being exiled in our own skins and places of living. How do local churches respond to these realities? How do we learn to create conversations about what is happening to us, our children, and our relationships?

Pluralism

The response was stunning and rapid when Rowan Williams, the archbishop of Canterbury and leader of the worldwide Anglican communion, proposed allowing certain elements of Islamic Sharia law into British law. Members of Parliament, the British cabinet, and the public all screamed their reaction to Williams's astonishing proposal. The intertidal waters of social and cultural transformation are reshaping one Western nation after another. *The new white waters are about the meaning of national identity and the role of religious law in the secular state.* Rowan Williams wasn't selling out the house of British identity and Christian belief; he was being a realist. Given current demographic trends in many European countries, including the UK, there will soon be far too many citizens of Islamic descent to ignore the Islamic sense of law and culture. This is simple mathematics and democracy. What does it mean to have more and more groups living side by side? We simply don't know! Pluralism has arrived with a vengeance, and we are not prepared for its implications.

Arriving at Pearson International Airport in Toronto, I enter anything but the Anglo-Saxon world in which the churches of that city once flourished. I am in a global, polyphonic culture of every people, language, and culture. I'm picked up by a Punjabi cab driver, taken to the Italian district for lunch, mix with a vibrant Chinatown crowd in the afternoon, and spend the evening in the midst of a multicultural audience at the theater. When I land back home in Vancouver, I drive along Granville Avenue toward the North Shore, passing block after block of stores and restaurants composed of polyglot nations. A Thai restaurant stands beside English Fish & Chips, which stands beside

Chinese, which stands beside sushi, which stands beside Italian. Every single one is the genuine article run by immigrants from these nations. Many of the street signs of my city are written in English and Chinese.

Pluralism is a child of modern technology (airplanes and computers). It is related to globalization, but the two are also in conflict. Globalization is based on a vision of a universal civilization shaped by the Western framework of a free market. At the same time, pluralism is the opposite and competing vision: a world in which no single power exercises hegemony and no single belief or ideology dominates.[3] A country or nation becomes a tapestry of alternatives and choices where the multicultural matrix is celebrated. Pluralism and globalization operate side by side, creating confusion and conflict. For example, globalization brings Iranians to Vancouver, and in their mixing with Chinese, European, Russian, and other ethnicities, there is created a pluralism of values that creates often unspoken conflict around how houses are sold or business deals are agreed to. It is a confusing place to live.

In a book summarizing a massive study of religious life in America, Diana Eck described the pluralistic changes reshaping religious life in the United States. "We are surprised to discover the religious changes America has been undergoing," she wrote.

> We are surprised to find there are more Muslim Americans than Episcopalians, more Muslims than members of the Presbyterian Church USA. . . . We are astonished to learn that Los Angeles is the most complex Buddhist city in the world. . . . Make no mistake: in the last thirty years, as Christianity has become more publicly vocal, something else of enormous importance has happened. The United States has become the most religiously diverse nation on earth.[4]

The pluralization of North American culture is having massive effects on the understanding and shape of Christian life here. A book by John Marks, *Reasons to Believe: One Man's Journey Among the Evangelicals and the Faith He Left Behind,* tells of his departure from the evangelical faith and his move toward a disbelief in God. In the introduction, he describes interviewing an evangelical couple in Texas about the *Left Behind* book series. One purpose of this interview was to go back over the places where his evangelical faith was formed to understand it from the perspective of his lost faith. Toward the end of that interview, the couple reached forward to ask Marks a final question: *When Christ returns, will you be left behind?* Marks felt the power of that question in a profoundly deep way. He is married to a woman who is a Jew, and they have a young son; the question implied that his wife and son were condemned to burn in hell. He was shaken to his core by the arrogance of the couple in asking such a question. We are faced here with the irreducible face of pluralism. Increasingly, the people in our churches are living beside, working with, and playing with people from outside the Christian narrative or from a radically different cultural tradition. The interactions and relationships between church members and these differing peoples raise questions about elements of their faith they have taken for granted. These questions are often being asked in silence because many Christians feel they shouldn't have questions about basic convictions of their faith. But many are wondering, and even asking out loud, if, for example, Jesus is really the only way to God. They are watching their Muslim or Buddhist friends and asking themselves if they can still believe what they're being told in church about the "other" who comes from a different faith or a radically different culture.

Pluralism comes in many forms. Most of us live in cities that are increasingly pluralistic. We inhabit time and places characterized by polychromatic national and ethnic composition. Everywhere, airports and malls are filled with the smells and symbols of multiple cultures. Housing developments and schools are gatherings of nations where multiple languages are spoken. Pluralism creates both richness and tensions. We live next door to other nations; we're engaged in conversation with people from all parts of the world, with customs and expectations vastly different from our own.

Beyond that, pluralism creates a dynamic that is far more complex than individual differences of language, customs, food, and clothing. The diversity of religious choice and openness to everything religious results in people crisscrossing religious boundaries as they construct their own personal spiritualities. Our churches are increasingly peopled with those who mix and match, no longer giving credence to the dogmas voiced from a pulpit or spoken from the prayer book even as they sit and listen or repeat the words. The veritable monopoly that Christianity once had in North America has ended.

Many Christians experience pluralism as loss. The metaphor of a religious center is replaced by that of a complex tapestry of divergent choices among a plurality of options. For example, Canadian national radio (CBC) no longer has a Sunday program series based around various Christian worship services. In the place of this long-established program is one called *Tapestry* that explores spirituality in all its multiple forms. Pluralism marks a shift from the idea of a national melting pot (where Christianity was the liquid into which all other ingredients blended) to a web of interrelated options in which no single option is privileged over any other. This is a new situation! Across North America, we can now see the rising buildings of Hindu temples or mosques along with a growing variety of buildings unique to other religions. In a spiritually hungry context, pluralism results in the loss of loyalty to Christian churches that for so long enjoyed a monopoly on religious life. People who attend Christian churches do not necessarily subscribe to a Christian perspective for all of life, or they may incorporate other strands of spirituality into their Christian practice.

As important as this notion of pluralism is, it is also a misnomer. It suggests the existence of clear choices between systems of belief. The reality is different. People now live off an amalgam of fragments they merge together into personal and idiosyncratic beliefs.[5] It is not unusual for a husband and wife to attend a well-established Christian church while also practicing Buddhism and belonging to a discussion group on self-actualization shaped by Taoism or other models of human development. All this spiritual picking and choosing of pieces and fragments of various traditions exacerbates the dilemma of leadership in the churches. What does it mean for those trained as pastors of churches to engage a society in which Christian culture is not at the center, when this was the assumption that has shaped church life? This is why many so-called successful, growing congregations are located in largely white, homogeneous suburbs, insulated from the reality that all around them, Christian culture is a waning influence.

The ethos of a pluralist culture is becoming the norm. In places of work, in our neighborhoods, at the local food stores, in places like Whole Foods or the malls recently refurbished to feel like village streets, and throughout the media, we are increasingly immersed in a pluralist culture and encouraged to taste the choices. We live with neighbors from differing ethnic and religious backgrounds who don't share our beliefs. The claims of Christian life, therefore, are silently questioned as many Christians become confused about their beliefs. Those in churches view Christian teaching not as norms for all peoples at all times but the points of view of the specific denominations to which they belong. In reaction, some form tight, ethnocentric communities to withstand the onslaught of difference. Pluralism represents another of the markers in this white water of transition in which we are now swimming. Christian life in North America was given its formative shape around denominations whose differences were claimed to be theological but were really differences of ethnicity and culture rooted in different parts of Europe and different expressions of the Reformation tradition. This established form of church life is hardly sufficient for guiding us in these tumultuous waters. We must become map-makers in the midst of an increasingly complex, confusing, churning environment. As one leader confessed: no one prepared me for this!

Rapid Technological Change

In the barren, inhospitable landscape of Afghanistan, along a graveyard for invading armies, small bands of men roam the countryside with cell phones communicating via satellite dishes directing bombers and guiding computer-driven missiles to selected targets. In small, isolated caves high in the mountains of that battered country, a small band of men shaped by a fanatical vision of religious life guide an underground war against the United States using exactly the same technology. Small bands of true believers, whether in Iraq, Afghanistan, Lebanon, or the West Bank, use e-mail and cell technology to communicate with each other and plan their attacks. The World Trade Center was brought down by such a group of men who used the powers of technology to turn the world upside down. In unknown offices across the world, faceless investors watch computer screens and are able to transfer, in an instant, huge sums of money around the world irrespective of the effects those decisions may have on the citizens of nations. Globalization and pluralism are driven by unprecedented technological change. Whole classes of workers disappear; work shifts from offices to homes; long-term loyalties are replaced by limited contract work.

The world is linked through an information highway that has become more and more ubiquitous. People meet on Facebook and share their inspirations on YouTube all the while Twittering to an assortment of friends. Groups of people at opposite ends of a continent or around the globe don't need to leave their own contexts in order to meet in real time and in video on Skype or some Webinar format. Telephones are no longer connected by wires in the ground but satellites in the sky that make them usable at all times, everywhere. E-mail means instant communication. The notion of "local" seems to be transformed into "anywhere at anytime." What does it mean for the formation of local churches and communities when people come to believe that "local" can mean anywhere?

This technological revolution is creating a world of amazing wonders. Who can deny the wonder of special effects in movies like *Harry Potter* and *The Matrix* or the power of an artificial heart to extend life, the ability to repair our bodies, change the DNA of food, or transport libraries at the push of a button. There is, however, another side to these technological advances. British sociologist John Gray describes technological innovations of the past two decades as something that makes "a new politics of insecurity universal" as traditional institutions unravel and careers and vocations that once seemed essential to a cohesive society disappear.[6] The technological revolution is both a wonderful gift and a radical uprooting of people at the same time. We are still not able to adequately assess what is happening in education, business, politics, or social life as a result of the technological revolution. The Internet allows a politician to raise more than $20 million in less than a week or turn an unknown like Ron Paul into a candidate for the presidency; it made the "change" mantra of Barack Obama into a national movement that took him to the presidency. It makes the revolutionary imagination of al-Qaeda available to Muslims around the world and turns more and more young people to places like Facebook to share their feelings and thoughts with people they will probably never meet. Technology is transforming the ways we live. Increasingly, those raised in the technological revolution are speaking a different language than our churches, in their print-oriented world. Technology makes communication across the street and around the world instantaneous, blurring the difference between the local and global. Social life is increasingly *delocalized.*

A class of seasoned pastors was asked to spend time in their neighborhoods. Those from the suburban churches complained that "neighborhood" is an urban concept that makes no sense in the suburban environment. They wanted to use the language of "networking" and "third spaces" (the idea that there are neutral spaces where people can meet without the imposition of someone's ideology) as the paradigms of relationship and communication in the contexts where they live and minister. They were saying, in effect, that there are no such things as neighborhoods in their worlds. This perspective is an expression of the ease with which we become captured by the impression that technology makes *place* irrelevant. Once we buy into this language of networks and third spaces, we are essentially buying into a conception of radical individualism in which we create, manage, and control spaces and time and where we intentionally attract (or avoid) particular kinds of people at the times most convenient for us. There is no accountability here because we can remove ourselves (switch away from the talk site or leave the third space) at any time we choose. The result is a pseudo-belonging because we don't have to struggle with the messiness of long-term relationships with the other, our neighbor, whom we may not like or have chosen.

The great thing about a third space is that I am in control. I can leave it whenever I please. It is utopia! People now embrace such notions as expressions of the new, technologically shaped world with little sense of how this approach to living radically undermines Christian life. This belief in a world where place is unimportant and people are increasingly physically disconnected flies in the face of the Incarnation because this most fundamental of Christian convictions confesses that place and people are inseparable and utterly central to human life. The interconnections and bonds that form a local culture (a neighborhood, for example) are being strained. The local is becoming more opaque and the global more pervasive and demanding on our lives.

The implications of technology stretch far beyond the ability to use PowerPoint or video clips in a Sunday morning service, beyond the ability to send e-mails to all the members of a congregation; beyond iPhones, Skype, and Facebook. The pace of change has not just picked up speed; it's become unprecedented and discontinuous. At one level, technology provides new ways of controlling our environment, and at the same time, just the opposite is true: technology represents the banishment of control. I talk with denominational executives and pastors who tell me that the Internet and cell phones, for example, mean they are more and more driven by the web of expectations, demands, and events that are coming at them from a multitude of contexts at the same time. Too many young adults tell the story of living in a job world of contracts. There are many others competing for the same contracts willing to work all the hours it takes to get the work done. With computerization, there is no longer any need for an office where one is accountable to a supervisor; rather, one is driven by the need to work all the time to keep the contract and fend off the competition.

Auto workers in the United States and Canada once thought their jobs untouchable, but technological innovation has made many of them lose out to the competing markets of the East, where people can live on much lower wages and transport their good for less cost per item. How do we make sense of these unknown, unpredictable, and unmanageable forces of the technological revolution? This is the new world of insecurity too many of people are facing.

The multiple ways technology is changing our world raise massive questions about the nature of leadership when it has been based on the ability to manage and control outcomes. The technological revolution undermines our capacity to do that. How do we make new maps where the technological revolution seemed to promise us more control but it ends up doing the opposite? The complexity of all the change doesn't stop here.

Postmodernism

"Postmodernism" is a confusing and misunderstood concept that has become a mantra, or catch-all label, to explain the new space in which we find ourselves. The language of postmodernism symbolizes people's sense that many of the elements of our ways of life have shifted, but we can't yet find the right language to explain what has changed or describe the kinds of skills, habits, and practices we need for this new space.

This postmodern turn is a way of summarizing a series of intellectual and cultural transformations that deconstruct many of the truth claims modernity took for granted as assumed facts. It encompasses philosophical and social movements that sought to explain and reshape the Western imagination after the horrors of the two world wars, the ending of colonialism, and the failure of the secular religions such as Marxism, National Socialism, the belief in the state as all powerful, the idea that the West was the apex of all human progress, and so forth. Although its roots go back to the late nineteenth century, its effects began to be felt during the 1950s and 1960s. The popular understanding of the postmodern shift views it functioning around three basic elements. The first is the so-called loss of confidence in the big stories of late modernity (the incredulity toward grand ideologies representing themselves as universal) such as communism, fascism, and democracy. In other words, the postmodern turn is a reaction to the dominant political ideologies that caused the horrors of the twentieth century as well as a growing conviction that Enlightenment claims of producing "facts" and "absolute truth" through the application of a universal method were fundamentally wrong.

A second element is the claim that there is no real connection between language (the words we use to describe things) and the world (the things we describe). What had been taken for granted as a normative understanding of our relationship to the world, namely, that our language names and is related to what actually exists (as in the biblical story of Adam naming the creatures of the earth), is displaced by the conviction that language tells us nothing about the world outside ourselves but is the form through which various groups exert power over the world and others. (This does not mean that people intentionally plot to use language in this way but rather that we cannot escape the fact that language reinforces a certain power structure.)

A third component of postmodern thought relates to how truth is replaced by ideologies of power. The idea of a consistent, understandable whole shaping human life (often called a *metanarrative*) is replaced by the idea of a *pastiche,* where our lives are actually characterized by a multiplicity of private styles, moments, experiences, and choices that we use to pick and choose our own self-definition. We construct meaning and the shape of our lives much as we select a clothes off a rack, dressing ourselves with completely different styles in order to accommodate our feelings or experiences at a particular time or place. The bipolar world of facts and values is rejected. It is increasingly seen as peculiar to suggest that there are actually frameworks, or ways of life, outside the self that ought to form the basis for social community or the character of a group. For example, the notion of absolute truth that emerged in the West through the Enlightenment is interpreted in a postmodern context as the language game Western people used at that time to ensure the hegemony of their particular metanarrative. In a postmodern reading of the world, people assemble their lives without reference to particular objective norms, rooting their values in personal preferences. It's not difficult, for example, to meet people who go to church from time to time not because it satisfies some criterion of truth but because a certain tradition or liturgy has an aesthetic appeal. People choose to enter a long-term relationship (whether or not they call it marriage) not because they believe they are making a covenant with a wider community and with God but because that is the choice they wish to make at that moment.

A pastiche carries with it the sense of imitation, of life borrowed or simulated; it suggests life lived on the surface, cobbled out of disconnected pieces of stories, traditions, and experiences. Technological change, globalization, and pluralization interact to produce a social context that disembeds people from basic social relationships. People do not feel connected to either a larger story or a social system that forms their identity. They shift about seeking pieces of stories and experiences with which to construct their lives.

Recent Canadian literature captures this new kind of postmodern individual. Anne Michaels's *Fugitive Pieces* deals with people whose social history and formative groupings in life have been torn apart through the terrible world wars; they are exiles and fugitives from their homes, searching out pieces from their past as they try to make new lives in their strange new homeland of Canada. Michael Ondaatje's novel *The English Patient* creates a similar picture. Working in the Italy of World War I, a Canadian nurse encounters a dying stranger, the English patient, who is not really English but someone totally other. He is an exile whose life and relationships have been blown to pieces by the horrors of war and the ideologies of powers. Yann Martel's *Life of Pi* is the story of an Indian boy whose immigrating family is shipwrecked, and he is set afloat with a zoo animal until finally arriving in Canada. The boy is another of the exiles, the displaced people traveling in a new land with strange imaginations about uncertain futures. These are all characters that express our confusion about a world that has changed; they inhabit a world where the old cartographies no longer work, where solid ground has evaporated into air to become only an illusion. They are living in places where all of life has to be made all over again.

Postmodernity is not so much a concrete marker sticking up in the white waters of change as a language that expresses our confusion and need to transcend the polarities and destructiveness the modern period has produced. This questioning of the modern has being going on since at least the last quarter of the nineteenth century. The postmodern turn has been developing in Western life from before the beginning of the twentieth century. It is a form of shorthand for the fact that we don't know where we are and we are having difficulty getting our bearings. It is a comment on the fact that few of us believe any longer that we in the West are the most "progressive" and "developed" people in history and that we have a privileged method that gives us access to truth unlike any others. These kinds of metanarratives and the hegemony we claimed for having truth under our control have been completely deconstructed. We know now that we live among a plurality of truths where there are no privileged positions anyone can claim to know more "truly" than any other group. This is what contributes to our disorientation, raising questions about the nature of Christian belief in a pluralist society. Postmodern language is a way of expressing this deep confusion and anxiety. Debates over correct definitions of postmodernity that would give us control and help us manage the right programs (for example, postmodern worship) will misdirect and are only examples of how we continue to think using modernity's maps as we try to navigate new terrain. Creating new maps requires creating spaces where people are safe to give voice to the lives they are really living. In such places, the Spirit brings forth new imagination. Definitions and formulas shut down such possibilities.

Staggering Global Need

In the summer of 2008, I was in southern Africa for meetings with missiologists from around the world to discuss the impact of globalization (and the export of the multiple modernities of the West) on the issues of leadership formation for the church. At those meetings, we perceived God calling forth a new world. As Christians from a variety of nations shaped by late modern, globalizing cultures, we all found ourselves in a place where none of us had been before. Our sense of calling was about forming leaders able to discern the mission of God by listening to the local voices of God's people and helping form Christian communities that can mediate engagement between the Gospel and these globalizing cultures. Approximately thirty people met together for five days. We had planned the consultation so that half of those attending were Africans.

As we met in groups to share our stories, it was stunning to realize that every one of our African friends told stories involving death in their families from AIDS—part of the terrible common story in all their lives. We sat with bright, vibrant men and women who shared with us what it was like to live with the virus in the midst of church communities that still denied its existence and made their own people feel like pariahs when they had the disease. This social reaction to AIDS is especially hard on infected women, who in the midst of poverty and ostracism must find ways of earning a living and staying healthy as they take antiviral drugs. Several of us church leaders from North America and the UK sat with a group of these women who told the stories of their struggles together. They were heartbreaking stories even as they revealed the strength, tenacity, and faith of these women, who had formed their own circles of support in the midst of grinding poverty. One young woman stood before us with a five-year-old boy. She told us he hadn't eaten for two days, that he had AIDS, and that there was no money to purchase either the food or drugs he needed. These women knew we were Westerners and had no compunction about bringing this little boy to us and asking for money. In their desperate plight, they would do anything to help the young in their midst. This child's story is one tiny example of the extent of human suffering and the massive global need that exists outside the West. And we can no longer pretend we don't know. The agonizing question, however, is what can be done. We know that these issues of poverty and AIDS must be tackled from other levels beside individual donations. But where is the will to make a difference? What does it mean when the economic and political systems we created in the Christian West seem unable to address the massive needs of huge parts of our world?

The African continent is dying, seemingly cast adrift by the powers of this world. Nelson Mandela has asked whether globalism only benefits the powerful, offering nothing to people ravaged by the violence of poverty. The answer seems to be a muted "very little"! Seventy percent of all new HIV infections occur in sub-Saharan Africa. Over 28 million men, women, and children are living with AIDS. The life expectancy of an African male has gone from sixty-two to forty-one. In Botswana, 44 percent of pregnant women are HIV-positive. These nations are losing their teachers, farmers, young professionals, and future leaders. We're in the midst of a human tragedy that, if left unaddressed, will approach the scale of killings in the world wars and genocides of the twentieth century and the Black Death of the sixteenth and seventeenth centuries.

AIDS in Africa is but one example of the scales of human tragedy confronting the world. The numbers of refugees and homeless people living in dislocation and abject poverty is rising at an astonishing rate. Around all the major cities of the non-Western world grow massive squatter towns composed of hundreds of thousands of people who can't hope to improve their subsistence living under current global conditions. The overwhelming majority are under fourteen years of age. Former United Nations Secretary General Kofi Annan stated that a quarter of the human race seems condemned to starvation.

Every day, the media (technology with its video phones and satellite communications) brings to us the immense human need confronting our world. We have created a global communication village in which we are brought face to face with staggering need at both the human and natural levels. Disease, exploitation, the displacement of peoples, and ecological destruction all increase the levels of vulnerability experienced by increasing numbers of peoples and the earth itself. Robert Kaplan, in his book *The Coming Anarchy,* does not envision a future in which the world experiences a lift (like a boat in a lock) through the expansion of economic globalization and communications technology. On the contrary, the metaphor he uses to describe the emerging order is dark: the world will be like a massive Soweto through which is driving a white stretch limousine carrying the comparatively few beneficiaries of globalization.[7] A complex world of need has emerged in which it is not easy to identify causes or to shape responses. The question that is raised in a muted way has to do with what it means to be the church in this world. Can we really claim to be followers of Jesus in Western churches when we largely ignore the massive suffering all around us and focus instead on seeker-sensitive services or self-help sermons that sound more like Oprah and Dr. Phil?

At first glance, the face of global need might not seem like a marker in the white waters of change where church leaders find themselves. At the very least, it presents an unprecedented challenge to our imagination as leaders, raising profound questions about people's very conception and practice of the Gospel in such a world. How do leaders cultivate local churches that begin to figure out how to live appropriately in this kind of world? This is a daunting question when most Protestant churches shaped out of the European and Reformation traditions are located in the affluent suburbs, embodying the very lifestyle that cannot be sustained if there is to be any kind of global justice. If we think for a moment of what it costs us to sustain the highly individualized lifestyles of the suburb where we have all our own resources, gadgets, and personal items, it becomes clear not only that very few people on this planet can afford this lifestyle but also that it takes huge amounts of resources and energy to sustain this style of life. Christian social life in the West, in terms of living styles, forms of consumption, and resource usage, does not represent the way in which global human life can thrive into the future. People in our churches vaguely know this, but it's easier to put this knowledge aside because there seem to be no obvious answers to the suburbs and the oil-guzzling automobile. What does it mean to make maps that transform the very ways we live as Christians in the West? How do leaders trained to engage and meet the personal needs of individuals form kingdom-based social communities that imagine together how to develop new ways of living and using their resources for the sake of the rest of humanity?

Loss of Confidence in Primary Structures

The Spanish sociologist Manuel Castells, who now teaches at USC, wrote a three-volume study of the technological revolution, identifying among its effects that the time in which we now live is characterized by a loss of confidence in the primary structures of modern life (political, juridical, medical, educational, religious, and economic). Fewer and fewer people believe that these institutions have the capacity to provide direction in the white waters of tumultuous change where we find ourselves. The presidential election of 2008 in the United States was characterized by the theme of change. Even while there is a renewed hope that the government of President Obama will forge a different and better future, there is a deep pessimism in the institutions that have shaped us, and while this is especially true of financial institutions, this pessimism goes to heart of the ways we have organized and shaped ourselves as a culture. It seems no longer possible to believe that the political, legal, and educational systems we have created have the will or capacity to address the global crisis we face.

As I sit in an airport and write this, I have just come from having lunch with a couple in their mid-fifties who have been church leaders for many years, serving in local church pastorates as well as Christian education. After a lifetime of commitment to the church, they are confessing that they no longer attend any church. "What's the point?" they ask. "What happens in those places is just disconnected from the realities of what people are experiencing in their everyday lives." I have heard this story in city after city across North America. We are witnessing the implosion of the existing church because growing numbers of Christians of all ages find its structures and the forms of its narratives irrelevant. This decline is not about people looking to have their "needs" met; it's about honest, committed Christians who just can't do church anymore. Many people, Christians included, sense that the primary structures of modernity in terms of education, politics, and religion are the sources of the massive human and ecological problems facing the world or at least have nothing to contribute to the solutions. This is a stunning shift in perception and conviction in a brief period of time. The young adults protesting the decisions of the Group of 20 as they met in France and Germany in April 2009 may have cheered Obama as a personal, charismatic leader, but they don't believe their governments have the capacity to shape policies that reflect the conscience of their people. They are more likely to listen to someone like the social activist Naomi Klein, author of *No Logo* and *The Shock Doctrine*, who argues that the primary structures that run our society are not serving us in ways that contribute to a resolution of our crisis.

The implication of this loss of confidence is that church leaders are faced with the reality that people have lost confidence in them as leaders and in the institutions of the church. Today, people form their commitments around small self-help and support groups to address their problems. They join loose networks rather than the social institutions that characterized the last century. Government is viewed as part of the problem, not the solution. Increasing numbers of parents opt out of public school systems to educate their children at home or in private schools. Churches become anachronisms with little to say about the pressing issues of life. In the heartland of Mennonite life in America, one leader described how numbers of his close friends are walking away from their church world to practice Buddhism for the sake of addressing the world's needs. They can no longer find hope in the church that formed them as children. Here is an incredibly difficult white water marker to negotiate for leaders. In the midst of all the churning waters of change, increasing numbers of Christians are simply leaving behind the boats that have carried Christian life for a very long time. What does a leader do in the midst of this massive shift?

The Democratization of Knowledge

Change is coming so quickly from every direction that it can't be monitored, managed, or controlled. The information and communications revolution means that knowledge has been democratized and is no longer governed by or limited to experts. We no longer need the hugely expensive computer systems few could afford that regulated access to information. The home computer is thousands of times more powerful than those that first directed men to the moon. Information technology that only a few years ago required enormous amounts of capital is now at our fingertips for very little money. As a consequence of the democratization of information, church systems that formed their identity on the control and distribution of knowledge now find themselves adrift. Some organizations still try to exert control over their staff in this new space through documents—letters, for example, that define what should be believed, taught, and practiced. If only it were that simple!

A side effect of losing control over the dissemination of knowledge is the erosion of prestige and power that came to professionals and the established leaders of organizations who served as the gatekeepers of knowledge and information. In practical terms, church leaders have lost their place as respected professionals who had the lock on certain forms of knowledge. Thanks to the Internet, everyone can access multiple networks that share information about church, theology, the Bible, and culture. All this knowledge is now in the public domain, open to any with the desire to follow the information highways. The leader has been decentered as the conduit of knowledge, and there are now multiple networks of knowledge within a congregation. Issues of ethics, morality, rules for life, and cultural practices can no longer be set by the brand name of the denomination or ordained clergy. The rules governing how systems work are changed through this democratization process.

This new space requires multiple forms of dialogue and negotiation. People come to issues with informed perspectives; any notion of leaders and experts as repositories of truth is losing its relevance. This democratization of information raises questions about a leader's identity and the skills he or she will need in this new space.

The Return to Romanticism

Whenever the waters of change are stirred, the perception grows that the dominant focus on management, predictability, and control is leading us in the wrong direction. This is exactly what happened from the beginning of the twentieth century up to the outbreak of the First World War. The reaction against the controls of rationalism resulted in a massive outpouring of Romanticism: a commitment to the moment, a trust in the connection and truth found in one's inner experience, a conviction that outside of ourselves existed another world, an ideal world we could grasp intuitively, which would be a clearer guide to the nature of life on this planet. Romanticism was a reaction to rationalism, with its commitment to method and use of reason alone and its belief that all of life could be explained in terms of scientific knowledge and purely materialist explanations. This gave rise to a corresponding crop of idealists who predicted or agitated for a new world order. What is happening in our time, in this new space, is no different. All the idealists, with their wonderful dreams of a new future and a different kind of world, are reemerging, telling us about the shape of things to come or presenting us with some past moment in history that gives us clues to how we are to function in the new space.

We must be aware of these responses to our turbulent time, particularly since they have infiltrated the ranks of professionals striving to help the church out of its current situation. Even books on missional life and change in the church have fallen prey to the Romantic fallacy. Some provide formulas (even to the point of providing equations in the form of $A + B = C$) for becoming missional churches without ever recognizing that this imposing of such a rational process is about control and management in a place were both are no longer possible. These promises of providing a formula that will produce the ideal of missional life are leading young church leaders down a road that will take them back to the future of modernity and management in the name of postmodern innovation. Such formulas suggest that someone has found the key, the hidden knowledge, the new postmodern technique that will usher in the organic, noninstitutional, nonhierarchical church. Such are the dreams of the new Gnostics. When our maps of the world no longer mark where we are, many will look for the Pied Piper who can lead them on the new "right" path. In this new space, looking for a mysterious stranger to provide all the answers is a beguiling temptation but nevertheless a false and unrealistic hope.

I am reminded of a nineteenth-century Romantic image: a painting by Casper David Friedrich called *Wanderer Above the Sea of Fog*. Friedrich portrays a solitary individual (himself) standing in the foreground of a massive, mountainous landscape. The immense bulk of mountains stand before him amid the fog of civilization and urban, industrialized life below. The fog represents the confusion and pollution of urban life that stands in the way of a clear vision. As the title of the painting suggests, however, Friedrich, as the paradigmatic

Romantic, has managed to stand above the fog in order to see the world from above it all. This is the kind of Romantic temptation I fear we can fall into right now. Like the wanderer standing alone above the swirling fog, we, in the midst of a strange new space, can be tempted to believe that we too can get above the fogs of confusion and see a new solution, find a new method for making the church work as it once did. The truth, however, is that at this point in time, there are no formulas that will give us back control and no ideals in the forgotten past that can become the means for making our worlds work.

CONCLUSION

This chapter has discussed some of the forces transforming our world. Others could be named, but these eight currents of change are sufficient to indicate the challenge leaders now face. At this moment, we are experiencing something like a perfect storm where a series of factors have come together at one time to change our world. This is why leaders have to become map-makers in our time, but to do so, we need to determine what is involved in leading in this place. We can begin to answer this question by examining the connection between the multiple complex changes shifting our world and something that has become a part of almost every level of our lives: the Internet. In this connection are the clues to how we should lead in this time.

CHAPTER SEVEN

LESSONS FROM THE FORMATION OF THE INTERNET FOR LEADING IN THIS NEW SPACE

In the March 2009 edition of *Atlantic* magazine, Richard Florida, author of such best-sellers as *The Rise of the Creative Class* and *Who's Your City?* wrote the lead article, titled "How the Crash Will Reshape America." His basic point was that the massive financial implosion of 2008–2009 won't be just a bad period or a bear market we all have to go through before we get back to normal. It will change the fundamental nature of life in America in ways we have hardly begun to imagine. Some cities will flourish, but others, some known as thriving centers of commerce throughout the twentieth century, will shrivel up and all but disappear. His concluding sentence at the end of the opening section is this: "I believe the financial meltdown marks the end of a chapter in American economic history, and indeed, the end of whole way of life."[1] Florida's point is that we will need to develop a new imagination about the world in which we live if we are to thrive in a place where most of what we've known about economic life for decades will have ceased to exist.

How do we develop such an imagination as leaders of churches caught in this new world? Chapter Six identified eight factors contributing to the turbulent "in-between" reality we are facing.

Additional reality-shifting transitions could include the following:

New nonstate actors. It wasn't too long ago that organizations like al-Qaeda, Abu Nidal, and Hamas were not part of our vocabulary. Today, they are in the daily news as new actors who threaten and attack the security of nations. What is different about these groups is that unlike our previous enemies, these have no address, no location where they can be nailed down or engaged with conventional means of fighting. They have propelled us into a new world of risk and insecurity.

A looming energy crisis. The competition for oil and the rising price of this commodity suddenly change the balance of power in the world, threatening to fundamentally undercut a way of life we have taken for granted and transform the very nature of our economies. Our suburban way of life is based on cheap oil. What do we do when it no longer exists? The majority of our middle-class churches are dependent on the internal combustion engine as the majority of their congregations drive to reach the church building. What happens when people have to cut out this drive each Sunday because of the cost of gas?

New insecurities. We once thought that a whole list of basic diseases had been eradicated, but we now face a new list of viral infections that threaten our lives. A few years ago, we had never heard of SARS, AIDS, or the bird or swine flu. Suddenly, the world feels a lot scarier and a lot less predictable.

This chapter makes the connection between these complex forces of change reshaping our world, the challenge of developing a new leadership imagination, and the development of the Internet.

UNDERSTANDING THE LEVEL OF CHANGE WE FACE

When we observe something we haven't seen before, we attempt to fit it into our own experience or repertoire of knowledge. That is how we work as human beings. This is also an example of how we translate something new and unexpected into something we know.

The Internet represents a radically changed way of thinking about how we function in the world; it represents a new space being created in terms of social networking, communications, the ways we learn, and the ways we create identities for ourselves.[2] At the workshops I host, I ask people (many of them leaders of local churches and denominations running major vision, mission, and strategic planning programs) to identify the center of control in this new space. I then ask them to meet in groups and develop a strategic plan for managing the Internet world. In other words, I ask them to think about how their learned world (their maps) of management, control, predictability, and preferred futures will work in this new space. It is at this point that for some, the reality begins to sink in that we just might be in a new space after all and the maps of modernity by which we were raised may not help us navigate this place. How did this world of the Internet come into being? The answer addresses our question about how we lead in a new space.

THE INTERNET: HOW DID IT HAPPEN?

When I considered the Internet's founding and development for the first time, I immediately understood in a new way why the challenges of leadership had become so hard and started to be able to visualize the ways we needed to address this new world into which we had tumbled.

The Internet is more than a bunch of computers talking to one another. It's like an ancient bazaar—a wondrous gathering of people talking, hosting, buying and selling, connecting, disconnecting, and communicating in a multitude of interactions, giving the ability to change people's imagination, spark a movement of hope, manipulate billions of dollars in a fraction of a second, or plunge innocent children into the hell of pornography. In terms of our modern maps for leading and planning, the Internet is nothing like the ordered, organized, managed world for which most of us were trained.

The 1960s marked the height of the Cold War between the East and West, with the threat of a nuclear holocaust a terrible reality staring people in the face. One of the concerns the federal government wanted to address was the protection of U.S. communications among its governments and military should Soviet A-bombs destroy major communication networks. Experts in the early stages of computer development (when computers were huge mainframes that filled rooms) tried to imagine how to create such a system. It seemed like an impossible task. Initially, the idea was born to place a number of computers in a number of locations across the U.S. Southwest (places like Los Angeles, Santa Barbara, Arizona, and so on in such a way that numbers of them would continue communicating with one another should several be destroyed in a nuclear attack. This is was the first experimental step in what no one anticipated—the formation of the Internet.

The Internet developed in three phases:

Phase 1: The Internet's beginning in 1969.

Phase 2: The Internet's transformation. Flowing out of phase 1 like a series of rivers are a number of lines representing some of the primary developments in the Internet's early growth that contributed to the transformation of its original design to something radically different.

Phase 3: The Internet in 1999. Clearly, something radically different has emerged that was not conceived of in the original design. Instead of a series of lines connecting boxes, what evolved looks like a dense series of ganglions and neurons with many, many connecting points.

Let's look at each phase in more detail to understand the changes that took place and then connect our understanding to the elements of cultural changed discussed in Chapter Six and the question of how we must lead in this new environment. It is this interconnection that will help us see how we might become map-makers.

Phase 1: The Internet, 1969

The world's first computer network was established as a research project with connecting sites across California, Arizona, and Utah. None of the creators had any thought or intention of creating the complex Internet we now take for granted.

The initial design of the Internet reflects the relatively linear, hierarchically ordered world of the 1960s, and it was an appropriate design given the particular needs and goals of the creators at the time. They could not have designed a different system: there was no way these initial designers could have imagined the implications involved in what they were developing, nor could they have foreseen what would emerge from their original work. It's fairly easy to describe the relationships between the computers in this diagram. Therefore, it is also relatively easy to predict how the system would function and what it could achieve in the not too distant future. Reality was structured in terms of manageable connections and identifiable hierarchies that ensured predictability. It was possible to define the role of the computers and the trajectories of the system. The initial development of the Internet could not have happened without this framework, consisting of the following:

Primary centers of focus
Series of controlled forces
Hierarchy, control, and predictability
Energy focused on a few fixed elements
A continual process of regulating and fine-tuning the whole system in order to maintain its stability and keep control over its functioning
People building on what they knew about the nature of how the world worked

When that first system was designed, no one imagined where it would eventually lead, nor could anyone predict the kinds of relationships that would emerge over the next thirty years.

Phase 2: Factors Transforming the Internet

As new elements were added to the original Internet, it unexpectedly started to shift out of a stable, predictable pattern and entered a phase of growth and disruptive change. This change was the result of experimentation and learning new ways of using the system. Quite quickly, all kinds of people and organizations saw the Internet's potential and began bringing many kinds of innovations and applications to its use.

As a wide variety of people experimented with the original design, its use broadened beyond the military purposes for which it was created. Universities, business, industry, and then broader public organizations and private groups saw the potential of the Internet's application across a whole range of areas, such as the ordering of communications across large organizations, its ability to gather huge amounts of data and apply them to everything from movie special effects to reading the delicate shaping of the heart to bringing disparate groups into instant conversation with each other. The possibilities seemed endless. Groups were quickly designing applications for their specific contexts, which meant new pressures to come up technologies and software systems to enable the Internet to integrate and absorb all this new potential. The result was an unplanned and unintended series of developments that in turn released their own unexpected forces. The laws of complexity and unintended consequences were suddenly at work in what was supposed to have been a simple, elegant system for communication in a nuclear war.

Then came a large increase in domain names (from 26,000 in 1992 to 5 million in 1999), the amount of usage time on the Internet (by 1999, there were some 17.6 million users in the United States alone), an increase in the average number of times someone comes online, and the number of people using the Internet. At one level, each factor by itself is a mundane thing. There is nothing radical, unique, or new in any of these things taken individually. It is what happened to them when they started to interact with each other that made all the difference. This was the development no one anticipated or had control over. There was no strategic plan at work here. In fact, the transformations happened in spite of the best management, predictability, and control systems that universities, governments, and the military could buy. For example, as the number of domain names being registered increased, there was exponential growth in online usage (the number of users online at any given time, the amount of time users spent on the Internet, and so on). The original design involved manageable functions within the overall structure with links and trajectories that had a limited scope. But as the Internet shifted out of a purely military environment into multiple settings of universities, governments, businesses, and households, the applications and effectiveness of the Internet changed rapidly. All these forces crowding into the Internet and its growth began to take on a life of their own. The shape, nature, and organizational form of the Internet moved out of any single group's control, becoming a new entity with increasing levels of complexity across all its interactions. No master designer planned that this would happen. No Wizard of Oz lurked in the background, plotting the steps and stages along the way to produce the present-day Internet. One of greatest sources of cultural transformation in our time did not come from a strategic plan or the alignment of resources. In what we might call an organic, almost spontaneous, uncontrolled way, the Internet grew and was transformed into something we would not have even imagined when it was first designed.

As phase 2 developed, the original Internet system shifted from a few to multiple centers of energy. The shift from singular to multiple centers is crucial for the transformation that eventually took place, since the system began to fluctuate around a growing number of variables. This in turn created multiple pathways that were initially distinct and separate.

Imagine, for the sake of explanation, that each of the factors I've discussed is the equivalent of a sound wave. I have no musical ability, but I am told that music happens because the sounds instruments produce are actually sound waves with different amplitudes. These sound waves, in an orchestra, for example, interact and in most cases produce a harmony of sounds. But these same sound waves, when placed under great stress and put in too much interaction, can produce a cacophonous dissonance. Various interactions of sounds waves can transform the nature of the music, just as various interactions of the forces of change can transform the nature of the system. This interaction can be illustrated in the following way. A sound wave can be shown as a simple wavelike line, like the ones in Figure 7.1. These are illustrations of simple, single waves moving at different amplitudes. We might think of the original Internet being composed of

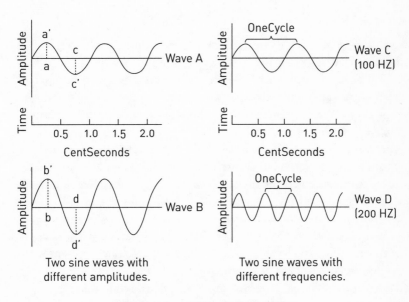

Figure 7.1.   A Simple Sound Wave.

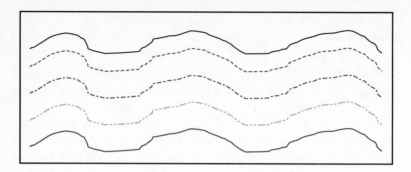

Figure 7.2.   A Series of Simple Sound Waves in Harmony.

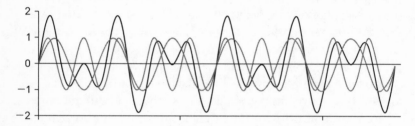

Figure 7.3.   Sound Waves Interactions with Each Other.

several separate waves moving at a level of amplitude that makes them work together in harmony, as depicted in Figure 7.2.

But as the frequency of Internet use increases and other factors start to grow exponentially, the waves begin to increase in amplitude. Now imagine an exponential increase in frequency caused by unparalleled growth in the Internet and its usage. The waves move more and more quickly, and the amplitudes get greater and greater. This causes them to interact as shown in Figure 7.3. The more intense the interactions, the greater the shift away from the expected ways the various elements were working with one another to something very different, as shown in Figure 7.4.

As more and more variables continue to interact, the process of transformation accelerates, which brings us back to the present maps of the Internet. What has emerged looks and acts completely different from the original Internet. How we understand and engage this transforming Internet will also need to change.

Figure 7.4.   Interactions Transform the Nature of the Sound Waves.

The Internet is no longer linear and distinct; it can't be predicted or managed. This transformation is unplanned, but it is not chaotic in the sense that everything is falling apart. Something radically new has emerged. The images in phases 1 and 3 seem to bear no relationship to one another, yet the latter has emerged out of the former. The imagination that conceived the Internet in phase 1, however, cannot be the imagination that will traverse the Internet in phase 3. A different map is required because the morphing Internet has created a new world, a new space. The transformation of the Internet is like the kind of change happening in the worlds of leadership and church life. Just as we needed to learn new ways of living with the Internet, so we have to learn new ways of leadership and church in our shifting world.

Phase 3: The Internet, 1999

It is obvious that in the shift from phase 2 to phase 3 a massive change has taken place. We are not dealing with the same realities, and yet the change occurred seemingly in a flash. A host of unexpected and uncontrolled factors converged to create an Internet that looks more like millions of interconnected nodes and nerve cells in an organism than a predictable, manageable, mechanical, hierarchical structure. A distinct pattern drawn as a series of boxes and lines blurs into an indefinable pattern where expected pathways disappear and we no longer see a structure that gives us control of the space.

Ask questions about this kind of Internet based on the established maps described in earlier chapters. Where, for example, is the center of control? There is none! How would one draw the lines of connection and relationship among all the elements? It would be impossible! How would one design a strategic plan to manage the movement and predict the outcomes of this new reality? It can't be done! In other words, so many of the rules, assumptions, and capacities that have guided us until now will not function in this new space of millions of diffuse yet connected nodes. Any notion of being able to form a plan and then align all the elements of this world to fit the plan is out the window.

This is a world that doesn't want to operate according to the rules and laws in which most of us were trained. And yet we are all aware that it is a world that is extremely effective in allowing people to communicate with one another, in creating space for creativity and innovation, for gathering information that changes the way nations relate to other nations and breaking down the barriers of time and distance. This is a world that has democratized information, creating a space where ordinary people have access to almost all the information that was once the domain of experts or the few people in power. This Internet is revolutionizing the world. And no one planned it that way—it emerged organically! There is no command center, no leader or group of leaders in charge, planning and directing everyone else. Here is a world free from control; it is self-organizing and cannot be managed. Business leader Charles Sirois points out:

> The speed of change brought about by the convergence of information technology and communications has transformed the predictable mechanical world, replete with automatism and relative stability, into an organic world in constant flux, one that moves fast in unexpected directions. . . . We can no longer predict the behavior of people or organizations with any reliability, because their interactivity on the network renders their behavior random and chaotic. At the heart of this change is the banishment of control. Change is coming quickly and from every direction; it cannot be monitored, managed or controlled.[3]

How do we lead and form churches in this kind of world when most of our competencies and skills are for a world that no longer exists?

WHAT WE ARE EXPERIENCING

Only a brief moment ago, the church enjoyed a favored status at or near the center of our culture. The church was like a wide, mature river flowing majestically through a settled, established landscape, providing identity, sustenance, and direction for those who lived along its banks. It shaped a culture; we took the river almost for granted. Like the Mississippi of "Old Man River," it just kept rolling along, providing a powerful point of reference and meaning for all. This world has suddenly disappeared! In its place is the experience of cultural shifts bombarding our lives and forming new patterns of being in the world.

Just as we could explain the emergence of the Internet in three phases, we can describe the emergence of this new space in three phases.

To clarify this shift, we will look at each of the three phases as they apply to our world.

Phase 1: The Known World

Modernity was the environment into which we were born and within which we learned certain skills of leadership and assumptions about how organizations and systems should work. Some (nation-states, for example) have not been discussed in this book, but my intention here is not to explicate every element on the list but to point toward the over-all nature of the "map" it represents, which has been the way we have learned to work and thrive up until very recently. This map told us we lived in a world we could manage through expertise and create the pre-dictability we wanted. We no longer live in this world. We have entered a different space. Phase 2 parses out the character of that space.

Phase 2: Liminality

The multiple elements of change we discussed in Chapter Six that have been moving across the geography of our culture for the past several decades are but a few examples of a process of discontinuous change that is accelerating rather than showing any signs of slowing down or returning to some prior period of stability and normalcy.

This transformational phenomenon is not limited to the Internet. Malcolm Gladwell's book *The Tipping Point: How Little Things Can Make a Big Difference,* provides insight as to why this is so.[4] Gladwell investigates why major changes often seem sudden and unexpected, suggesting that such transformations are dependent on small num-bers of people and patterns that can't be predetermined. In our everyday life, there are sets of emergent patterns over which no one has control but in which lots of people play a part, even if they don't recognize that they are involved in a level of patterning and change that can transform their reality. The Internet itself is an example of this. The result, in Gladwell's language, is that a series of factors that may seem disconnected or inconsequential to what we are doing at this moment eventually come together in ways that produce a "tipping point." A series of unconnected, unforeseen events or forces converge, gather momentum, and produce what is experienced as a sudden, massive, unexpected transformation in the way we live or see reality. Hence the Internet!

Gladwell's notion of a tipping point goes a long way toward accounting for why we now find ourselves in a new space where our established maps for navigating the world no longer correspond to the topography. The reality of this tipping over into a new world has more to do with the crisis facing church leaders and church systems than arguments that Christendom or institutions or clergy are the problem, explanations that reflect our need to fit our experience into our current categories or maps rather than actually helping us identify what is happening.

Independently, each of the forces contributing to the transformation of North American culture (summarized in Chapter Six) is not sufficient to account for the massive levels of discontinuous change we now experience. The academic and urbanologist Richard Florida, whose book *The Rise of the Creative Class* was a best-seller, describes this tipping-over process as our being at the end of a whole way of life. The convergence of a series of differing forces in a compressed moment of time (the past quarter-century) has tumbled us into a new space where our established maps no longer make sense of where we find ourselves.

This is why the church, among many other systems foundational to modernity, has been thrown into sudden, massive, unexpected change. The transformation of the Internet helps us understand how to address this new context. It suggests how we might lead and create new maps for the mission of God in our churches, a world in flux, as depicted in the phase 2 image. Again, no one intentionally planned for this to happen, but this is where we are, and we cannot ignore it.

Phase 3: The Emergent Future (New Space)

We don't know what is emerging or what the new forms of church and mission will look like at this point. This is why we have to become map-makers. We are in a place of adaptation, a new space that is the gift of the Spirit. We are in this place of confusion where our maps no longer serve our needs not because of unsolvable world changes but because the God of creation wants to call forth in us a new imagination as God's people.

ADAPTATION AND DISCONTINUITY

What confronts us are multiple, accelerating forces of discontinuous change that require us to learn adaptive skills to shape communities of faith and witness. Adaptive leaders know they no longer have the answers but are ready to become map-makers. The experience of the Internet suggests the ways in which we might become these kinds of leaders in our churches, as we shall explore in Chapter Eight.

PART TWO

THE MAP-MAKING PROCESS

CHAPTER EIGHT

CULTIVATING A CORE IDENTITY IN A CHANGED ENVIRONMENT

T he chapters in Part Two present a series of four steps for doing missional planning or developing the skills of missional map-making in local churches. The intent is to provide an overview of how to go about missional map-making in the hope that leaders will be able to adapt the specifics to their own traditions and their local contexts. The first two steps are covered in this chapter, step 3 is treated in Chapter Nine, and step 4 is the subject of Chapter Ten.

STEP 1: ASSESS HOW THE ENVIRONMENT HAS CHANGED IN YOUR CONTEXT

Use the descriptions presented in this section to ask questions about your own environment, about the ways in which the context has changed, and about how people are responding to this changed environment. The experience I describe may not be the same as yours, so what are the specific experiences in your own context?

As I pastored several congregations in Canada over a number of years, I began to recognize that something fundamental was changing church life with relation to the cultural transformations we would come to describe as globalization and postmodernism. One indicator was that the people turning up at the various churches I pastored were coming from other churches. I was also aware of the ways in which the forms of church life we were practicing required a number of full-time staff and volunteers to attend to a set of factors shaping the inner workings of the church (worship, small groups, children and youth programs, discipleship, and so on). Those of us in leadership bought into an implicit expectation that focusing on these internal factors was what brought success and growth. What became clear to us was that by attending to these variables, our congregation did draw new people, but they were almost always Christians from other places. The people in the church were all good and energetic people, but their basic focus was shaped by this centripetal force, what later came to be described as the attractional model of church. I realized that leaders could work with these variables by measuring how people felt about them in the church, even adding a variable called outreach or evangelism, but all this measuring and comparing would not change the fact that the people feeling good about the health and growth of our church were longtime Christians coming from other churches.

As I walked about the neighborhoods in Toronto in the 1980s connecting with people, several other things became clear to me. First, Canada is a country that has been shaped into a secularized, pluralist, postmodern society far faster and more extensively than most areas of the United States. The people in these neighborhoods—representing a huge array of nationalities and ethnicities, professionals and blue-collar workers of all ages—were never going to turn up at church on Sunday morning no matter how good or healthy our worship was, and they were never going to sign on to our great ministries and programs. Something had changed in the culture! I don't know how else to say this.

A while ago, I was having lunch with a couple of people in Denver, one of whom, Marcia, runs her own business as a designer. She described a workshop she had been to a few weeks earlier on the use of color in interior design. She said, "Something has changed out there. People have been talking about going green, but something has happened: there is a deep change going on in our culture right now that is going to change everything, and it's symbolized by the color green." That's not a scientific statement backed by a series of published studies from a prestigious university, but Marcia's observation is catching what people are feeling, just as you know when a weather pattern changes through the sense of air pressure dropping or different smell in the air. I think many of us would intuitively agree with Marcia's observation; we know the environment has changed even if we don't have all the words and studies to support this sense.

Jeb Brugmann, secretary general for the International Council for Local Initiatives and a member of the Cambridge University Program for Industry, recently wrote a book, *Welcome to the Urban Revolution: How Cities Are Changing the World,* about the ways cities are changing both human and natural environments. His argument is not simply that more and larger cities are coming to shape our world but that just like the development of the Internet, something about the nature of cities themselves has changed as a result of this exponential growth, bringing with it all the variables this kind of growth produces. According to Brugmann, we have entered a world not just of big cities inside national boundaries but of something radically different that is revolutionizing our social and political realities. First, a set of networked global urban centers is starting to emerge: "Cities . . . not countries or individual corporations, are the new . . . centers of a world City system" in which cities have morphed into a weblike network of interconnectivity that is different from and greater than nation states or even multinational corporations. This city system represents a new kind of global, urban reality, and uniquely, it is shaped more by bottom-up, local interactions than any top-down plan, an "urban revolution," largely beyond the control of governments and nations. Brugmann argues for us to make an imaginative shift in the way we think about cities, their influence, and the shape of our future on this planet: "Today our world has been fundamentally reorganized by the Urban Revolution but we discuss it almost cryptically, through demographic trivia. The media have been keen to report that 'half the world's population now lives in cities,' but we are overlooking the main event: half the world *has become* a City." Like the Internet, what has emerged is a world city system where urban life is radically changing the relationships between local and global affairs. When half the world becomes an interconnected city, "local conditions and events, even at the margins of a provincial town, are amplified into global events and accelerated into global trends, often overwhelming the systems and strategies that nations, corporations, and international institutions use to manage their affairs."[1] Brugmann uses the example of the Indian city of Tiruppur, a city of 52,000 in the 1990s but more than half a million now. It has become one of the world's top manufacturing centers for cotton clothing, competing well with megacities like Mumbai. But its industrial rise is not about high-tech machines; rather it comes from the local traditions of the Gounder caste, who applied traditional approaches to sourcing and organizing a village to build a worldwide, just-in-time knitwear industry. Brugmann summarizes the meaning of this example in the following way:

> From their small production units, this urban migrant community developed a tight network of five thousand local firms and thousands of other small supporting units, which together produce and export goods worth more than a billion dollars each year for companies such as Wal-Mart, Tommy Hilfiger, and Reebok. Tiruppur's knitwear industry can't really be understood as a "global" corporate phenomenon in the tradition sense. It is based on deep and, until recently, undocumented local traditions of seasonal agricultural production and labor management. Through the Gounder community's urban migration and its member's grassroots investments in their adopted city, they have been giving real shape, as in Machala, to a more diverse and unpredictable kind of globalization than the popular notion suggests. In a world that is fast becoming a City, the local realities of places like Machala and Tiruppur are gaining increasing global significance.[2]

Brugmann provides many other examples of this emerging, interconnected global city that no longer operates according to the assumed rules of how urban or commercial life ought to be. He notes that Irvine, California, didn't even exist in the 1950s but became the center from which global action came to address the depletion of the earth's ozone. It was Irvine's mayor, Larry Agran, and an internationally known chemist, Sherwood Rowland, who lived in the new city, who mobilized a worldwide, urban response. In the emerging global city, small districts, remote provincial towns, and entirely new cities are playing major roles in world affairs and changing the concrete order of the world. More and more, it is the unmanageable, unthinkable, and unpredictable events at local levels in cities that shape the future of our life on this planet rather than national governments or multinational organizations. To get a taste of this world city system and its effects, think of the origin and spread of the SARS epidemic of several years ago or the more recent outbreak of swine flu. Each began inside the world city system, each quickly spread around the globe, and each originated among small groups of city dwellers living within the radius of a few blocks. Think of the situation in Iraq just months after the U.S.-led invasion when the coalition assumed the war was all but over. Small, unknown, undetectable bands of urban dwellers living within a few blocks of one another in urban centers like Fallujah changed the nature of the entire conflict with their creation of improvised explosive devices (IEDs). Think of the movements of youth in Iran after the summer 2009 elections. More than 60 percent of Iran's population is under thirty-five and living in the cities. They are not powerful people, but their responses to their leaders over the coming few years will transform the nature of relations in the Middle East and therefore around the globe. The reason for this is the world city, with its forms of interconnectivity and communications that make the small actions of unknown people in cities like Tehran more important and influential than political and economic leaders.

In moments of revolutionary change, when environments shift, most people don't notice what's happening at the time. We understand the significance of events only in retrospect, as Brugmann illustrates with the Industrial Revolution, which began in the mid-1700s but was only recognized and named some eighty years later. People were debating and arguing about what was happening long before the concepts of industrialization and modernization became clear and acquired labels. "European society had already been fundamentally reorganized by industrialization before the new phenomenon was given a name," Brugmann writes.[3] Just as the Internet, over a thirty-year period, went through a radical transformation that has affected just about everything in our lives, and the urban world has entered a similar shift, transforming some of our most basic assumptions and categories about power and the sources of change, so has the church entered its own period of radical transformation in which the assumptions and categories that made it successful no longer reflect the new realities.

By the late 1980s, it had become clear to me that the environment in which church functioned had changed; it was like a weather pattern that had held for a very long time suddenly being swept away by winds off the lake; we were in a new atmosphere. The simplest way I could describe that transformation was to say that all our attention to the internal variables of church life no longer helped us understand and engage this changed context. That didn't mean they were unimportant; it meant they no longer correlated or connected to what was happening in the lives of the people of the neighborhoods and communities in which we lived. I was starting to realize that

I needed a different imagination for what it means to be a church in a community and what it means to lead in such a church. One of the things this growing realization meant was that it would be possible to be a faithful community of God's people only by reengaging the neighborhoods and communities where we live and learning to ask what was happening among the people of the neighborhood, attending to their stories, and cultivating receptiveness to being surprised by what God might already be up to among all these people who aren't thinking about church or even God. How would I do that?

I was also observing that the pluralist and postmodern turn in the culture was raising massive questions among people both inside and outside of church about the meaning of some pretty basic stuff like the nature of marriage and relationships. The sexuality conflicts in churches these days are one of the signs of this confusion, as is the remaking of boundaries and categories related to sexuality and the meaning of religious commitments and narratives. Where might the values for creating peace and justice be found among all the competing claims and counterclaims one now hears in the local neighborhood? In the Dalai Lama and Buddhist ways of life? In Jesus' call to love and peace? In some secular notion of a common good? The reshaping of our culture because of the factors introduced in Chapter Six was creating confusion and anxiety as people tried to negotiate both personal meaning and their relationships with one another. (See, for example, the 2009 movie *He's Just Not That Into You,* which explores these issues among the generation in their thirties and forties. The movie is an amazing statement about how hard it is for young adults to navigate the once taken-for-granted waters of relationships, trying to create new maps that will assist them in this navigation.)

In the midst of these reflections, I also became aware that the questions, confusion, and anxieties wrought by cultural change were not limited to the so-called secular world. George Hunter's *How to Reach Secular People,* written in the early 1990s, describes the characteristics of "secular people."[4] His list described most of my church.

Secular People

- Are ignorant of basic Christianity and are often biblically illiterate.
- Seek life before death. They think more about life this side of death—how to find it, salvage it, give it meaning and purpose—more than they think about life after death.

- Are conscious of doubt more than guilt. They see themselves as victims and do not think they are responsible for their actions. Instead of guilt, they are skeptical and full of doubt, especially when it comes to believing in absolutes.

- Have a negative image of the church and doubt its intelligence, relevance, and credibility.

- Have multiple alienations: work, nature, government, jobs, and one another.

- Are untrusting.

- Have low self-esteem, compounded with divorces, dysfunctional homes, and so on.

- See the world as out of control, with political unrest, the AIDS epidemic, and so on.

- Experience anything in their personalities, families, and lives that they can't control as a problem.

- Are lost and cannot seem to find God on their own.

There was really no basic difference between the issues facing people who had left the church behind and those who still belonged to local churches. All the upheaval and confusion of a world moving through the massive changes outlined in Chapters Six and Seven was not just "out there" in the culture but also in the church. The change in the environment in which our churches are location has been dramatic. A first step in missional planning involves taking the time to become aware of this incredible change in our own contexts. Our tendency as leaders is to rely mostly on such tools as demographic data or internal assessments about how people in the church feel about certain programs (worship, youth, evangelism, and so on) but not attend to these environmental changes. Without attending to these transformations in our environment, we will miss what is happening in our world, and our planning will continue to reach Christians from other churches rather than the people in this new world. I began to recognize that leading in this new environment required a different approach from what I had been trained to do as a pastor. As I looked more closely at how change had transformed the Internet, I began to see how we might go about missional map-making in a local church.

STEP 2: FOCUS ON REDEVELOPING A CORE IDENTITY

The first step in becoming missional map-makers in this environment is to be convinced this is the nature of the landscape, not just of the neighborhood, but of the church, too.

The second step in becoming missional map-makers is learning how to cultivate environments that re-create a core identity among the people of a local church.

The image of the Internet I described in Chapter Seven became for me a new way understanding what had happened in the midst of all the transformations that had shifted us into a new space. I began to see that the world could no longer be framed in terms of a series of predictable, manageable categories that, if we just got them right, would translate into new levels of effectiveness. Just as the Internet had morphed into something structurally and organically different, so had the church and the surrounding community become different creatures than those I once knew. If I was going to lead in this new space, I needed to develop a different kind of imagination. As I began to understand the depth of the change the Internet represented, I recognized our neighborhoods, places of work, local churches, and relationships to those within and without what we consider our networks or communities were also becoming more and more diffuse, unpredictable, uncontrollable, interconnected webs of relationships. It is no longer possible to put everybody into neat categories (secular and churched, spiritual and unspiritual, insider and outsider). It is more fluid than at any time in my life and becoming ever more so. Someone in the church can belong to a great variety of what the journalist Ethan Watters called "urban tribes" (small groups of young adults who have created meaningful and sustaining networks of relationships outside of any organizational systems) and be shaped by a series of interconnected networks of which the church is but one among many. The web image has become far more the reality of the local church and the communities in which it is located. Missional planning begins with this reality rather than with a mission and a vision statement. These may well come later, but we need a different place to start in becoming map-makers in this new world. The starting place has more to do with how we form people in this environment than it is about developing the traditional mission statements for a church.

We have entered world where clear, identifiable differentiations between groups are disappearing. One cannot manage, control, or predict the relational and communicative points of connection throughout the system. The Internet illustrates the fact that in modern and postmodern North America, there has been a radical breakdown, a shattering, of an ordered, stable world of common meaning in which the church once functioned at the center. What has emerged is a social context without a center. In the place of any claim to a center there are now multiple nodes of energy, with people moving in and out of relationships with one another (and in and out of churches) around these nodes in a continual process of dissolution and recombination of social, moral, ethical, and religious choices.

In *After Virtue*, Alasdair MacIntyre argues that we can't even claim to live in pluralist world. Pluralism implies that there are a series of coherent options and frameworks from which people choose. For MacIntyre, we no longer live out of cohesive narratives but are living off fragments, bits and pieces of religious belief. In this new reality, social meaning and ethical content are gathered from a wide variety of sources and assembled, Lego-like, into a lifestyle. We live in a social context where coherent frameworks of religious and ethical meaning are collapsing, and in response, people form their religious and ethic commitments from bits of this and that. Disembedded, self-authenticating individuals now live off these bits in continually shifting combinations. In the place of a coherent narrative are privately chosen combinations, selected fragments from an assortment of religious offerings in the marketplace of personal faith and spirituality.

What are the implications for a local church and for leadership in this place? Figure 8.1 represents a local congregation set within the social context I've just described. The dotted line indicates that congregations no longer can imagine themselves as closed or bounded set communities.[5] An often unspoken assumption we make is that our churches, with their traditions and commitments to the biblical story, are more like bounded sets: they have a clear core identity, and most members know the rules and convictions of the church at the boundaries and agree to abide by them. This was the normal assessment of church identity for most of the twentieth century. Denominational branding and statements of beliefs and practices (for example, the *Book of Order* of the Presbyterian church or the constitutions of Baptist churches) were what distinguished one church group from another and from the community in which it was located.

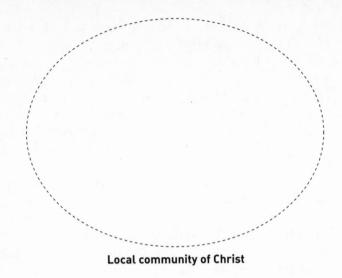

Local community of Christ

Figure 8.1.   Boundary Between Local Church and Local Cultures
No Longer Distinct.

These distinctive factors served as boundaries that defined a church's identity, with relation to all other groups. In this new space we inhabit, the distinction between inner and outer worlds that once formed the bounded sets of church identity is dissolving,[6] even though most pastors and church boards continue to function as if these constitutions and rule books will ensure their identity and distinctiveness. The boundaries between our local churches and our present culture, shaped by fragments and the loss of common narrative, are blurring and even disappearing. The "outside" is also now very much "inside." The biological equivalent in the life of an organism is its loss of cellular integrity. It is as if the semipermeable membrane of the cell has broken down to such an extent that its unique, distinct identity is lost, and the organism's DNA has dissolved into fragments through some unknown, unanticipated virus. When this happens, the cell's functionality and life are called into question. This is the situation of our churches, as well as the neighborhoods and communities where these churches are located.

In the center of Figure 8.2 I have added the term *Core Identity*, indicating that in this new space, one of the most critical leadership skills is the capacity to cultivate an environment that enables the re-forming of Christian life around the core identity of the Christian narrative.

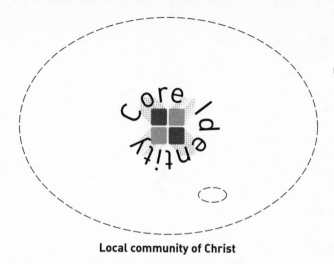

Local community of Christ

Figure 8.2.   Redeveloping Core Identity.

Forming a *core identity* as one of the first steps in missional map-making, or missional planning, will seem counterintuitive to those raised with modernity's methods of mission and vision statements and strategic plans. To cultivate a people in our local churches who are asking questions about what the Spirit is up to in their neighborhoods requires a church environment where people feel safe enough and encouraged to learn to listen to God and one another as a basic habit of their lives. Missional map-making requires an environment in which the ordinary people of God are invited to reexperience the biblical narratives in the conviction and confidence that they can hear and discern the ways of God among them as a people. Core identity also involves rediscovering some basic habits and practices of Christian formation critical for discernment and the capacity to name what we are seeing God do in our time and place. We need to cultivate environments in which this way of life can reemerge in local churches. It will be among the ordinary people of God that the ability to discern what needs to take place in their neighborhoods and communities must emerge. The new maps come from among the people. This discernment is far more a bottom-up than a top-down process. In most cases, the imposition of vision and mission statements by church boards and pastoral staffs shuts down the critical processes of discernment and misses the fact that most people in our local churches today no longer pattern their lives after church traditions or the biblical stories.

Cultivating a core identity requires leaders skilled in the art of cultivation; they must be adept at tilling the soil that calls forth and energizes a core identity in the local church. This core identity is the equivalent of redeveloping the DNA of an organism that has, through some great shock, lost its cellular integrity. Map-makers in this new space, therefore, are artisans relearning ancient skills of working in and with the ordinary soil of people's everyday lives, the earthed, grounded ways of Christian life where the local church is situated. Chris Erdman, pastor of University Presbyterian Church in Fresno, California, is doing this by sharing the journey of his own pilgrimage with his people and others in a little book called *Returning to the Center: Living Prayer in a Distracting World.* He uses the illustration of his own life to invite people into ordinary practices of prayer for discernment. In the book, he invites people to become apprenticed to a practice of Christian listening and discernment that has been largely lost in our culture.[7] The point here, however, is that in a new space, the people of our local churches cannot begin to imagine or plan for missional engagement without recovering some of these core skills of Christian identity and formation. What's involved in tilling the soil? How does a practicing leader like Chris Erdman go about this cultivation task in his own local church? How do leaders go about preparing the ground to form missional communities of the kingdom?

In the first place, Chris has taken the time to build a deep level of trust and confidence in himself as a leader. He has done this in a number of ways. First, he understands that basic to trust is competence in the field of expected work. When Chris was called to University Presbyterian, he was expected to do the standard work of any clergy person: preach, teach, manage the church, visit the sick, and care for people's spiritual lives. Chris could quite easily have written a volume on how so many of the expectations that lie buried in these functions were just expressions of an old Christendom or an attractional model of church that was outdated. But he didn't take this easy road. He understood that trust meant beginning where people are, not in some vision or mission statement about where they should be. So Chris worked at preaching well and attending to the spiritual needs of his people. Over time, this built a deep sense of trust in Chris as a leader. Because he attended to the basics and the deeds people expected of a pastor, they were ready to listen to him in other areas of their lives as well.

Second, on the basis of this trust, Chris was granted access to people's minds. He developed a series of programs and held conversations with people that invited them to tell their stories. The result was an environment in which people were beginning to sense that not only did he want to hear their stories but that their stories where crucial to understanding what God was up to among them. All of this took time, of course. It was not forty days of listening to people's stories and then coming out with a new vision statement. Nor was the process of listening to people's stories a tactic Chris used to get something else done; he was introducing a way of life into the church. To do this, he needed people to know that their stories were important; he needed to focus on these stories and bless people in their telling of them. The reasons for this are because most people in our local churches don't feel it's safe to share their own stories and longings, and just as important, they have lost any sense that in their stories lies the Spirit's creative possibilities for their communities and neighborhoods. Chris created the kinds of safe spaces where these stories began to emerge and people slowly started to believe that it was among their stories that the Spirit's future might be discerned.

When working with his board, Chris did not try to dissuade them from projects and ideas they wanted to initiate. He was always working from the conviction that to love a people and create an environment within which to rebuild core identity, one had to begin where they were, not where he wanted them to be. Early on, board members wanted him to come up with a vision statement and a strategic plan for the church. He didn't argue against this or declare his unwillingness to do these things. Instead, he agreed to these proposals (not because he believed they would change the church but because that was what these leaders expected at that point), but he also did other things. He spent a lot of time meeting individually with the leaders of the church, listening intently to their reasons for wanting strategic plans and then inviting them to share their stories about their own lives and journeys. He also invited them to join him in experiments around prayer and some of the simple practices to be introduced in Chapter Nine. In retreats together, they continued the conversations about planning and discernment. In all of this, Chris was, again, working at creating environments of safety within which the underlying stories of the people could emerge. By gently connecting those stories with biblical narratives and prayer, there emerged in the church an environment of trust in which people felt a new kind of safety to risk their own stories; there gradually emerged a new kind of conviction, that the Spirit of God could actually be at work in the ordinariness of their lives. This is what is involved in cultivating the kind of environment within a local church that creates the space for redeveloping a core identity.

The recovery and reintroduction of Christian identity require leaders who attend to the soil of their local churches in the ways Chris Erdman has done for almost a decade. The soil in which most of our churches have grown is a product of modernity. It's more like the packaged soils one buys from garden centers that are crammed full of chemical compounds that will ensure vigorous growth without any trouble whatsoever. The parallel in so many churches is that the "soil" in which they are planted is all about strategies for growth in numbers or meeting individual needs or shaped around some form of worship or programs for multisite church life. This kind of soil has been developed to yield church members who serve in programs and agree with the vision, mission, and goals of a church staff or board. Such soil does not produce environments in which people believe the Spirit is shaping a new world through the ordinary lives and imaginations of the people themselves. The soil we have to cultivate needs the nutrients that give back to our people the conviction that church is a safe place for them to be who they are, to dream and to believe that from within their lives can come forth the imagination of the Spirit for their communities and neighborhoods. This isn't all that will be required, but without preparing this healthier kind of soil, it will be practically impossible to form mission-shaped communities.

Missional map-making will also involve cultivating environments in which the people in a local church come, once more, to believe they have the capacities hear God in the biblical narratives. Cultivating this kind of environment is not, however, about a leader doing more teaching. If increasing teaching were the answer to transformation, churches across North America would be transformed. For generations, seminaries have been teaching centers shaping our leaders in their own image—as teachers. The reintroduction of a Christian core identity into a local church calls for more than this standard approach. What Chris Erdman did was listen to the narratives of his people and then introduce biblical narratives into the midst of their stories not as answers and solutions but as alternative stories that invited engagement with the people's stories. This created an environment in which people were wrestling with Scripture rather than taking notes about dates and times and meanings and predetermined answers. This is about giving the Bible back to the people of God in the conviction that they can hear the Spirit in the midst of this wrestling. The work of leadership here is what I have described elsewhere as the work of the poet.[8]

What I propose here goes beyond extra effort placed on teaching or biblical exposition. I propose a full-scale reengagement with the biblical narrative involving focused attention on the catechetical ministry of the church. Several years ago, Mennonite missiologist Alan Kreider published a little book called *The Change of Conversion and the Origin of Christendom* in which he pointed out that the transformation of the Roman world by these early Christians was made possible by the ways they were able to take a massively disparate set of peoples shaped by many competing narratives and religions and resocialize them into an alternative community known as the church.[9] This happened most clearly in the first four centuries and prior to the time of Constantine. Conversion to the narratives of the kingdom of God was a lifelong endeavor, requiring the engagement of the whole community and a set of processes that shaped people around certain habits or ways of being God's people together in the midst of the real contexts in which these young churches were forming. (The nature of these habits will be discussed in the next chapter.) The formation of the churches' DNA in those early years was as much about practices as it was about what we have come to identify as the teaching role of the pastor in a church. In Protestantism, the great bulk of the emphasis on formation has been placed on the teaching and preaching roles of the pastor. But as important as they are, those roles largely omit the most critical element of transformation in the early church: learning and living a new set of habits and practices.

In our day, cultivating an identity around a biblical narrative will need to be done within a framework like the one encountered by the people of God in Babylon. The single most significant element in that period of the Exile was the people's emerging capacity to reclaim their primary stories from a context of loss. The removal of the Jewish people from Jerusalem and its environs by Nebuchadnezzar along with the destruction of the Temple and the flattening the city's walls precipitated a crisis of massive proportions for Israel. The very meaning and nature of their beliefs and practices were called into question at fundamental levels. The Jews had been torn from their dominant, what Walter Brueggemann calls, "royal religion" of Jerusalem that had given them security and been thrown into the strange world of Babylon. Babylon raised the question of whether it was even possible to worship God in that new space, where the maps of Jerusalem had ceased to have any relevance. The narrators of these stories in Scripture are clear that God created this crisis of identity in order for the Jews to reexamine their founding stories and again be able to discern the ways of God. The implication of the Babylonian captivity stories is that as long as these people remained inside the royal religion of Jerusalem, they would never be able to remember their stories or know what God wanted to do in the world through them.

It is easy to miss the point of these Babylonian captivity stories, with their psalms of loss and lamentation. Notice that in Jerusalem, the sacred aspects of Jewish life had been reduced to paying attention to the categories of temple worship, feast keeping, and the like—which would have given them a high score on any test of health by modern church leadership standards. However, in Jerusalem, the people of God had lost their essential DNA; they had strayed from the real story of God's work in the world, even while they packed into the temple and kept the festivals.

In our own situation, we need more than increased efforts to teach Bible courses or extend the amount of preaching in a Sunday sermon. Such tactical strategies miss the point. If the Christian narrative has been largely lost in the ending of modernity and the new pluralisms of our neighborhoods with their disparate spiritualities, then there is a massive need for practices and habits that re-create a Christian identity. This cultivation of our DNA is one of the core leadership activities needed at this moment in time.

CHAPTER NINE

CULTIVATING PARALLEL CULTURES OF THE KINGDOM

Chapter Eight introduced the first two steps in becoming missional map-makers in a new space.

Step 3 is presented in this chapter. It is about how we go about forming people in the practices and habits that make the local church a parallel culture in the neighborhoods and communities where its people live.

STEP 3: CREATE A PARALLEL CULTURE

What do we mean by the idea of creating a parallel culture in our local churches?

This is a way of life that has been understood by Christian communities through the history of the church. The early Celtic communities in places like Lindisfarne in the UK or the beginnings of Benedictine life in Italy in the late Middle Ages are illustrations. What is proposed in this chapter is that the third step in forming missional life in this new space involves the resocializing of Christians into certain kinds of practices and habits of Christian life. This work of resocializing will involve missional map-makers in forming local churches as parallel communities of Christian life.

What will be involved in this third stage can be gleaned from the story of Václav Havel's experience under communism in the last decades of the twentieth century. Before becoming the Czech president, Havel was an internationally renowned writer and playwright who grew up in a wealthy, politically connected family. Havel expresses his experience of living under communism as that of needing to form a *parallel culture.* Before becoming president of his country, Czechoslovakia, in 1989, while it was still under Communist rule, Havel participated in and witnessed events in which average citizens did some very ordinary, practical, normal things that resulted in the transformation of that country at the end of the Cold War. These ordinary people were factory workers, artists, teachers—men and women from all forms of life who felt they were caught in a system that would never change and from which they could never escape. They had no part of power blocs or elites but gradually developed habits that formed this parallel culture in the midst of the dominant Communist government. What happened was unexpected and unplanned. There was no grand strategy; rather, people began doing simple things that changed their reality. In coffee shops and other meeting places, a few would bring short original poems or commentaries and share them with others. These were not politic tracts but personal statements about their experiences under communism. They were not intended to change the political or social situation but merely to articulate inner convictions. Mostly, these texts made it clear that the writers didn't believe in communism anymore. Their compositions were passed around; others read them and wrote their own pieces or created music. Again, none of this was a planned strategy but became a habit or practice among people. This was the slow, gradual creation of a parallel culture in which more and more people found ways of confessing that they didn't believe in communism anymore. Havel's conviction is that when enough people entered this parallel culture, communism could not be sustained and collapsed from within.[1]

Ordinary people discovered and practiced disciplines of resistance as they wrote poems and brief essays (for example, some people wrote of children trusting their parents in the midst of a public culture that encouraged children to spy on their parents and report on their activities; they were not overtly political but told the story of another reality). It was this kind of storytelling among people, even while the Communist mantle seemed unshakable, that created the parallel culture. Such acts of imagination require courage. At the beginning, there must have been a sense of uncertainty and strangeness as people tentatively edged their way toward something none of them could clearly articulate. It was hard work, but eventually communism crumbled, and Czechoslovakia was transformed into the multiparty democracy of the Czech Republic and the independent republic of Slovakia.

A parallel culture develops as ordinary people feel the loss of the capacity to make sense of their lives. In this state of flux arise those revolutionary moments when ordinary people find something awakening in them that begins to reshape the nature of community and society. This reawakening to the possibility of reshaping Christian life in local contexts is the calling of the church in the new space we inhabit. Parallel cultures do not come into being without careful attention to the practices and habits that shape a common life. Havel described this happening in his own country through a small, relatively insignificant group of men and women whose alienation ran deep; they sensed the profound disconnection between the demands and values of their sociopolitical context (state communism) and their own sense of what it might mean to live in a community that cultivated life and creativity. Gradually, but with determination, ordinary citizens experimented in developing simple habits, such as writing poems or songs, that formed them around this other dream or imagination of flourishing in freedom. What is fascinating about Havel's description is that these people were never able to take political action to change institutions and organizations. They were shut out of these systems, but in consistently and intentionally taking action on a small scale in their everyday lives, they discovered that the political systems and institutions, with their hierarchies of elites, professionals, and experts, didn't have the power to transform their environment. Social transformation required something radically different: the simple and intentional habits of everyday people that gradually established an alternative. Similarly, the early Christians did not transform their world through political action in and of itself; they did it through cultivated practices and habits that shaped them as communities of faith.

Life among the early Christians involved such practices of formation as giving hospitality to others, pledging to keep the marriage covenant, caring for widows or the dying, and sharing with people in need.[2] Men and women from the diverse Roman Empire were brought into the church through a process of catechesis that involved resocialization into a parallel culture, achieved through simple but powerful practices that formed the ways these people lived in their communities, ultimately giving them a DNA that transformed the world. Christians in our context know of these practices but have largely lost the ability to practice them.

Some form of parallel culture is what map-makers in a new space must cultivate. If cultivating a core identity of Christian life requires reexamining the biblical narratives from the experience of crisis and loss, then local churches will form these identities through the cultivation of practices and habits. What has characterized our identity until now, and what kinds of practices should shape our identities going forward?

Since the middle of the twentieth century, the small-group movement has shaped congregations. Such groups, by and large, have had little to do with forming people in practices of Christian life. In churches today, small groups usually exist for people to connect on a personal level to find spiritual forms of intimacy in a lonely world. The Bible serves as little more than a springboard for conversation about each other's lives. These groups do little more than reflect how the metanarrative of modernity, with its focus on autonomy, intimacy, and personal needs, has taken over the imagination of the church. The current use of small groups in churches serves to deepen the captivity of the church to expressive individualism and trivializes the biblical narrative by reducing it to a means of engaging personal experience and feelings. From its start, the small-group movement was shaped mostly by the human potential movement. Its frameworks tended to be those of psychology, with its focus on the expressive needs of the self rather than the formation of parallel communities. In response to this pervasive expressive individualism, some movements are emerging that seek to recover the catechetical practices of the early church in an attempt to form parallel Christian communities in local neighborhoods. The New Monasticism is one example. Groups like the Mustard Seed with Tom and Linda Sine in Seattle or The Simple Way, a community of Christians shaped around the work of Shane Claiborne in Philadelphia, identifying themselves as a web of subversive friends conspiring to spread the vision of "Loving God, loving people, and following Jesus," are other examples of these emerging movements. In Edmonton, Alberta, people like Howard Lawrence and Greg Brandenbarg are forming neighborhood-based churches shaped around common practices and finding people in these neighborhoods hungry for the community these Christians are creating through their practices of hospitality. These kinds of movements understand that at the core of a missional engagement with our culture is the stark need to form communities shaped by practices of Christian life. These are emergent attempts to create parallel cultures of the kingdom. What are some of the habits and practices that can reform the DNA of our churches?

PRACTICES FOR A NEW DNA

Jesus formed a community of disciples as a parallel society, a light on a hill, whose commitment to one another and their world would transform their culture by the end of the fourth century. Like the Hobbits in Tolkien's *Lord of the Rings,* the church is sent on a journey into strange lands; the travelers found themselves in an in-between world where little of what they encountered was worked out in neat categories or settled into easily managed programs. One suspects that this will need to be the way of life for missional communities for a long time. Our task is to form local churches as environments in which that journey might begin all over again. Too much of our current church life is focused around meeting the needs of expressive individuals. Those who argue that meeting needs is a strategy to get people into the church miss the point. If we communicate a Gospel that says at the front door that Jesus is all about meeting my needs (remember, most of the time we are talking about middle-class expressive individualists who are already the most pampered generation on earth), then at some point we are going to have to tell them that in fact the opposite is the case. Jesus actually came to call them into a life that requires them to let go of their needs. We created congregations full of little Hobbits who crave nothing more than their comfort and having their needs met. Some of those Hobbits have discovered that the world beyond their narrow range of vision is in terrible distress, and they have to go on a journey that will take them far away from every need and want they ever had. The rest of the Hobbits are still in the dark.

Shaping people committed to living out the will of God in our current congregations requires the cultivation of practices. Even leaders themselves must be committed to a new imagination and a new way of life. Leaders will initially have to invest a great deal of their time in a relatively small number of people, as they begin to cultivate these intentional practices of faith. Like the cultivation of an herb garden where one starts small and goes slow, leaders will need to begin slowly by inviting small numbers of people into some simple experiments in Christian practices. This is a way of seeding the ground and providing safe demonstration plots for others to see what this parallel culture might look like. Small experiments rather than wholesale change is the way we form people in practices of Christian life. Whole-church programs that try to get everyone on board may have some short-term effect, but like a plant growing in dry soil, these programs begin with great energy and enthusiasm but then wither away and die. The most effective ways to develop a parallel culture is to begin by forming some demonstration plots. Starting slow and small also provides the leader with an opportunity to learn by doing. Experimenting means becoming a both learner and leader. The journey might begin as the leader forms a group who agree to live by a set of practices for six months. Meeting times would be shaped around reporting to one another their engagements in practices that week. This kind of group, with intentional accountability regarding practices, is a departure from the way most small groups function. *Accountability* is a hard word to use in churches these days when it comes to practices of Christian life. As a local church leader asked a recently, "Why does my denomination have no problem creating accountability protocols for pastors around things like sexual boundaries but screams loud about coercion and becomes highly resistant when some of us suggest that pastors should also be held accountable for their spiritual life and practices?"

What follows is a brief description of several practices essential to reformulating a church's DNA. Figure 9.1 continues filling in the diagram showing that the essential work of missional mapmakers will involve cultivating practices of Christian life among the people of a local church.

They can be introduced into a number of groups ready to experiment together but should not be introduced as a program for the whole church. The intentional cultivation of such practices is an important step in inviting a local church to discern those new forms of life that the Spirit seeks to shape in our new space, and none of us can anticipate or plan for them without going on this journey of living into practices of faith. Remember, introducing these practices needs to be done in the context of what was presented in Chapter Eight. As people in a local church are able to give voice to the ways the environment in their context has changed and as they feel increasingly safe to live into their narratives, engage with the biblical stories,

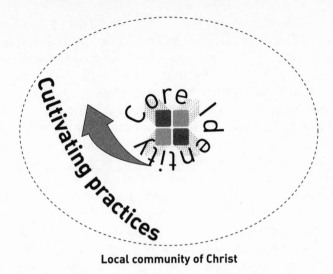

Local community of Christ

Figure 9.1. Cultivating Practices of Christian Life.

and come to trust that the Spirit is at work in and through them, only then, with that groundwork in place, it is possible to introduce these practices as a way of life.

The Purposes of Practices

While guarding against simplistic attempts to return to another time, we can learn a great deal about how to form our parallel communities from the history and experiences of the church. In other times (especially those seminal periods between the fifth and seventh centuries), Christian life was formed around orders. At the time of their founding, they were experiments in which small bands of people had instincts about what might be involved in forming a parallel culture. Celtic and Benedictine orders were formed in cultures radically different from our own, and yet they were also formed in times that had affinities with our moment. For the Celtic missionaries, the world was in flux, with little sense of solidity and direction. Peoples were in movement all across Europe as the Pax Romana that had provided a context of stability and predictability dissolved, creating an uncertain and insecure world for many. The Celts formed their movements of transformation in what for them were new spaces where the world seemed to be coming apart and everything was shifting and changing.[3] We can't re-create their ways or how they shaped their practices in their context, but how they went about shaping a parallel society offers us insight in conceiving practices for our day.

The use of practices has a dual aim. First, we simply need to learn again some of the habits and practices that Christians have developed over the centuries to shape a parallel society in the midst of massive change. Although counterintuitive to the modern, Western imagination, it is the daily application of practices, not great ideas or big ideals (preaching and teaching doctrine), that reformulates the DNA of a community and changes our reality. This may sound strange, but anyone who has worked with people who have to rehabilitate broken limbs or recover from a stroke know that these challenges are overcome by the simple yet arduous work of day-by-day practices. I can talk and read all I like about losing weight; I can watch every *Oprah* TV show on weight control with the best, most sensitive "experts" telling me how it's done—but none of this will change the reality of my life. Only when I act by exercising regularly and eating smaller portions each day will my reality change. In Havel's Czechoslovakia, it was the daily patterns, the habits put into practice month after month and year after year of telling stories and writing poems or essays or music that literally produced a parallel culture that rejected the Communist narrative. When that happened, from the inside out and from the bottom up, the political and social system of communism could not survive. This is how cultures are changed and DNA is transformed. Practices are the key ways to enabling people to discover new maps in the strange, new spaces where they find themselves. The practices and habits that once formed Christians as parallel societies with a distinct DNA have been largely forgotten. We have just lived through a long period of the church's history in the West when we simply assumed that most people were Christians; we assumed that just by the fact of living in this culture, we were formed as Christians. Most of us now realize that it was never quite like that and that we have lost the habits and skills of Christian formation.

The second purpose of practices is somewhat more difficult to describe. As we rediscover and reapply practices of Christian life in a local church, they give us the capacity to discern some of the ways in which Christian life has been shaped and deformed by our cultural context. When Israel was in Babylon, or out in the desert on the other side of Egypt, the people began to cultivate new rhythms of life (the ways they worked in an alien land, their regular dependence on God to give them daily bread in the desert, the need to discover new forms of worship and community in Babylon through the formation of the synagogue). Within these new rhythms they came to see the ways Egypt and Jerusalem had deformed them as God's people. That discernment resulted, in each situation, in the development of codes (the laws of Leviticus or the reforms of Josiah) intended to shape the DNA of this people in new situations.

In our situation, the way this discernment develops is through corporate practices and what we will describe as rhythms of life. The learning of the church through the centuries is in the recognition that in such practices lies the possibility of unmasking our enmeshments and forming ourselves as a parallel society. These are the ways we reformulate the DNA in a local church today. The gift of the disruptive transformations moving through late modern culture is that this turbulent moment in time has propelled us into a new world and in so doing has given us the opportunity to see again how we might be formed as God's people in local neighborhoods and communities. It is as if the Spirit is opening a window for the church and we are looking into a new world being invited to risk discovering what God might want to re-form and make within us as God's people. It is a wonderful moment in the life of the church.

Practicing the Offices

Monastic communities intentionally formed their lives around the practice of offices. The word comes from *officium*, meaning the duty of Christians to pray daily for the whole church. Such communities ordered each day around specific times when bells rang, calling the community from its diverse occupations to gather for a brief period of Scripture reading and prayer. These times in the day shaped Christians in a local area as a parallel society by reminding them that their life and allegiance belonged to God. The offices of prayer and Scripture would also continually ground them in the biblical narrative.

Why is the practice of offices important for missional formation? It creates a context in which two critical things happen. First, for those of us who have learned again this daily way of life, as we regularly practice the daily offices, we are being reshaped in the imagination that our lives are gifts from and belong to God. We come to experience in a new way that none of us are self-made; we receive our life every day from God as gift. Imagine what this kind of character would do as witness to and transformation of our culture, with its focus on the individual as self-made? Imagine what might happen in our neighborhoods and communities when the people of a local church live for the other in their lives rather than themselves? I am struck by how deeply we have been formed in North America by the objectivist philosophy of someone like Ayn Rand, with her exposition of self-reliance and self-made individuals who are the center of their own worlds. While listening to Alan Greenspan explain the economics of the past two decades that led us to our current crisis, I could not help recognizing how this man's imagination was shaped by Rand's work. He has practiced her principles all his life, and they came to shape his economic policies, which in turn shaped our global economy in ways that have been terrible for many around the world. The practice of the daily offices forms a local community of Christians in a radically different set of habits and consequently creates a different imagination. The daily offices shape our understanding of grace and gift and embed in us a recognition that we do not make life happen; life is a gift to be embraced, a vocation to be lived in the presence of God and others.

Consider what happened a few years ago in rural Pennsylvania when a man drove up to an Amish schoolhouse and shot teachers and children. It was a terrible tragedy. The media were quickly on the scene, trying to interview parents and get the raw edge of the tragedy on film for the evening news. Media pundits began talking about the ways in which people process such awful events through anger and the need for revenge. When neither of these characteristics appeared among the Amish parents or within their communities, experts on morning TV shows began taking about what denial does to a community. A friend of mine, a sociologist at a university in Pennsylvania, grew up in the Amish community and still knew many of the people in the community where these children had been murdered. He said to me, "Alan, what the media don't get is that every day, three to five times a day, these people in their daily lives say the Lord's Prayer to themselves. So when they come to the words 'Forgive us our debts as we forgive our debtors,' these are not just nice ideas but a part of the very core of their lives. Yes, these people are grieving terrible losses, but they also live by a different story, and most people in America have no idea about that story, even if it does go to the core of the Christian story."

Second, the offices assist us in becoming aware of how easily and incessantly other narratives enter one's own and the community's life, recasting us in ways incongruent with the Gospel (how else, for example, could the church in America come to the conclusion that the Gospel of Jesus is about meeting the needs of affluent, middle-class men and women?). The New Testament describes the church as a people formed by the cross; it is a journey with a cost attached. The cross remains at the center of the DNA of Christian identity. It confronts us with the continuing recognition of how deeply the narratives of my culture control the way I live. In the practice of the offices, we remind ourselves and each other of the cost of our commitment to following God; corporately, we learn to discern how we crowd out the Lordship of Christ, which should be the one essential focus for our lives as a people.

What might the use of these offices look like in practice? Few of us want to become monastics. We work hard in our vocations and have extreme demands placed on every aspect of our lives. In the language of sociologist Kenneth Gergen, we are saturated selves with so many conflicting demands that we become not a single person but many selves who appear and disappear, depending on the place and role demanded of us.[4] This advocacy of practicing the daily offices is not an argument for withdrawal from our worlds into separated, monastery-like gatherings. While that is an option for some, the offices described here are for formation in local churches. One group of church leaders began this at the staff level of their church. Several on staff became aware of how their lives were so shaped by the busyness of multiple demands that they could rarely practice the disciplines of listening and discernment. They agreed to an experiment: committing themselves to a period of time in which they would practice stopping at designated times of the day for Scripture and prayer. They used a small guidebook organized around the seven days of the week, each focusing on a central element of Christian life (Resurrection, Creation, Incarnation, Spirit, Community, and Cross).[5] Each day is divided into four short sets of liturgy built around Scripture reading and prayer. The commitment involved keeping two of these offices each day. They did not need to be together to do this. Wherever they found themselves at the agreed times, they would practice the office. At first, it was an energizing adventure. Members of the group felt keenly in touch with something that gave shape and meaning to life. But within a few months, something else began happening. The times of office keeping would pass and they would realize that the events of the day had so shaped their time that the office was neglected. It became difficult to keep this simple practice. Here is where discernment begins. This experiment with a simple, corporate practice exemplified how hard it is in our culture to shape life around an alternative story; incarnating that commitment into actual practices is very difficult.

We are so deeply embedded in a context where busyness and the demands of daily life drive us to the extent that we feel like the proverbial mouse on a treadmill. We live in a culture where increasing numbers of people in our congregations feel incredibly insecure about their future and are watching the number of hours they must work increase. Technology has not lightened our load but made our work a 24/7 reality. Where are the places where we can be formed by an alternative story? Is there another rhythm of life that is a counterstory to this dominant narrative? What do we do when we become aware that despite our greatest longings, our lives are driven by narratives contrary to the future Jesus called into being? The practice of keeping daily offices is a subversive activity in this culture. It confronts us with these kinds of questions. Keeping the daily offices is not meant to induce guilt. If feelings of guilt are the result, then one does not grasp the nature of grace or the purpose of the offices. It is only as we enter into and struggle with the offices that we discover the challenge of the journey that we face in shaping ecclesial communities in America. At the same time, it is only the practices, with their daily rhythms, that will reformulate the DNA of our churches in the midst of our new space.

Practicing Hospitality

Creating new maps in our new space involves the recovery of hospitality, an ancient practice of the church, whose purpose has been largely forgotten.[6] Hospitality is not an evangelism strategy but a genuine welcoming of the stranger as part of the family, as embodied in ancient Middle Eastern cultures. In a culture as isolating and fragmenting as our own, people have become strangers to one another. Today, the stranger can easily be the person next door, the widow whose children live far away, or many of the young people who crave conversation and acceptance from an older generation.

Hospitality, a profoundly Christian habit, is a radically alternative practice in a culture where people feel like strangers to one another in their own neighborhoods and where we are too often turned into commodities that others want to use in order to sell their goods (we are all quite used to the telephone calls where the friendly voice on the other end of the line seems to know our name and is interested in us but quickly turns out to be some anonymous voice from a call center halfway around the world trying to sell us something). Our antennae are attuned to the fact that almost every situation in which we find ourselves has attached to it some means of using us as a commodity. How many of us are familiar with the endless stream of surveys that now confront us wherever we go? In shopping malls, over the telephones, passing through airports, well-dressed men and women want us to stop and answer a few questions about this and that. These are methodologies for discovering people's likes and dislikes. We are used as objects and commodities to improve a product or service that will sell. Such experiences cause us to put up our guard against almost everyone who is different or unfamiliar. The stranger in our culture is viewed as a threat or a danger, and we hesitate to extend our welcome. Modernity was birthed in suspicion, and we are socialized to be suspicious of everyone outside a small circle of people. The Neighborhood Watch program is an example of what has happened to people in the urban and suburban neighborhoods of North America. The sign "This is a Neighborhood Watch Community" at the entrance to a neighborhood indicates that we live in contexts where neighbors no longer know one another. To protect goods and children from the stranger, these "neighbors" must now create a program to wall off the outsider because the outsider is dangerous. Schools create regulations to ensure that no adult can enter this public, social space without passing through a well-monitored world of secretaries and cameras. Grandparents and friends are not allowed to pick up children after school without the express written permission of the parent who presents that permission in writing to the school; phone calls are not sufficient. People no longer know one another in our society.[7] Trust is low, and fear of the stranger is high. We create more and more ways to safeguard ourselves from the stranger, which does nothing to strengthen our sense of belonging or community. In fact, our lives keep fragmenting.

The DNA of the Gospel calls Christians into a way of life that addresses this fear and suspicion of the stranger. People hunger to be welcomed, to be recognized and given worth in a culture that moves in the opposite direction. Welcoming the stranger is a revolutionary act in the formation of a parallel culture. The Bible speaks of a day when there will no longer be strangers. The imagery of the consummation of God's salvation is of a great banquet. God welcomes the stranger. All who were not my people (1 Peter) are invited to the great banquet table of life. Jesus speaks in parables of the great feast resulting from his entering the world. His disciples are urged to go out into the world and find the strangers, those who do not fit into the normal structures of the culture and who are looked at with suspicion, and invite them to the banquet. What is disarming about these images is the absence of agendas to make people into something. The stranger is invited to experience the hospitality of God. Hospitality is a way of practicing the eschatological future by welcoming the stranger to our table as honored guests. In the biblical stories, God uses the stranger to introduce the strangeness of the truth to the community of faith (Jesus' walking with the two disciples on the road to Emmaus has much to do with how the stranger can be the bearer of God's presence and how the stranger can open our eyes to God's truth). To remain aloof from and fearful of the stranger by building walls of protection against such people (we are reminded of the anachronism of gated communities in our day) is to build walls against the possibility of encountering the disturbing realities of God's truth. Parallel societies welcome the stranger into their midst. Map-making in the midst of our shifting time requires us to rediscover this essential practice.

Missional environments are formed as a group adds the practice of hospitality to the keeping of the daily offices. In learning to practice hospitality, those in a local church begin by setting aside one evening a month to welcome the stranger into their homes. The stranger is someone other than a friend or church member, such as a neighbor, work associate, or acquaintance from a coffee shop or sports team the children play on. Our culture's fear of the stranger is so high that inviting someone too far outside the circle of such acquaintances is too great a first step. The purpose of these invitations is to treat the stranger as a guest, inviting the outsider to experience the gracious table of God. This is how one group of Christians began practicing hospitality in Edmonton, Alberta. Realizing that their church community was absorbing almost all their time, Greg, Howard, and their wives began inviting several people on their street over for cookouts and suppers, and out of this rhythm emerged a decision to create a neighborhood church on the few blocks around their homes. They understood that by welcoming the strangers in their midst, they were transforming their community, block by block. New bonds were formed, and a new imagination emerged for being church.

Why is hospitality an important practice? Practicing hospitality requires us to stop busy, demanding routines for a period of time and focus attention on the stranger for the stranger's sake. By practicing this simple act of faithfulness and witness, we quickly start to see how conditioned we are to experience changes to our routine as interference. Hospitality forces us to confront the ways our lives are driven by agendas and demands that push away relational encounters with others.

Creating a gracious table does not include an agenda to "convert" the stranger but to create space to listen to the stranger, nothing more. Hospitality is best expressed in the unspoken code Middle Eastern people have about the stranger who comes to their door: if a visitor comes to your door, feed him, rest him, and care for him; only after three days may you ask what he wants. What a gift to give people in this day and age, and what a radically transformative action this would be in the suburban neighborhoods of most congregations! As this simple practice develops in a local church, when the people come together in small-group meetings, part of the conversation is shaped around what people are experiencing in this practice of welcoming the stranger. In the initial months, it is experienced as an imposition on busy lives. This is the natural process of awakening to our own captivities, the cultural lies about what is important and essential. In the practice of hospitality, we confront our own need for conversion to the Gospel of the kingdom.

What is welcoming the stranger ultimately about? The New Testament tells a wonderful story of Jesus coming to meet two distraught disciples after his crucifixion. They are on the road, returning home to their former lives. They are bereft of hope, for in the execution of Jesus, their world has fallen apart. A stranger meets them on the journey and walks with them on the way. In their grief, they have no thoughts about the possible identity of this stranger, who is of course the risen Jesus. The man speaks about hope, expectation, and the promises of Scripture, and yet they still have no sense of who this stranger might be. Finally, as night is falling, they naturally extend an invitation to the stranger to eat with them. At the table, sitting beside each other in this place of sharing, the stranger breaks bread, and their eyes are suddenly opened to the truth of who is sitting with them. The truth about the stranger becomes visible at the table. The truth about the people in our neighborhoods, communities, and culture is experienced in relationships around the table. The truth about the creation of a new kind of culture is experienced in the practice of hospitality.

Receiving the Poor

I suspect that it will be very difficult to become map-makers in this new space without habits directed toward overcoming our isolation from those who are pushed to the bottom. Readers of this book are most likely well-educated, middle-class men and women who have learned to manage the systems of their culture. When Jesus spoke about the difficulty of entering the kingdom, he was describing people who had achieved a place of power and entitlement. His comments were not meant as a judgment but as a description of how hard it becomes to see the kingdom when we are the privileged. This is a fact of life. Unfortunately, affluence often makes it hard to embrace the parallel culture of the kingdom. Václav Havel's friends formed a parallel society out of their experience of loss; the captives in Babylon could hear again the stories of being God's people because they were no longer lulled by the controlled security of Jerusalem.

Middle-class Christians find these things hard to understand. They tend to live in homogeneous neighborhoods where everyone looks the same. Witness what happens when newcomers to these neighborhoods do not keep the unwritten social contract—putting up a fence that doesn't match the others in the area, painting their homes in colors not on the "approved palette," or failing to cut their grass often enough. Think about our responses in these situations in our own homogenized living areas. Even here we discover the extent of our unwillingness to engage with difference. North Americans are continually bombarded with messages telling us that the purpose of life is to meet our own needs. Likewise, the Christianity preached in churches has been tailored to meet our needs. Jesus' words are filtered; we do not hear them addressed to us.

As North Americans, we are part of the metanarrative of social democracies that tells us that there are separate spheres of life. Religion and commerce are separate worlds that don't interfere with each other. We believe that an invisible hand governs the global economy (except when the invisible hand is seen as so greedy and self-centered that it must be managed by government intervention, as in the current financial meltdown) and that if each of us, within limits, follows our own economic self-interest, everyone, especially the poor, will benefit.[8] This perspective is part of the modern story. Economic systems are an important and necessary way of shaping human life. Cultivating parallel communities of the kingdom involves economic values, the use of money. The middle-class North Americans attending most suburban churches do not have a lot of disposable income. On the contrary, they are often caught on an economic treadmill that keeps both parents at work full time just to earn enough to pay for the mortgage, the cars, and the children's education. Many are caught in the myth of the suburban dream; they feel there are no alternatives to holding on and working harder.

Economic discipleship is not a side conversation for the Christian. How might we engage the ways we are held captive by values that block our ability to live more fully as kingdom people? How might we discover ways of being God's people that involve economic accountability and sharing? Cajoling Christians into some form of tithing is not the answer. That is like asking for a tax without giving any better reason than that God requires this or providing the most anti-Gospel reason, that tithing is a part of God's plan for blessing us economically. Simply giving money to the church does not address the question of forming communities of the kingdom where people grow in their awareness of the economic powers controlling their lives. A dual barrier exists to this kind of missional witness. Middle-class Christians feel increasingly chained to an uncertain economic juggernaut that controls their lives. At the same time, while experiencing a significant economic collapse that has created massive anxieties about our personal economic lives, there is also an accelerating disparity between the poor and the rich. Today, this disparity goes beyond class, sex, and race to involve generational inequality too. Larger and larger numbers of young adults find themselves facing a world that does not offer them the prospects of their parents.[9]

Cultivating a missional environment calls for the practice of intentionally nurturing a listening friendship with someone outside one's own economic world, which goes beyond taking on people as a project or volunteering at a rescue mission. While these are important activities, what I advocate as a practice is building actual friendships. Many of us in middle-class churches do not live in proximity to the poor and don't know how to develop such a relationship. Building friendships is threatening and destabilizing because it takes people beyond their comfort zones. Furthermore, it seems an impossible request in their already busy lives. How does one fit another relationship into the schedule? These are real and legitimate questions. This kind of practice can only begin after the first two practices have become a regular part of one's life and have helped us confront and challenge how we live in light of the values we claim as followers of Christ.

Learning

Local churches are characterized by people with little sense of the Christian story as a whole. People have bits and pieces of the story, but individuals in congregations have a diminished sense of the God's great story for all creation that is found in Scripture. Corporately, congregations have a diminished sense of the overall purpose and direction of the biblical narratives. A parallel society is one that learns to live at the crossroads, or intersections, between the biblical narrative and the multiple modernities and postmodernities now shaping this new space.[10] Such crossroads, for example, are the multiple belief systems and cultural values that can exist in a single neighborhood as North American society grows more and more diverse and nations live alongside one another. Another practice that will need to be cultivated in this space is that of being a learning community. The urbanologist Jane Jacobs wrote a book exploring the reasons why great cultures that seem to flourish suddenly shrivel and die.[11] Part of her argument is that the reason cultures die, or enter a dark age, is that they begin to lose the memory of their story. Her point is that once a community has lost the ability to know and tell its story, it will very quickly lose its identity and die. This is especially so in our increasingly pluralistic neighborhoods characterized by multiple and often competing stories about the nature and meaning of life. The situation of the church in North America is that people know pieces of the story or have their favorite texts that bring personal meaning to them, but corporately, they've lost the basic memory of what God is up to in the world, of how this great, capacious story from Genesis to Revelation is actually forming a narrative about the nature of the world.

After a sermon, a man who had been attending church for about three years told a friend that it was one of the most helpful sermons he had heard. When asked why, he said he'd never known that the book of Acts was written after Paul. Though on its own an insignificant event, this man's reaction indicates the loss of our coherent sense of God's story. If we are to recover the DNA of Christian identity in this new space, local churches must become centers of learning that are shaped by the environments in which they are located. These centers of learning are places where ordinary people are invited to wrestle with how God's story might engage the multiple stories of our neighborhoods. This means that local churches are becoming locations for serious and long-term learning, local seminaries of sorts, where people can turn serious attention to the learning of the story. Nurturing the DNA of Christian identity requires building into the lives of those taking on Christian practices the habit of intentional learning. In Washington, D.C., the Church of the Savior has practiced this way of life with its members for years. Known as the School of Christian Living and the Servant Leadership School, it invites people into a process of lifelong engagement in learning. The school incarnates the kinds of missional learning practices, such as learning how to listen to the stories of their context and how to listen to the ways the biblical story connects, that need to shape every church on this continent. Anyone familiar with the story of the Church of the Savior knows the massive impact this small church has had on thousands of leaders across America over the past fifty years. Out of their learning process, ordinary Christians have formed mission groups that work with children on the streets, provide hospital care for people who cannot afford to look after themselves, bring together opposing political groups to seek the good of the city, and many other experiments in missional life.

SUMMARY

Cultivating local communities of the kingdom in the midst of this new space calls for leaders who know how to form churches around practices of Christian life. This chapter has outlined a number that seem essential at this moment. These practices are not intended to add new burdens but rather to create an environment in which people begin to understand and challenge the ways their lives are controlled by values in the larger culture. The practices represent practical ways of living out the implications of Romans 12: the transformation of the whole self toward God's kingdom. Commitment to these practices takes time to develop; they are never intended to be another set of religious rules. Leaders need to discern which church members are ready to begin living these practices and set about doing so in small ways. At the same time, as we discussed in Chapter Eight, they are continuing to cultivate the soil and shape environments of trust that give others the time they need to learn by seeing others work with these practices and come to believe they are not another burden the church wants to lay upon them.

My intention in this chapter was not to provide an exhaustive list of Christian practices but to describe the contours of a few practices that will help leaders shape missional environments in the midst of discontinuous change. Experiments in these forms of discipleship have been practiced throughout the history of the church. Leaders are called to cultivate such environments by recovering and translating into this moment the resources of our great tradition.

To this point, we have discussed three of the steps in becoming missional map-makers. This is a developmental process in which leaders need to move slowly through each step gradually introducing each one, interpreting to people what they are doing while they continue to build trust by carry out with excellence the pastoral care, preaching, and church management for which they were first called. By following this process, the local church is gradually being shaped as a people who are becoming a listening community (they are coming to believe that the Spirit can speak in and through the ordinariness of their lives), and as such, they are growing in their discernment of what the Spirit is calling them to do in the neighborhoods where they live with the capacities to name (out of their engagements in practices and the biblical narratives) what God is up to, and this will lead the people of a local church to corporately name what they can do together in the name of Christ. This is what we turn to in the next chapter.

MAP-MAKING PARTNERSHIPS BETWEEN A LOCAL CHURCH AND NEIGHBORHOODS AND COMMUNITIES

Chapters Eight and Nine outlined the first three steps in becoming missional map-makers:

Step 1: Assess how the environment has changed in your context.
Step 2: Focus on redeveloping a core identity.
Step 3: Create a parallel culture.

These steps create a listening community that believes that the Spirit speaks through the ordinariness of their lives and invites them to discern how they are being called into in the neighborhoods where they live. This chapter discusses the elements involved in step 4, identifying what they will do together as a local church in the neighborhoods where people live.

STEP 4: FORM PARTNERSHIPS WITH THE SURROUNDING NEIGHBORHOODS AND COMMUNITIES

As discussed in Chapter Nine, our neighborhoods are no longer the quiet, homogeneous contexts they may have been a generation ago; they are now diverse places subject to a never-ending barrage of ideas and data from our information society, flowing from the people across the street and, through the Internet and the media, from around the world. One of the challenges to missional life in this context is cultivating missional life in an information-overload world. Another is creating and leading experiments in mission in the local context. Experiments are the critical bridges to a community's developing a missional ethos because we can never achieve that through programs focusing on whole-system change or big strategies that involve everyone in the church.

Cultivating Missional Life in an Information-Rich World

We are living in the midst of a communications revolution. The quantities of information coming at us from many quarters is already massive and increasing every day. In Figure 10.1 the arrows directed into a local church community represent the multiple amounts of information coming into people's lives in our congregations. In fact, to be accurate these would represent hundreds and thousands of points of information coming into people's lives all the time. One can expect, for example, that while the Scripture is being read or a sermon given people are receiving and sending twitter messages that are communicating levels of information and data outside what a leader might imagine is the primary information being given from the front of a church or in an information bulletin on a Sunday morning. The weekly church email is but a miniscule point of information within myriad e-mails and other information pieces a church attender receives in a week. Most of the time, this information-overloaded world of people is carry multiple narratives, many of which are in direct competition with much of the Christian imagination. This is the information-rich world in which leaders must seek to form mission-shaped life. Figure 10.1 also indicates a series of smaller circles inside the larger circle representing a local church. These indicate that inside the local church there

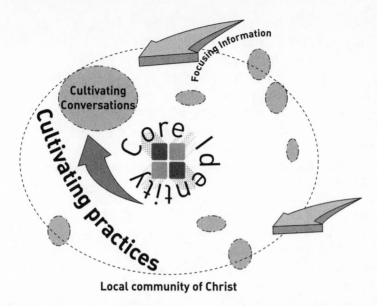

Local community of Christ

Figure 10.1. Attending to Narratives—Focusing Information.

exist multiple ways in which people are coming together (formally and informally) to wrestle with the many stories and narratives seeking to shape their lives. It is by attending to how these narratives are at play among people and learning to cultivate a dialogue among people and with the Biblical stories that leaders find ways of cultivating a mission-shaped direction among their people.

Missional map-makers must be cognizant of the power of this information revolution to affect people and also to overwhelm them as they look at the world. How do we understand the dynamics of conversation and communication in this new world of the Internet and information networks? A way to get at this question is to use the illustration of Garrison Keillor's movie *A Prairie Home Companion,* about the fictional last performance of the stage presentation of *A Prairie Home Companion* as it was broadcast live over the radio each week. At one level, the movie is about the events on stage. But at a whole other level, it's about what is happening offstage. In the movie, for example, are two sisters, played by Meryl Streep and Lily Tomlin, who are wonderful singers. They perform a wide range of songs before the live audience, belting out favorites that delight their listeners. One gets the sense that they've done this for most of their lives and it's second nature to them. To watch them perform onstage is a tremendous delight. But this onstage performance is only a part of what is happening in the movie. In fact, it's not even the most important part. When they're not performing, we see the sisters in their dressing room or conversing with other performers in the corridors backstage. It is these offstage dressing room and corridor conversations that reveal to us the real human drama of their lives as they argue, cry, and pour out their hearts to one another. If all we did was focus on the onstage performances, we would miss most of the story of their lives.

This distinction between onstage and offstage is crucial to the nature of the communications revolution that has resulted in our Internet world. It has to do with both the direction of information within a church (from the stage to people or among the people themselves) as well as how people are being helped to sort through the massive amounts of often conflicting information and data coming at them all through the week. Attend Sunday morning worship services in most local churches and ask the about the nature of the communication. Where is it coming from and who is in control of the information? Methods of delivery may have changed (video announcements, overhead projectors, PowerPoint, and so on), but the basic assumptions about communication remain the same as they have for generations: communication is "onstage." What does this mean? What I still witness in practically all the churches I visit in my travels is a public, onstage discourse that says the local church is about a set of preestablished programs and events that people in the church (and perhaps in the community) have the opportunity to join. Before the Internet and the communications revolution, the programs and events were probably the primary ways people did communicate and work with one another. Not so today! The problem here is that most pastors believe that what they have to say—the programs the church has created and the values and priorities they have developed—are the most important pieces of information that need to be communicated. Part of the reason for this one-way communication is that it has actually been the norm in most of our churches, so these pastors are simply communicating as they always have. While this may be true, it fails to take into account that in the communications revolution, the whole nature of communication has been transformed. In a networked, multichannel, Facebook world, one-way communication cannot be the norm. Furthermore, to be fair to pastors, they feel pressure and demands from people in their churches to manage programs and ensure that the church is being run properly to the point that they don't feel they have the time or the freedom to engage this communications issue. Why, I continually hear pastors complain about being overworked just sustaining the expected programs of the church; they claim to have little time or energy left over for anything else. Whether or not their perception is accurate, my point here is that church leaders, by the nature of the system, are focused on making the programs work and therefore come to assume that measuring these "onstage" programs (worship; discipleship; youth, adult, and children's ministries; mission trips; and so on) actually measures the life of the church. It doesn't! Further, pastors are convinced that if the church is to develop a missional life or engage in a process of change, the leadership will need to find new programs and events to make this happen, which is why pastors feel tension when it comes to questions of transformation. They feel caught between uncomfortable (and ultimately ineffective) choices about which programs to keep and which to let go of in order to initiate new programs for transformation or the cultivation of mission-shaped life in the new space.

Their problem is their perception. The formation of a new imagination and the cultivation of a mission-shaped community have little to do with programs, existing or yet to be created. But this is where leaders spend almost all their time and attention. They still assume that if they align and organize the boxes in the right way, the church will thrive as a mission-shaped community. This is just not the case, because this is not how the world works anymore and its not how people communicate with each other in this new space. The onstage world of programs and events that defines the life and work of pastors is not where the future is being formed. The future is taking shape in the offstage world of conversations and communication.

In the summer of 2009, the British Labour Party was imploding. Its leader, Gordon Brown, had been prime minister for almost two years and faced an election in 2010. Brown presented to his party and Parliament programs for managing the global financial crisis in his country. In his caucus, he outlined the details of his program and emerged claiming his party's support. In the meantime, offstage, increasing numbers of Labour Party members in Parliament were text-messaging and talking with each other on platforms such as Facebook with an entirely different set of narratives than those being spoken in the onstage world. The Internet had created a world with multiple channels of almost instantaneous communication where conversations outside the public discourse were shaping the outcomes of people's political lives—and it was all happening offstage.

This is the new world we have entered. Our onstage programs are no longer shaping people's lives. When Barack Obama was running for president of the United States, he promised to tackle the question of health care reform. He won the election, in part, on a mandate for change and through an extensive engagement with the Internet world of text-messaging and other forms of communication that connect people these days in networks of conversation none of us can map or manage. Then as president, in the spring of 2009, he determined to engage the issues of health care reform as they were being discussed in Congress and the Senate. But he chose not to do this by designing a program and then seeking to convince representatives and senators to sign on to it. Instead, he created space in each house for conversations across partisan lines. He sought to push diverse people into talking with one another, knowing that this was how the world was now operating. At the same time, quietly and behind the scenes, his staff started forming conversation groups on health care reform across America. In living rooms and chat rooms, they created offstage spaces for dialogue without presenting any specific program for people to debate, to agree or disagree over. At the time of writing, the outcome of these initiatives is still not decided. Many variables will come into play that will shape and reshape the conversations President Obama and his staff have started across the country. The point here is not what the specific outcome will be but the fundamental recognition that in a networked world of multiple communications channels, pushing programs and conclusions has become the least likely way to transform a community or achieve buy-in to a set of ideas. Transformation and innovation come not from programs presented by leaders but from the myriad ways ordinary people come together in dialogue. And that dialogue can no longer be mapped or set into a series of prescribed meetings (after Sunday services or in small-group meetings). The communications revolution and the Internet have recentered control of communication and connection away from the onstage and into the offstage world.

Pastors and church boards don't have control of communications anymore. This is why media groups like CNN create multiple venues for ordinary people to engage in conversations (through e-mails, blogs, or Twitter) and to become the reporters of events in their own local contexts. Only when we as church leaders understand that the future is forming offstage and outside the programs will we grasp the implications for the reshaping of our life in this new space: recognition that leadership in the local church is less and less about creating and managing programs and then trying to get people into them and more and more about creating the environments that foster interconnections and conversations among people. Earlier chapters in this book have described some of the massive shifts remaking our culture and the fact that we are no longer in a world of management, control, and preferred outcomes. We are now in this "unthinkable" world where our programs cannot help us imagine a new future. In an unthinkable world, it's not the programs but the conversations that matter. Over the past several years, a conference of churches in the Midwest have been working on the question of how they take their conference and its denominational tradition and reshape it as a missional conference. For a time, they worked at reshaping the constitution and organizational structures of the conference, coming up with new diagrams and designs for creating a missional conference. This took a good deal of time and no lack of energy debating what needed to be changed and what had to stay the same. As these conversations moved forward and a new structure was introduced and then approved by the assembly of church delegates, it started to dawn on some of the conference leaders that all that work had achieved almost nothing in forming a missional conference. People just poured their established habits and ways of working into the new structures; they were functioning pretty much as they always had—only the names of the organizations and systems had been changed. Fortunately, some wise leaders were able to acknowledge this reality. They also realized that after all this work, they themselves still didn't really know how to get from where they were to becoming a missional conference. In other words, they came to see that it wasn't primarily about structures, and they also sensed that they were trying to manage change in a world that kept changing under their feet (one example of that was the unanticipated financial meltdown that cause them to reduce conference staff on short notice). What they became convinced of was that the Spirit was among the people of their churches, and therefore, if they were to figure out how missional change would take place in this unthinkable world, they would need to engage in a whole series of conversations among the people. That is what they did. Over a four-month period, they held a series of well-designed listening conversations among the people.

As they listened to and reviewed these conversations, a sense of excitement grew that they were hearing that God was up to something among them. At their regional assembly in the spring, they shared the results of these listening conversations with the five hundred delegates and invited them into more conversations. These were beginnings. These initial conversations didn't suddenly transform the conference into a missional system. But the energy that has started to emerge, the sense that in the conversation are the clues to God's future, has taken hold of people in this system. They now believe that in an unthinkable world, communication is about conversation. Missional map-making calls for leaders who attend to the "offstage" conversations of their people. It involves creating safe spaces where ordinary people engage in more and more conversations about what is happening in their lives and what God might be up to in their neighborhoods. The role of leadership is to learn how to nurture these places of conversation and dialogue within and across churches, inviting people to believe again that their own stories contain clues about what God may be up to among them as a local church.

I have written elsewhere about my basic conviction that the Spirit of God dwells among the ordinary people of God.[1] I have described how, by extension, God's future is among these people, not with boards and leaders with vision and mission statements. The imagination for what a local community of Christians might be doing in their neighborhoods is found among the people themselves, not in programs designed for another era or deemed by leaders as essential to the inner life of a church. The unthinkable, unimaginable new things the Spirit is gestating in a local church will be called forth in conversations among the people. This is why the role of leadership is that of cultivator rather than program planner, a shaper of dialogues rather than a cheerleader for established programs. Missional map-makers do not go about looking for people to fill the programs of the church but become detectives of divinity listening in on conversations, attending to what the Spirit might be birthing, ready to be surprised rather than bent on fitting people into predetermined categories. These are some of the new skills leaders must develop in this new space. The map-makers are in our local churches; they are ordinary people in whom the Spirit is gestating all kinds of unanticipated futures for the kingdom. Mission-shaped leaders create environments of permission-giving and experimenting in which these ordinary dreams might be birthed.

Thanks to the explosion of the communications revolution, local churches are less and less like closed systems where the primary information people receive comes from the church or a narrow array of organizations. This is why presbyteries and conferences and dioceses struggle to discover how they can communicate effectively about themselves in this new space. It wasn't too long ago that the plans, programs, and communications of these mid-level judicatories were the shapers of local church life. Not anymore. We are all now immersed in a complex sea of multiple meanings where huge amounts of information continually make claims and counter claims upon everyone's life. People in our congregations are wide open to the information revolution and are being influenced by it in ways we have barely begun to imagine. They are swimming in a world of overwhelming, ubiquitous information. Information has always been present, flowing in and out, back and forth across the membrane of congregational identity. Today, the nature and form of information is different and far more complex. Until the late 1960s, information was increasing, but it tended to remain within the boundaries of dominant cultural frameworks most people took for granted. (People would, for example, be conversant with their national denominational newsmagazine—and notice that practically all of these magazines disappeared in the last two decades of the twentieth century.) Information today moves in many different directions at once. Look, for example, at the *New York Times* online, or *Wired* magazine or *Esquire.* These are no longer about one-way communication or simply the passing on of packaged information. Not only do they provide links that take a person into multiple levels of communications around various aspects of an article, but they also invite the reader to participate in the actual construction of information, images, and communication. It means, in part, that people are moving about the information highway at high speed, dismissing a huge amount and focusing on a few things that are of immediate interest. Information and communication are less about how I get *my* information across and more about how we invite people into a multichannel conversation. The tidy dissemination of controlled information is what has been exploded in the current information revolution.[2]

A powerful agent of change in a system is the introduction of new information (Barack Obama's use of the Internet to introduce conversation about health care reform, for example). The people in our congregations are being bombarded with information at an accelerating rate in the postmodern context. It is impossible to control the sources and flow of information into congregations or manage its diversity and ubiquity. But to cultivate missional environments, leaders must learn how to attend to information, understand its power, and develop the capacity to help congregations interpret and filter it in the light of their commitments. This is not about telling people what to believe but inviting them to ask questions about their information environment in the light of God's story. Thomas L. Friedman in his book *The Lexus and the Olive Tree* provides an excellent discussion of one way a reporter learned new skills for managing the information revolution and discovering how to attend to certain types of information in an age that has radically democratized information and decentered the role of experts.[3] Friedman was trained as a political reporter but in the 1990s learned that something was happening in the world that meant it was no longer possible to be an expert in one particular area of reporting and to actually understand what was happening in that area. In politics, for example, he discovered that he needed to learn about economics, social movements, and communications processes if he was to be in a position to report on politics. He needed to increase his knowledge in other areas, not to be in control of a subject but to filter out relevant information from the data assaulting him on all fronts. This is what leaders forming mission-shaped communities in this new space need to cultivate in themselves—knowing how to help people reflect on information within the biblical narrative.

What are some ways in which leaders can do this in their local churches? Some of these proposals will seem obvious but no less important. First, it is still about the depth to which a leader is willing and ready to listen to his or her people. By attending to the "offstage" conversation, one can learn a great deal about the information and communication that is shaping the lives of people in a local church. This is one area where church leaders are supposed to have high skills sets, attending to and listening to the narratives of others. What has been repeated throughout this book is that this kind of listening can be achieved only when the leader moves away from the need to promote strategies and visions and becomes present to people. It will mean a hard assessment of how time is spent in order to set aside hours in a week for being with people. This is the humble, old-fashioned skill of practicing presence. But one practices this presence with a focused desire to hear what the other person is saying, to call forth the person's stories, to be the detectives of divinity that are hungry to sense what God is up to in the other. In this kind of attentive listening one will hear the ways in which the multiplicity of information is affecting people.

One pastor would do this by setting aside time each week to connect with people in a local coffee shop (any place where people gather on a regular basis will do). In so doing, he connected with a collage of stories: he learned what kinds of information were affecting these people and how they were engaging that information (anything from Michael Jackson's death to the beatings of young males in a local community to the importation of food from a particular part of the world). What he did with this information was ask himself what biblical narratives connected with these stories and the questions they were raising for people. He didn't use the Bible to give people answers but rather to invite them into more conversations about how the pieces they were discussing and the biblical narratives might be connecting.

Another leader looked at the whole process of communication in the church, recognizing that it was all a one-way, onstage process. What she did (slowly at first) was invite people in the church to share a bit of their own story in announcement time. People started to look forward to hearing from one another as the stories moved from little packets of formal information (how long someone had been in the church or how a person came to join the church) to people sharing stories of what they were experiencing in their neighborhood and with their neighbors. This simple act began to create an environment in which people took ownership for sharing stories and information with one another. It meant cutting the sermon down some each Sunday and leaving out a chorus or two, but the trade-offs where worth it. This pastor quickly learned that as stories were shared among people, she had the new and energizing role of bringing elements of the biblical narratives to these stories and putting simple questions before people.

The conference that created listening conversations is another example of how one group began to empower the narratives and their people so that communication started moving in multiple directions across the network of churches. This didn't all happen serendipitously, as if it needed no planning or organization. Of course it did. People needed time, for example, to learn some simple skills of how to have listening conversations with other people (it seems strange to write this, but people really do need training and encouragement to engage in these kinds of conversations). As the conversations started to take hold, leaders also needed to help churches share with one another what was happening as a result of these conversations. This took communication skills, telling the stories of how churches were responding, offering people assistance in creating these conversations for themselves.

I think of how some friends who are younger leaders and far more aware of the communications revolution than I go about this. One such leader listens to the stories and chatter of his people (think about Facebook and other venues where people are communicating with one another about events and news). He would then skillfully use music, video, and other forms of media on a Sunday morning to frame the ways his people were commenting on and engaging the information that was important to them. He would bring elements of the information world into Sunday morning then, working with biblical texts, ask questions about the communication that people where sharing in their Facebook or blogging or Twitter world.

If you want a really out-of-the-box, creative way of thinking about how to engage the biblical narratives with this new information world, the story of several colleagues in the UK is worth telling. Several years ago, Colin Greene (an Anglican theologian) and Martin Robinson (a church planter for the Churches of Christ in the UK, church historian, and director of Together in Mission, a network for training missional leaders in the UK) were both working for the Bible Society in the UK. They knew that in this new space of the communications revolution, printing more Bibles, creating Bible tracts, or developing one more video on why the Bible is important just wasn't cutting it with the growing generations of nonchurched, media-savvy people in the UK. They decided it was time to think outside the box. Through a set of wonderful circumstances, they came into dialogue with some writers for *Vogue* magazine who wanted to do a fashion shoot (this certainly doesn't sound like a religious subject or something the Bible Society would be interested in). Colin and Martin wondered about information, communication, and the Bible. What could the interface be between this magazine and the Bible? Over several months, an idea was hatched. Working with the magazine's designers, writers, and photographers, Colin and Martin told stories of women in Scripture (not all of them perfect and pure). With great integrity, the magazine staff, together with the Bible Society staff, created a story and an amazing fashion photo shoot based on women of the Bible for the UK millennium edition of *Vogue*. One might ask, What's the point? The point is that this interface between a primary artifact of the communications age and the Bible created a space for conversation and dialogue about the Bible and its relevance in a postmodern culture. The magazine staff were so excited about the possibilities of partnering with Colin and Martin that they wanted to do a second piece. Unfortunately, there was too much resistance from the Bible Society to risk another round.

One of the elements of the communications revolution Colin and Martin understood in this project (we will learn these kinds of things only if we are willing to risk and experiment) is that in the communications revolution, images and icons have become more important in connecting people than written pieces (which is not to say that written pieces are no longer important but rather that they are not what first connects with people as much as they used to). For example, we are more likely to connect with the image of the Berlin Wall than a long story about it; we see a picture of the burned remains of the twin towers, and we are immediately inside a world; we see a picture of Michael Jackson doing the moon walk or some step out of the *Thriller* video, and a whole generation is immediately taken into a set of narratives. Another generation will see the image of a young, screaming, naked Vietnamese girl running down a dirt road and immediately recognize that it was that image, more than all the protests and sit-in, that ended the war in Vietnam. Why, then, don't we read the Bible with this perspective in mind? In preparing to communicate with people about the Christian narrative, why not spend time in a particular story asking what the images are that communicate the story just as my colleagues risked and experimented with the people of *Vogue* magazine? I remember several years ago, the Academy Awards were later in the year than usual and Easter came quite early. That year, Sophia Loren presented the Oscar for Best Picture to the Italian producer of the movie *Life Is Beautiful.* I'll never forget his response to her announcement. He literally jumped up from his seat and, rather than walking down the aisle, stepped across the tops of the rows of seats, shouting his delight, as he got to the front of the hall as fast as he could. It was an amazing moment of communication, his utter joy and exuberance at hearing his movie named Best Picture, the energy with which he responded, and the abandon with which he kissed an icon of the movie world, Sophia Loren. Everyone in that Los Angeles theater and the millions around the world watching shared that moment with him—it was brilliant communication in a communications world. I was fortunate enough to know someone in Vancouver who is a member of the Academy of Motion Picture Arts and Sciences (the people who vote on who is awarded Oscars each year). I was planning for Easter Sunday, and I immediately knew what I wanted to do. I called my friend and asked if he could get a video clip of that portion of the Academy Awards for me, and he did. On Easter Sunday, we met in a large, darkened auditorium, entering a room that symbolized the death of Jesus. Someone began a mournful song in the dark from somewhere in the room. Other joined in; it was a song that raised the question of what had happened to Jesus and what was to be done now that he was gone. Then, as the lights slowly rose, another person in the auditorium started reading the texts where Jesus appears to Mary and she runs so fast to tell the disciples and they run in disbelief, encountering Jesus. As the words poured out and the lights were still dim, I stood up and asked the question, What must it have been like to hear that news that terrible morning? Then the screen came on, Sophia Loren made her announcement, a skinny man shouting Italian jumped from his seat and raced across the tops of other people's seats, screaming his joy. There was no need to say more! In our gathering, the lights came up, the music started, and we rocked, we rocked with liturgy and confession around the Creed. We knew that he was alive! There are endless ways of engaging this amazing time in which we live.

Connecting Conversations and Inviting Experiments

In this context of multiple streams of nonlinear communication, where fitting people into established programs will never connect with the flux and change of our neighborhoods, how do leaders cultivate mission-shaped life in a local church? Mission-shaped life involves a series of interacting factors that need to be cultivated together. First, it requires creating an environment within the local church where a high value is given to attending to the conversations among people and giving voice to their stories and narratives.[4] Second, it involves bringing those narratives into conversation with the biblical narratives; that is, leadership is not so much about telling people what the Bible has to say as it is about inviting people to discover how their stories connect with the biblical narratives. This is where the leader is less a pedagogue and more a poet.[5] Figure 10.2 expresses this process

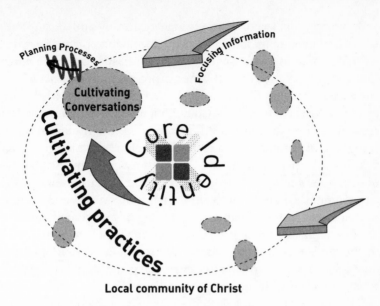

Local community of Christ

Figure 10.2.   Forming Experiments.

in a local church where the small circles, as discussed in reference to Figure 10.1, represent the ways people in a local church find themselves, formally and informally, in the midst of conversations. These kinds of "off-stage" conversations, however, usually aren't occurring in the formal programs of the church, which is why leaders need to discover ways of attending to the nonprogrammatic and more informal narratives of people in their church. These circles are intended to represent numbers of conversations and interactions across the system in which people are learning to tell their stories and read the Bible through these stories. It will be out of these interactions that people will start to tentatively name experiments they would like to test in being God's missionary people in their community. In this way, we begin to frame new maps.

Managing and planning an overall mission strategy from the center outward will no longer work. Neither will using demographic studies of the congregation's context to create an overall, centralized strategic plan for mission prove a great help in this new context. Understanding of a church's changing context is not unimportant, but these kinds of processes tend to be shaped by the assumption that it is possible, by measuring and objectifying the context, to plan and predict a preferred future. Linear planning and alignment of the system with a predicted future are contrary to the realities of an emergent, discontinuous context such as ours, which is characterized by uncertainty. Truth be told, among their members, local churches already have most of the information they need to know what is happening in their communities. Church members are in touch with the context because they are in it. They may not use the social science categories of demographics, with their cohorts and highly specific definitions of people types and groups, but among the ordinariness of their common life, congregations have a cumulative sense of their communities. Often the problem is that leaders have no idea of how to creatively call forth that understanding or how to cultivate environments that allow the imagination of the people to connect with their experiences of their context. As a result, they place a premium on using expert information or centralized planning. We are in a time when a radically different imagination is required.

The steps outlined in Part Two so far suggest that mission is not a centralized plan captured in a mission statement and developed in a strategy that aligns the congregation's resources and people around a common set of actions. Rather, the work of leadership requires capacities to cultivate listening conversations and dialogues around people's "offstage" narratives and bring them into conversation with the biblical narratives. Linked with the practices of Christian life as outlined here, tentative but wonderful imaginations for engagement in the neighborhoods will emerge from among the people. This process of dialogue is not shaped around some central plan but involves small, at times unplanned engagements among people over coffee, supper, or in groups shaped around the practices.

In a period of discontinuous change, it is impossible to control, manage, and centrally plan this kind of process. But as people are invited to engage with common practices, as they intentionally reenter the biblical narratives from places of confusion and exile, as they become aware of and understand a missional ecclesiology of God's reign, and as they process the continuous flow of information about the neighborhoods, workplaces, and the world where they live and work, the potential for new imaginations and innovations for mission will emerge. These will emerge from among the people themselves, as people experimentally and tentatively test the nudging of the Spirit and gradually become confident that the Spirit of God is really up to something among them. Above all, mission emerges out of our collective struggle to understand what it means to be God's people in this kind of world.

The great reality of the church is that by the Spirit, God's imagination for the future is already among God's people, and so the work of leadership is in the cultivation of the environment that will allow this imagination to gather energy. In this time of radical discontinuity, the key theological notion guiding our path is that God calls a people, and among that people, the imagination for a new future can be born. The new maps for missional life emerge from the interconnections and interrelationships that form between members of a congregation. They emerge from among the diffuse, noncentralized nodes of energy and creativity continually swirling among people.

Cultivating Planning Processes

Remember when I said that strategic planning wouldn't work? That's because traditional models of church leadership start with strategic planning, with articulating a vision, forecasting a future, and working to secure support from the congregation. The missional planning model flips the old model on its head. There is a place for certain forms of strategic planning, but these are now found not at the beginning or coming from the center but toward the end as people initiate experiments in mission. When a sense of calling emerges from among a group of people, it needs to be translated into actions that require resources and a careful delineation of how the mission will be carried out. In Washington, D.C., for example, a mission group meeting in a troubled area of the city with high levels of unemployment saw a desperate need to provide care for young children. These children were left to themselves on the streets during the day with little direction and often sparse amounts of food. This mission group was part of a larger church that practices the steps outlined in Part Two of this book. Gradually, people in the group became convinced God was calling them to respond to the needs of these children. They didn't know what to do but decided they would create an experiment over several months in what we would normally call a day care program. Once this sense of calling had emerged, they needed to plan how to do it. That is where standard elements of strategic planning became important. The people in this group had taken all the appropriate actions: recognizing the changed elements of their context, reengaging the biblical narratives, working with practices of Christian life, asking questions about what God was up to in their neighborhood, and identifying what they could do together. Now they needed to set goals, look at resources, plan further actions, and ensure that their strategies would be effective. This means that strategic planning happens at a micro-level across the diffuse and dispersed experiments being conducted in the neighborhoods. The people themselves are taking on the responsibilities of strategic planning. Leaders can be available to assist and facilitate, connecting people with resources, and so on, but this is a genuine work of the people that emerges from among their common life of discernment. The role of the leadership is to continuously cultivate the environment that enables people to gather energy and imagination for mission at multiple points of experimenting. The work of cultivation is not about defining or identifying the missional actions ahead of time but rather about creating the practices, habits, learning, and safe spaces for all the offstage interactions to occur. But as mission emerges, as groups of people start to gather and shape the ways they will engage their context in witness and with kingdom life, there is a need for some strategic planning. As a mission emerges, people need to be able to plan their activities, define the steps they will take, align their energies and resources with the vision, and so forth. In this sense, mission becomes a radically decentralized process.

The role of leadership is to cultivate the core identity of the system, its DNA, to support the practices and habits that infuse the system's life and identity throughout. But the action of mission and life can no longer be discussed in terms of center and periphery; it now consists of multiple nodes of energy and imagination, creating centers of missional life that cannot be predicted or planned in advance. In this way, a local church shapes itself for vital life in a time of rapid, discontinuous change.

This is the context in which the new maps emerge. Leaders are no longer CEOs with overarching vision and mission statements tied to a centralized plan built around key programs. They are cultivators of an environment in which God's future emerges because that future lies within the people who comprise the congregation. God's future lies within his people; the role of leader is to create an environment in which it might be called forth.

In these last stages, missional map-makers don't simply sit by in some passive mode. Leadership within a local church is vital at this juncture, but again, the leadership skills required are not about command and control but the continual encouragement, cultivation, and support of people. For some, it is about walking beside groups of people who are moving into experiments. Like teaching someone to ride a bike or build a project for the first time, the role here is mentor and booster, providing the kind of background support that helps people continue in their initiating work. The leader also functions as an interpreter who bridge communications between the experimenting groups and the rest of the church, especially groups such as church boards that can sometimes become concerned that people may be stepping outside the bounds of protocols or assumed expectations. This is where the leader continues to cultivate an environment of trust and expectation among people. Above all, the leader is doing what I call a "this is that" form of communication. This means that the leader is continually functioning as an interpreter, pointing out how and where these experiments connect with, come out of, and are shaped by both the biblical narratives and the core values of the tradition to which the local church belongs.

The missional map-maker is key in each of the steps outlined in the chapters in Part Two. They are very active, giving form to these steps, working with staff, boards, and many kinds of people across the church in learning together how to initiate and embed these steps in the church's life. The energy of the leadership is in calling forth the experiments from among the people. In one church, a group determined it wanted to create an experiment in developing transitional housing for women in the neighborhood. The pastoral staff of the church had been intimately involved in the processes leading up to this decision. This did not mean leading the group or being a prime decision maker. Rather, it was the relational presence in the dialogue, providing insight and guidance where requested, interpreting what was happening to the board, connecting the group with others in the church who were growing in their interest, and ensuring that the group had thought through the details of resources, costs, and time commitments. All the time, the leader was blessing the group members in their work. At the same time, this leader was also connecting with others across the church who, because of the transitional housing group were themselves starting to ask questions about experiments and connecting with their neighborhoods. In these early stages of exploration, the leader might walk with people through their neighborhoods or suggest guidelines for how they might do this.[6] The leader's work as an environmentalist is to attend to the whole system and how these experiments are being understood, developed, and interpreted to others and creating new moments of dreaming about being God's people. And underneath all of this, building into the liturgies, biblical narratives, and conversations of the church, are conversations about what God is up to and how people continue to learn about shaping church life into a new world. Much of this work is informal. It is not about organizing experiment groups into committees or placing them somewhere in an organizational church. In these initiating times, everything needs to be held lightly, and this requires calm, wise leadership that helps shape these environments of expectation. As experiments begin, others in the church begin to catch on to what lies behind the steps I have outlined—this is a time for ongoing interpretation, for encouraging others into experiments. In other words, the leader is functioning at multiple levels at once— encouraging, interpreting, and at the same time continuing to ensure that all the expected functions of the church are accomplished with excellence. These are the ways leadership functions at the beginning of the experimentation period.

POSTSCRIPT: MAP-MAKERS AS CULTIVATORS OF ENVIRONMENTS

Throughout these steps, one of the underlying activities of a leader involves what I have called cultivating environments. This final section looks more closely at this ancient practice of cultivation. Missional map-making in a new space is, first, about the ability to cultivate a certain kind of environment.[7] In *Missional Church: A Vision for the Sending of the Church in North America,* Inagrace Dietrich comments, "The future of Christian life in the Spirit does not spring forth without intentional cultivation."[8] Cultivation is an ancient word that was related to the world of agriculture. It has to do, therefore, with the soil in which things grow. The way we attend to the soil will determine the types and the vitality of the vegetation that grows there. So healthy environments are critical to the thriving of any kind of life. We see this, for example, in modern cities faced with the problem of air pollution, an environmental imbalance that results in an increase in lung disease or asthma. A parallel can be made in terms of local churches faced with a changing community or rapidly changing attitudes toward spiritual life in a society. If the church has spent a good many years developing its own internal environment around specific programs that are focused on its inward life, then it has probably grown out of touch with its community and neighborhood. Its environment is able to read and adjust to its own internal needs (worship styles, types of programs, or ways of meeting) but doesn't have the same ability to read the environment in its neighborhood and community. In the context of the changes discussed in this book, it becomes essential for churches to learn how to attend to their external (local community) environment. While this sounds like a simple proposal, it requires a huge change in imagination. My experience is that a majority of churches know that the world outside their doors is in the midst of a huge transformation. But the way they want to address this transformation is by working hard to improve on the internal environment of the church. No amount of internal enhancement will result in a church's ability to engage the changing context, because the people living in these neighborhoods are less and less prepared to go to a church. The purpose of map-making is to assist the people of a church in discovering that they need to attend to the environment in their neighborhoods even more than in their churches. This practice of cultivation needs to be rediscovered as a rich resource for framing the work of leaders in this in-between period of massive transition.

The problem is that few of us have any direct experience with the practice of cultivation. While the hobby of gardening is growing in many urban contexts, the ways of soil and plants remain largely a mystery to most of us. Most of us have lawns. We cut and weed the grass at the front and back of our homes. But these activities are usually the opposite of cultivation. We take a gas-driven, polluting motor to which is attached a steel blade, and we basically slash the top growth of the grass down to a level of acceptable homogeneity. Following this cosmetically justified destruction, we spread small pellets of poison mixed with nitrogen in order to control what we don't like and create a predetermined coloration that we deem satisfactory. For most of us, this lawn maintenance ritual represents the extent of our experience with cultivation; we'd like to do more, but our busy lives dictate that gardening is a relative waste of time on the economic scale of life and therefore far from most of our imaginations. Therefore, for many leaders (and I count myself among these), our unfamiliarity with the rhythms and habits of cultivation means that we are entering a world that has become profoundly alien to us. We need to wrestle with the call to become cultivators even while we acknowledge that we are all being initiated into a strange process. Map-making in this new environment is not simply about creating something new off some clean sheet or *tabula rasa;* rather, it invites us to rediscover traditions and habits we have lost.

Cultivation originally encompassed the tending of animals and crops, and it is worth reflecting a little on what this practice meant to people prior to the modern period. It involved learning skills through repetition, habit, and devoting time and attention to a field, soil, a plant, or a group of animals. At its core, cultivation entailed the readiness to bother with the ordinariness of soil or the stubborn dumbness of an animal because in that patient commitment to the ordinariness of these things, the richness of the earth or the goodness of the animal was brought forth. In plowing a field, a farmer was breaking open the earth. Something was being started; a process was being initiated that was more like a covenant with the earth than a mechanical set of actions designed to produce a predictable outcome or product. It's hard to even make sense of this concept in our day. Undoubtedly, the earth was tilled and cultivated in order to produce food to feed hungry mouths, but far more was going on. The festivals and liturgies of church life that marked the seasons suggest awareness that in this cultivation of the ordinariness of the soil, there was a covenant between God and the earth and the people of a community.

These are difficult ideas for most of us shaped in modernity, especially in urban environments. When I planted an herb garden several years ago from seeds cultivated in tiny little bowls in the basement, the shoots of green lay buried beneath the soil for a period of time as they were being called forth by a mysterious interaction of earth and rain and seed. In that planting process, I was making something, not by the imposition of my will, but by working with and becoming part of a process that was much greater than myself and my tools. Cultivation is a process that is, at its heart, profoundly mysterious. When I use those herbs in my cooking, it is with a sense of pride and wonder at what I have made, but also with a deeper sense of entering and becoming part of a larger reality in which I am a participant. Those who cultivate do not make but call forth what is already inherently present. This activity of cultivation goes to the very nature of creation and therefore the nature of God.

My limited experience with a small herb garden makes it clear that the act of cultivating requires working with what is there rather than imposing some external meaning or agenda. In the garden, meaning is already present in the potential of the seeds or young plants to grown into healthy, mature versions of themselves. To cultivate the herbs in ways that bring out their best and fulfill their purpose requires my cooperation. Certain herbs must be contained or their roots grow throughout the garden, choking off the life of other herbs. Some herbs can't be allowed to develop toward the flower stage or the wonderful aromatic smells and flavors they give off are muted or lost. All this tending must be carried out by listening to and understanding the nature of each herb. It is like entering a sensual relationship with the garden in which, as the scientist and philosopher Michael Polanyi describes, one becomes focally attentive as there emerges a personal knowledge impossible without patience, time, and relationship.[9] As a cultivator, I enter a world, in this instance the world of the herb garden, in which I am shaped as well as I give shape. If I am to participate well in this world, there are practices and habits to be learned and limitations to be honored.

Cultivation involves placing oneself within a set of habits and practices appropriate to a particular world. Such habits and practices are formed out of and within a relationship with whatever is being cultivated. Indeed, there can really be no way of life, no world formed, without accepting and taking on both the limitations and the practices of the world being cultivated. Only by accepting and working with both is there a possibility that the world will move toward its *telos.* This kind of life journey is not about power over something or even control of it; it is more at the level of being invited into and confronted by a mystery. One chooses to engage that mystery in order to discover, along the way, the purpose that is simultaneously embedded within and also in the process of unfolding After working in the herb garden over multiple seasons, I can predict the shape and outcome of the mystery and its *telos.* But I suspect that in our period of discontinuous change, we are all called into the cultivation of something that is as yet unformed and unclear from our perspective. Our task is to enter into this world and learn habits and practices that emerge from engagement with this new context and with one another. Here there is a high potential for failure and error, a great need to unlearn old habits and risk new ones. But we enter this process with an understanding of mystery and without the hubris that we can control or manage what is taking place. We have a much humbler task of cultivating in a time and place where the gardens are quite different and a new kind of herb or flower is emerging. Our role is not to make the pattern that will emerge but to be like midwives at a birth, tending the process and providing encouragement along the way. We nurture something that is not ours, recognizing that we are neither the makers nor the creators but those who work alongside.

Paul illustrates this process in his correspondence with the house churches in Corinth. In chapter three of the first letter, he rebukes the Corinthians for the ways they have turned the Gospel into power issues about who is following the best leader or which group has the best handle on the truth. Paul is clear and articulate about not only the nature of Christian life but also the character of those called among them as leaders. The cross pervades the letter. It is the source of foolishness to the Greeks and a stumbling block to the religious who have a well-developed sense of how believers should work for God's righteous approval. The metaphor Paul uses to counter the Corinthian images of leadership is significant: Peter, Apollos, and he are the ones who cultivate a garden. Consistent with his cross-shaped ecclesiology, he makes it clear that none of these leaders is responsible for making the Corinthians: it was neither their power nor their eloquence but the mystery of the proclamation and demonstration of cross-shaped lives that called into being these little communities of the kingdom. The role of these leaders in the formation of missional communities is that of cultivators of a garden—some plant seeds, others water the young plants, and some, like Paul, wrestle with errant growth and discipline the plants in directions they were intended to grow. Left to themselves, the plants will grow wild and misshapen and will miss the nature of their calling and formation. Gardeners are cultivators, men and women bending down low, kneeling in the dirt with hands deep in the muck, their arms and faces pushed into the growth to prune and shape and form a people through the use of practices and disciplines. This is the nature of cultivation; it is the form leadership must take in this period of massive, discontinuous change. We cannot predict or control what lies before us. We are in a different world and must learn a new set of practices. How do we cultivate communities of God's people in this time and place?

Such cultivating enables a continuing conversion to flourish in the discontinuities and forms of communities of difference.[10] Sister Mary Jo Leddy, who founded the Oscar Romero Center in Toronto and now teaches at the Jesuit Regis College in that city, describes this cultivation of Gospel life in a reflection on the writings of Václav Havel.[11] It is appropriate to end this book by again referring to the life of that amazing man by completing the story he told about the formation of a parallel society. Havel was president of Czechoslovakia (1989–1992) then later became president of the Czech Republic (1993–2003). For the eastern states of Europe, trapped as Soviet satellites in the decades preceding the end of communism, it seemed as if communism and the totalitarian state were a pervasive, immovable presence in everyone's life. Communism did not exist "out there" in the structures of government and power as if it were external to the minds and spirits of the people. It was so pervasive, wrote Havel, that it was also "within" each and every person who had been born and grew up in the system. In this sense, it seemed totally oppressive and impossible to overcome.

As recounted in Chapter Nine, in the decades before its fall, people began to do something that would lay the groundwork for the end of communism many years hence. This was the tentative beginning of a parallel society. None of them had a notion that they were engaged in activities that would have this result; they did not imagine that their actions would contribute to the end of communism. People began to ask how they could live the truth in a culture based on a fundamental lie. What made it so difficult was that the lie was not just "out there" in other people or the system; it was in their heads. In small numbers, through letters, novels, poetry, plays and conversations, people started to tell each other, in seemingly insignificant ways, that some element of the reality under which they lived was a lie. On its own, each small action seemed inconsequential to the overwhelmingly pervasive presence of communism. But as more and more people quietly participated in the process, a difference began to emerge. People saw more and more of their life under communism as lies, and they stopped believing the lies. When these simple actions of resistance grew in number, like increasing numbers of sound waves interacting with one another, communism's power started to crumble from the inside.

This was the inadvertent formation of a parallel culture Havel described so eloquently. The people could not form an alternative culture, he argued, because the power and reality of communism was so strong, it infected all of life, and it was impossible for the people within it to step outside its environment and influence. But it was possible to slowly create a parallel way of life within the monolithic fact of communism. This is the kind of environment missional map-makers cultivate in our discontinuous new space. It will be done in ways that reflect the wise words of Wendell Berry when speaking about the devastations to our natural environment: "We must begin by giving up any idea that we can bring about this healing without fundamental changes in the way we think and live. We face a choice that is starkly simple: we must change or be changed."[12]

NOTES

Introduction

1. Richard Florida, "How the Crash Will Reshape America,"*Atlantic,* Mar. 2009, p. 28.
2. Lesslie Newbigin, *Foolishness to the Greeks: The Gospel and Western Culture* (Grand Rapids, Mich.: Eerdmans, 1986), p. xx.
3. Darrell L. Guder, ed., *Missional Church: A Vision for the Sending of the Church in North America* (Grand Rapids, Mich.: Eerdmans, 1998). This book is just one in the Gospel and Our Culture Series published by Eerdmans.
4. At the Allelon Web site (http://www.allelon.org), you will find a series of video interviews and essays under the theme "What Is Missional Church?" that provide a rich resource for those interested in exploring the missional question further.
5. *Thirteen Days* (New Line Cinema, 2000). The movie's title is borrowed from the book by Robert Kennedy, *Thirteen Days: A Memoir of the Cuban Missile Crisis* (New York: Norton, 1968). The comments in the text are based on the script of the movie rather than Kennedy's book.

Chapter One: Maps Shaping Our Imaginations in Modernity

1. See Garrett Green, *Imagining God: Theology and the Religious Imagination* (Grand Rapids, Mich.: Eerdmans, 1989), pp. 66–74.
2. Rabbi Harold M. Schulweis, "Darfur Meditation," © 2006 Valley Beth Shalom. Reprinted with permission.
3. An excellent exposition of this perspective as it emerges first in Descartes and then fixes itself as one of the central features of the modern imagination can be found in Roger Lundin, Clarence Walhout, and Anthony C. Thiselton, *The Promise of Hermeneutics* (Grand Rapids, Mich.: Eerdmans, 1999), pp. 6–62.
4. Alasdair MacIntyre, *After Virtue,* 2nd ed. (Notre Dame, Ind.: University of Notre Dame Press, 1984). This discussion is based on aspects of Chapter 15,

"The Virtues, the Unity of Human Life, and the Concept of a Tradition" pp. 204–225.

5. Ibid., p. 204.
6. This is part of what the postmodern turn rejects in modernity. See Zygmunt Bauman, *Intimations of Postmodernity* (New York: Routledge, 1992). Structuralism argues a contrasting view, namely, that human beings are born into and are already part of existing systems of meaning and narratives that shape us in our particularity and specific history.
7. An army officer seeking to lead a church meeting first wrote *Robert's Rules of Order* in the 1870s. This was at the height of the Industrial Revolution, when people were searching for new ways of ordering and organizing the new types of societies emerging under laissez-faire capitalism. What seems to be missed by church groups using this form of structure today is that it emerged from a particular social formation at a particular time in the late nineteenth century and that it expresses a way of organizing the world based on an emerging class of freely associating societies in England. There is little engagement of theological critique of these rules based on the context in which they emerged or the assumptions about how people organize and form social life. This industrial age mechanism for human interaction continues to shape the practices of many churches.
8. Manuel Castells, *The Rise of the Network Society,* Vol. 1, 2nd ed. (New York: Wiley-Blackwell, 2000).
9. James Cowan, *A Mapmaker's Dream: The Meditations of Fra Mauro, Cartographer to the Court of Venice: A Novel* (New York: Warner Books, 1996).
10. Ibid., p. 40.

Chapter Two: Leading in an In-Between Time

1. Joshua Cooper Ramo, *The Age of the Unthinkable* (London: Little, Brown 2009) page 114.
2. See, for example, Paul Klugman, *The Return of Depression Economics and the Crisis of 2008* (New York: Penguin, 2008).
3. See Stephan Chan, *The End of Certainly* (New York: Zed Books, 2009) as one clear, informed example.
4. G. K. Chesterton, "Five Deaths of the Faith," *Everlasting Man* (Part 2, Chapter 6), http://www.worldinvisible.com/library/chesterton/everlasting/part2c6.htm.
5. Hannah Arendt, *Between Past and Future* (New York: Penguin Books, 1993), p. 9.
6. Ibid., p. 26
7. Alasdair MacIntrye, *After Virtue,* 2nd ed. (Notre Dame, Ind.: University of Notre Dame Press, 1984), p. 213.

8. Ibid., p. 215.

9. Ibid.

10. Ibid., p. 216.

11. See David Bodanis, $E=MC^2$ (New York: Walker, 2000).

12. Frijof Capra, *The Turning Point* (Toronto: Bantam Books, 1983), p. 76.

13. See Brian Greene, *The Elegant Universe* (New York: Vintage Books, 2000).

14. Louis Dupre, *The Passage to Modernity* (New Haven, Conn.: Yale University Press, 1993), pp. 6–10.

15. Ibid., p. 10.

16. Lesslie Newbigin, *The Gospel in a Pluralist Society* (Grand Rapids, Mich.: Eerdmans, 1989).

17. Ibid., p. 8.

18. Lesslie Newbigin, *Proper Confidence* (Grand Rapids, Mich.: Eerdmans, 1995), p. 4.

19. Ibid.

20. Ibid., p. 6.

21. Brueggemann, *Texts Under Negotiation: The Bible and Postmodern Imagination* (Minneapolis: Fortress, 1993) pp. 18–19.

22. Arthur Kornberg, "Invention Is the Mother of Necessity," *Globe and Mail,* Nov. 4, 2000, p. A13.

Chapter Three: When Common Sense Is No Longer Common

1. Huston Smith, *Beyond the Post-Modern Mind* (New York: Crossroads, 1989), p. 3.

2. Alanna Mitchell, *Sea Sick* (Toronto: McClelland & Stewart, 2009).

3. Portions of this discussion are adapted from Michael Fulks, "Gestalt Theory and Photographic Composition," *Apogee Photo Magazine,* http://www.apogeephoto.com, 1997–present.

4. Dava Sobel, *Galileo's Daughter* (New York: Penguin Books, 2000).

5. Ibid., pp. 153–154.

6. Richard T. Pascale, Mark Millemann, and Linda Gioja, *Surfing the Edge of Chaos* (New York: Crown Business, 2000).

7. Ibid., p. 22.

8. Thomas L. Friedman, *The Lexus and the Olive Tree* (New York: Farrar, Straus & Giroux, 1999).

9. Joshua Cooper Ramo, *The Age of the Unthinkable: Why the New World Disorder Constantly Surprises Us and What We Can Do About It* (New York: Little, Brown, 2009), p. 8.

10. Ibid., pp. 175–176.

11. Alan J. Roxburgh, *The Missionary Congregation, Leadership, and Liminality* (Harrisburg, Pa.: Trinity Press International, 1997).

12. Parker J. Palmer, "Change, Community, Conflict, and Ways of Knowing: Ways to Deepen Our Educational Agenda," Maricopa Center for Learning and Instruction, http://www.mcli.dist.maricopa.edu/events/afc99/articles/change.html. 1993.

13. See Avery Dulles, *Models of the Church* (New York: Doubleday, 1974).

14. Lesslie Newbigin, "Christ and Cultures," *Scottish Journal of Theology*, 1987, *31*, 3. See also Lesslie Newbigin, *The Open Secret: Sketch for a Missionary Theology* (Grand Rapids. Mich.: Eerdmans, 1978), ch. 9.

Chapter Four: From Playing Pool to Herding Cats

1. Thomas Petzinger, *The New Pioneers* (New York: Simon & Schuster, 1999), pp. 18–19.

2. René Descartes, quoted in Frijof Capra, *The Web of Life* (New York: Anchor Books, 1996), p. 67.

3. Marshall McLuhan, *Understanding Media* (New York: McGraw-Hill, 1964).

4. I understand that this form of strategic planning has been called into question and that the business world is itself undergoing massive transformation. This is evidenced in the work of people like Peter Senge (*The Fifth Discipline*) and Margaret Wheatley (*Leadership and the New Science*). These themes will be addressed in this book. At this point, my intention is to be descriptive of a process that remains generally the case for leadership across the spectrum of the churches.

Chapter Five: Why Strategic Planning Doesn't Work in This New Space and Doesn't Fit God's Purposes

1. Colin Greene and Martin Robinson, *Metavista: Bible, Church and Mission in an Age of Imagination* (Milton Keyes, England: Paternoster, 2008), p. xx.

2. Thomas Petzinger, quote in Cecily Ross, "Paradigms Lost . . . and Gained," *Toronto Globe and Mail*, Mar. 13, 1999, p. D11.

3. Petzinger, *New Pioneers*, pp. 19–20.

4. Margaret Wheatley, *Leadership and the New Science* (San Francisco: Berrett-Koehler, 1999), pp. 29–30.

Chapter Six: Eight Currents of Change and the Challenge of Making New Maps

1. See, for example, John Gray, *False Dawn: The Delusions of Global Capitalism* (London: Granta Books, 1999), and Karl Polanyi, *The Great Transformation* (Boston: Beacon Press, 1957).

2. John Gray, "Where There Is No Common Power,"*Harper's,* December 2001, pp. 18–19.

3. In another sense, however, globalization thrives as pluralism shifts into a culture of second- and third-generation immigrants who live off the fragments of their traditions and cultures. The more people live off these fragments, the more their identity becomes opaque and amorphous. The more this happens, the more people of all traditions buy their shifting identities off the rack, so to speak, of the global market. This is a complex relationship. It is possible also to observe the reverse, where the disembedding forces of globalization create a context where people reappropriate their traditions and specific cultures, sometimes in some frightening ways.

4. Diana Eck, *A New Religious America* (San Francisco: HarperOne, 2001), pp. 2–4.

5. See Jonathon Wilson, *Living Faithfully in a Fragmented World* (Harrisburg, Pa: Trinity Press International, 1997).

6. Gray, *False Dawn,* pp. 19–20.

7. Robert Kaplan, *The Coming Anarchy* (New York: Random House, 1999).

Chapter Seven: Lessons from the Formation of the Internet for Leading in This New Space

1. Richard Florida, "How the Crash Will Reshape America,"*Atlantic,* Mar. 2009, p. 48.

2. Not everyone is enthralled with the Internet and all its incredible claims about reshaping our social worlds. See, for example, Lee Siegel, *Against the Machine: Being Human in the Age of the Electronic Mob* (New York: Spiegel & Grau, 2008).

3. Charles Sirois, *Organic Management: Creating a Culture of Innovation* (Toronto: HarperCollins, 2000), pp. 17–18.

4. Malcolm Gladwell, *The Tipping Point: How Little Things Can Make a Big Difference* (New York: Little, Brown, 2000).

Chapter Eight: Cultivating a Core Identity in a Changed Environment

1. Jeb Brugmann, *Welcome to the Urban Revolution* (Toronto: Viking, 2009), pp. 5, 10, 12 .

2. Ibid., pp. 5–6.

3. Ibid., p. 10.

4. George G. Hunter III, *How to Reach Secular People* (Nashville, Tenn.: Abingdon Press, 1992), pp. 44–53.

5. See Guder, *Missional Church,* p. 205. In a bounded-set organization, the rules are made clear at the boundary (the point of entrance into the community, like reading the contract before you sign the agreement to use a Visa card), whereas a centered set invites people onto a journey shaped by a basic conviction (for example, by the worship of God or a rule of life such as availability and vulnerability), and the "rules" are discovered along the way.

6. This distinction between inner and outer worlds is fundamental in all cultures. In the biblical world of the ancient Near East, this was a powerful metaphor for describing social distinction and meaning. See Richard Sennet, *The Conscience of the Eye* (New York: Norton, 1990). Here we are dealing with the issue of boundaries that distinguish and differentiate.

7. For more information, contact Chris Erdman at chriserdman@upcfresno .org or check out this resource at Roxburgh Missional Network.

8. See Alan J. Roxburgh, *The Sky Is Falling: Leaders Lost in Transition* (Eagle, Idaho: Allelon, 2007).

9. Alan Kreider, *The Change of Conversion and the Origin of Christendom* (Harrisburg, Pa.: Trinity Press International, 1999). See also Walter Brueggemann, *Cadences of Home: Preaching Among the Exiles* (Louisville, Ky.: Westminster/John Knox Press, 1997).

Chapter Nine: Cultivating Parallel Cultures of the Kingdom

1. Václav Havel, *Open Letters: Selected Prose, 1965–1990* (London: Faber & Faber, 1991).

2. For further discussion, see Wayne Meeks, *The Origins of Christian Morality: The First Two Centuries* (New Haven, Conn.: Yale University Press, 1993).

3. See Martin Robinson, *Rediscovering the Celts: True Witness from Western Shores* (London: Fount Press, 2000).

4. Kenneth Gergen, *The Saturated Self: The Dilemmas of Identity in Contemporary Society* (New York: Basic Books, 1991).

5. See David Adam, *The Rhythm of Life* (Harrisburg, Pa.: Morehouse, 1997).

6. See Patrick R. Keifert, *Welcoming the Stranger: A Public Theology of Worship and Evangelism* (Minneapolis, Minn.: Augsburg Fortress, 1992).

7. See Richard Sennet, *The Fall of Public Man: On the Social Psychology of Capitalism* (New York: Random House, 1978).

8. See Gray, *False Dawn.*

9. See Heather Menezies, *Whose Brave New World? The Information Highway and the New Economy* (Toronto: Macmillan, 1995).

10. See Michael W. Goheen and Craig B. Bartholomew, *Living at the Crossroads* (Grand Rapids, Mich.: Baker Academic, 2008).

11. Jane Jacobs, *Dark Age Ahead* (New York: Random House, 2004).

Chapter Ten: Map-Making Partnerships Between a Local Church and Neighborhoods and Communities

1. See Alan J. Roxburgh and Fred Romanuk, *The Missional Leader: Equipping Your Church to Reach a Changing World* (San Francisco: Jossey-Bass, 2006).

2. See Castells, *Rise of the Network Society.*

3. Friedman, *The Lexus and the Olive Tree,* ch. 2.

4. For a helpful illustration of how this happens, see Mark Lau Branson, *Memories, Hopes, and Dreams* (New York: Alban, 2006).

5. See Roxburgh, *The Sky Is Falling,* and Roxburgh and Romanuk, *Missional Leader.* For readers who wish to explore this theme in more detail, see Paulo Friere, *Pedagogy of the Oppressed* (New York: Herder & Herder, 1970), and Gerald A. Arbuckle, *Refounding the Church: Dissent for Leadership* (Maryknoll, N.Y.: Orbis, 1993).

6. See the field guide "How to Read a Community" at http://roxburghmissionalnet.com/index.php.

7. See Guder, *Missional Church.*

8. Ibid., p. 149.

9. Michael Polanyi, *Personal Knowledge: Towards a Post-Critical Philosophy* (Chicago: University of Chicago Press, 1958).

10. There has always been a tension within Christian traditions around the Christian identity in relationship to the culture in which Christian life is lived. Some Mennonites, for example, describe themselves as a *contrast* society. The meaning of such "difference" in this discussion refers to the ways the practices of Christian life we have discussed shape communities of faith in ways distinct from the broader culture in which we live.

11. Mary Jo Leddy, "The People of God as a Hermeneutic of the Gospel," in Craig Van Gelder, ed., *Confident Witness, Changing World: Rediscovering the Gospel in North America* (Grand Rapids, Mich.: Eerdmans, 1999), pp. 303–313.

12. Wendell Berry, "Conservation and Local Economy," in *Sex, Economy, Freedom, and Community: Eight Essays* (New York: Pantheon Books, 1993), p. 12.

THE AUTHOR

Alan J. Roxburgh is president of Roxburgh Missional Network (http://roxburghmissionalnet.com). He is an author, conference speaker, and consultant to churches and denominational systems around the world. He has pastored congregations in a small town and the suburbs and has assisted in the redevelopment of a downtown urban church. He has directed an urban training center and served as a seminary professor. His books include *Reaching a New Generation, Leadership, Liminality and the Missionary Congregation, Crossing the Bridge: Leadership in a Time of Change, The Sky Is Falling: Leaders Lost in Transition, Introducing the Missional Church,* and *The Missional Leader.* He was also a member of the team that wrote *Missional Church: A Vision for the Sending of the Church in North America.*

Roxburgh also works with Allelon in the formation of leaders for the missional church in the Mission in Western Culture Project, a multiyear project that addresses the question of mission in Western cultures from the perspective of the local church and its context and the implications for leadership development, and with Allelon Training Centers, a partnering program with Together in Mission (UK) that trains mission-shaped leaders.

When not traveling or writing, Roxburgh enjoys mountain biking, hiking, cooking, and relaxing with his wife, Jane, and their five grand-children, as well as drinking great coffee in the Pacific Northwest.

He can be contacted via e-mail at alanjroxburgh@gmail.com.

INDEX

A

Accountability, and practices of Christian life, 148
Acts 11, 21
Acts, book of, 160
Afghanistan, 29–30, 97
Africa, xxii, 103–105
After Virtue (MacIntyre), 9–10, 26–27, 135
Agran, L., 130
Agrarian civilizations, 12–13
AIDS, 103–105, 112
al-Qaeda, 112
Alignment, concept of, 64–65, 84
Annan, K., 105
Antioch, and early church, 21, 36
Arendt, H., 24–25, 30, 37
Associational organizations, in industrial age, 13–14
Atom, concept of, 28–29
Atomistic view, of world, 10
Attractional church, xiii, 128
Autonomous individual.
    See Individualism

B

Babylonian captivity, 141–142, 150–151, 158
Baptists, 14

Belief statements, and core identity, 135–136
Benedictine order, 143, 149–150
Berlin Wall, fall of, 49–50, 90, 175
Berry, W., 188
Beyond the Post-Modern Mind (Smith), 41
Bible Society, 174–175
Biblical narrative: and communication, 173; and core identity, 136–137, 140–142; ending of, xx; need for engagement with, 36–37; and offstage communication, 176–179; and parallel culture, 160–161; and people's stories, 139–140; relevance of, xviii; and small-group movement, 146; and *Vogue* fashion shoot, 174–175
Biomedical technology, emergence of, 38–39
Bosch, D., xviii, 84
Brandenbarg, G., 146
Brown, G., 167–168
Brueggemann, W., 37, 141–142
Brugmann, J., 129–131
Buddhism, 96, 107
Bunyan, J., 22–23
Bush, G. W., 55, 91
Business models, use of, 68–69

C

Canada, 128
Capitalism, 90–91
Castells, M., 15
Cat-herding analogy, 59–60, 69–72
Cathedral, medieval, as map, 8–9
Celtic communities, 143, 149–150
Change: assessment of, 127–133; and democratization of knowledge, 107–108; and emergence of new space, 120–123; forces of, 89–110, 112; and global need, 103–106; and globalization, 90–93; level of, 112–113; and loss of confidence in primary structures, 106–107; and pluralism, 93–97, 135; and post-modernism, 100–103; resistance to, 88–89; and return to Romanticism, 108–110; and technology, 97–100; and tipping point, 122
The Change of Conversion and the Origin of Christendom (Kreider), 141
Chesterton, G. K., 21
Christendom, concept of, 44
Christian culture, waning of, 94–97
Christian life, and third space concept, 99
Christian narrative. *See* Biblical narrative
Church of the Savior, 161
Churches: as associational organizations, 14; attractional model of, xiii, 128; and change, xiv–xvii, 21–23, 47, 131–133; and core identity redevelopment, 134–142; and early church, 34–35; and individualism, 147; and leaders for in-between state, 34–39; missional type of, xix; neighborhood-based type of, 146–147; and numerical growth as success measure, 68; organizational culture of, 44–45; and planning, 62–64; and resistance to modernity, 17; role of, 32–33; and standard indicators, 30–31; status of, xii–xiii, 120–121; and strategic planning method, 65–67; and

tipping point, 122. *See also* Strategic planning
Cities, nature of, 129–130
Claiborne, S., 146
Climate change, 25, 42–43
Cold War, 49–50, 113–114, 144–145
The Coming Anarchy (Kaplan), 105
Commerce and religion, as separate worlds, 158–159
Commodification, of people, 69, 91, 155
Communication, 165–176. *See also* Internet
Communism, 100–101, 144–145, 186–187
Communities, 31–32, 164–188
Computer, as way of knowing, 62
Computerization, and nature of work, 99–100
Constantine, 141
Consumption, and global need, 105–106
Control: and Internet, 115, 116; and laws, 64–67; and modernity, 75; and Newtonian mechanics, 79–80; and return to Romanticism, 108–110; and technology, 99–100
Conversation, 165–179
Core identity, 134–142, 153
1 Corinthians, 186
1 Corinthians 1:28, 37
Cowan, J., 15–16
Cross, and core identity, 153
Cuban Missile Crisis, xix–xx
Cultivation of environments, practice of, 182–188
Culture, 6–11, 32–33, 43–45, 94–97. *See also* Parallel culture
cummings, e.e., 43
Czechoslovakia, 144–145, 150, 186–187

D

Darfur, 8
Default maps, 53, 55, 82
Democracy, loss of confidence in, 100–101

Democratization, of knowledge, 107–108
Demographics, preoccupation with, 81
Denominations. *See* Churches
Descartes, R., 9, 22, 23, 62, 63
Dialogue, communities of, 31–32
Dialogue on the Two Great World Systems (Galileo), 22
Dietrich, I., 182
Discernment, discipline of, 153, 154
Discourse on Method (Descartes), 22
Diseases, as new insecurities, 112
Dupre, L., 33, 34

E

Early church, 34–37, 36, 141, 145–146, 149–150
Eck, D., 94
Economic systems, 4, 106–107, 159–160
Educational structures, loss of confidence in, 106–107
Einstein, A., 61
Emergent church, xvii, 17
Emergent future, new space as, 122–123
Energy crisis, implications of, 112
The English Patient (Ondaatje), 102
The Enlightenment, 9, 101
Environment, 127–133, 182–188
Epistemology, concept of, 54–57, 60–67
Equilibrium, 46–55
Erdman, C., 138–139, 140–141
Eschatology, 68
Europe, 12–13, 22, 32
Experiments, forming of, 176–179

F

Facebook, 97, 174
Faith, and modernity, 67–69
Fallujah, Iraq, 131
Fascism, loss of confidence in, 100–101
Final causes, notions of, 68
Financial structures, loss of confidence in, 106–107
Fish harvesting, model for, 51–52
Florida, R., xv, 111, 122

Foolishness to the Greeks: The Gospel and Western Culture (Newbigin), xviii, 67
Frederick the Great, 61
Free-market capitalism, 90–91
French Revolution, 13
Friedman, T. L., 49–50, 172
Friedrich, C. D., 109–110
Fugitive Pieces (Michaels), 102

G

Galileo, G., 22, 23, 47–48
Galileo's Daughter (Sobel), 47–48
Gated communities, 156
Gender equality, ideas of, 6–7
Genetics, revolution in, 38–39
Gentile Christians, 36
Gergen, K., 153
Gladwell, M., 121–122
Global need, and change, 103–106
Global warming, 25, 42–43
Globalization, 50, 90–94
God, Spirit of, 76–77, 170, 178–179
Gorbachev, M., 50
Gospel and Our Culture Network (GOCN), xviii–xix
Gravity, and Newton's worldview, 61
Gray, J., 98
Great Britain. *See* United Kingdom
Greco-Roman world, and early church, 22
Greene, C., 75, 174–175
Greenspan, A., xv, xvi, 43, 152
Growth, as success measure, 68
The Guns of August (Tuchman), xx

H

Hamas, 112
Havel, V., 144–145, 150, 158, 186–187
Hawaii, 49
Heisenberg, W., 28–29
Henlein, P., 62
He's Just Not That Into You (film), 132
Hinduism, 96
Hizballah, 50
Hospitality, practice of, 154–158

"How the Crash Will Reshape America" (Florida), 111

How to Reach Secular People (Hunter), 132–133

Human beings, commodification of, 69, 91, 155

Human potential movement, 146

Hunter, G., 132–133

I

Icons/images, importance of, 175–176

Identity, 7–9. *See also* Core identity

IED (improvised explosive device), use of, 30, 50, 131

Images/icons, importance of, 175–176

Imagination, role of, 7–11

In-between state: and church leaders, 34–39; and communities of dialogue, 31–32; and emotional turmoil, 53–55; and failure of established categories, 50–51; and liminality, 52–53; and maps of modernity, 28–31; and need for new categories, 41–43; reasons for, 24–25; and role of culture, 43–45. *See also* Change

The Incarnation, 35, 99

Independent object model, and modernity, 28

India, 129–130

Individualism: and modernity, 26–27, 33, 63; new form of, 102; in North America, 152; radical form of, 99–100; and small-group movement, 146, 147; views of, 9–11

Industrial Revolution, 13–14, 131

Information age, 14–15, 97–98, 164–176

Inner maps. *See* Maps

Inner/outer worlds, distinction between, 136–137

Insecurity, sources of, 97–100, 112

Internet: and communication revolution, 165–176; and democratization of knowledge, 108; development of, 113–120; and rapid technological change, 98; significance of, 134–135;

sound waves analogy for, 117–119; transformation of, 115–120

Invisible hand theory, of Adam Smith, 61, 90–91, 158–159

Iran, 131

Iraq, 7, 29–30, 55, 97, 131

Irvine, California, 130

Islam, 50, 96

Isolation, in North America, 69

J

Jackson, M., 175

Jacobs, J., 160

Jerusalem, and early church, 21

Jesus: and nature of God, 76–77; and parallel culture, 147; and receiving the poor, 158; and strangers, 156, 157–158

Jewish Christians, 36

John 15:1–7, 77

Judaism, 7, 21–22

Juridical structures, loss of confidence in, 106–107

K

Kant, I., 63

Kaplan, R., 105

Keillor, G., 165–166

Kennedy, J. F., xviii–xx

Kennedy, R. F., xiv

Key maps. *See* Maps

Kingdom of God, and strategic planning, 76–77

Klein, N., 107

Knowledge: concepts of, 9–11; democratization of, 107–108; and modernity, 27

Kornberg, A., 38–39

Kreider, A., 141

L

Laissez-faire capitalism, 90–91

Language, nature of, 101–103

Lawrence, H., 146

Laws, and predictability and control, 64–67

Leadership: and connecting conversations, 176–179; and control, 64; and cultivation of environments, 182–188; as expression of maps, 62–63; and forming experiments, 176–179; and measure-predict-manage methodology, 60–67; in medieval period, 33–34; and missional planning processes, 179–182; modernist map of, 6; and Newtonian mechanics, 80; role of, 77–79, 170, 172–173, 174; and trust, 138–139

Learning, as practice, 160–161

Lebanon, 50, 97

Leddy, M. J., 186

The Lexus and the Olive Tree (Friedman), 49–50, 172

Life Is Beautiful (film), 175–176

Life of Pi (Martel), 102

Liminality, 52–53, 121–122

Listening, 153, 159–160, 173–174

Loneliness, in North America, 69

Lord of the Rings (Tolkien), 147

Lorenz, E., 71

Luther, M., xiii

M

Machala, India, 130

Machine, as dominant map of modernity, 61–63

MacIntyre, A., 9–10, 26–27, 135

Management: and Internet, 115, 116; and modernity, 75; and Newtonian mechanics, 79–80; and return to Romanticism, 108–110

Mandela, N., 104

A Mapmaker's Dream: The Meditations of Fra Mauro, Cartographer to the Court of Venice: A Novel (Cowan), 15–16

Maps: challenges to, 4–5; concept of, xi–xii; making of, 37–38; and modernity, 9–11, 60–67; nature of, 6–9

Marks, J., 94

Marriage, nature of, 4, 132

Martel, J., 102

The Matrix (film), 98

McLuhan, M., 62

Measure-predict-manage methodology, and leadership, 60–67

Medical structures, loss of confidence in, 106–107

Medieval period, 33–34

Mennonites, 17, 107

Metanarrative, concept of, 101–102

Metavista: Bible, Church and Mission in an Age of Imagination (Greene and Robinson), 75

Metrics, and churches, xiv–xv

Michaels, A., 102

Milton, J., 22

Mission description, and strategic planning, 83

Missional Church: A Vision for the Sending of the Church in North America (Guder, ed.), xix, 182

Missional church, concept of, xix

Missional life, in information-rich world, 164–176

Missional model, of strategic planning, 179–182

Mitchell, A., 42–43

Modernity: and assumptions of strategic planning, 79–82; basic concepts of, 9–11; beliefs of, 33; challenges to, 28–31; development of, 12–15; and dichotomy between public and private, 67–69; emergence of and map-making, 15–16, 33; and importance of understanding, 35; and independent object model, 28; and individualism, 26–27, 33, 63; key maps of, 60–67; as known world, 121; and machine as dominant map, 61–63; nature of, 24–25; as primary map, 6–9; problems with, 25–27; and reality, 63–64; and role of church, 32–33; and universalizing principle, 76

Mumbai, India, 130

Mustard Seed, 146

Mutually assured destruction (MAD), 50

N

Narratives. *See* Biblical narrative; Offstage communication; Stories

Needs-centered ministry, xiii

Neighborhood: and church location, 146–147; concept of, 98–100; partnership with, 164–188; watch program in, 155

Networking, concept of, 15, 98–100, 107

New Monasticism, 146

New space, 121–122, 122–123, 136–137

Newbigin, L., xviii, 34–35, 57, 59, 67, 69, 81, 84

Newlove, G., xi

Newton, I., 60–67

Newtonian mechanics, 60–67, 79

No Logo (Klein), 107

Nonlinearity, 51–52, 71

North America, 12–13, 32–33, 69

Numerical growth, as success measure, 68

O

Obama, B., 98, 106, 107, 168, 171

Objectification, 63–67, 76–77, 78

Objectivist philosophy, 152

Offices, practice of, 151–154

Offstage communication, 166–172, 173, 176–179. *See also* Stories

Ondaatje, M., 102

Online usage, 116

Onstage communication, 166–172, 173

Orders, and Christian life, 149–150

Organization, and Newtonian mechanics, 80

Outer/inner worlds, distinction between, 136–137

P

Palmer, P., 54–55, 56, 62, 69

Paradise Lost (Milton), 22

Parallel culture: concept of, 143–147, 186–187; and hospitality, 154–158; and learning, 160–161; and offices, 151–154; practices for, 147–161; and

purposes of practices, 149–151; and receiving the poor, 158–160

Parish system, status of, xii–xiii

Partnerships with communities: conversations and experiments in, 176–179; and cultivation of environments, 182–188; and information-rich world, 164–176; and planning processes, 179–182

Pascal, B., 62

Passover, 7, 24–25

Pastiche, concept of, 101–102

Paul, apostle, 36–37, 186

Paul, R., 98

1 Peter, 156

Petzinger, T., 79

Physics, changes in, 28–29

Pilgrim's Progress (Bunyan), 22–23

Place, as irrelevant concept, 99–100

Plagues, in Europe, 22

Plankton, death of, 42

Planning. *See* Strategic planning

Pluralism, and change, 93–97, 135

Polanyi, M., 185

Political structures, loss of confidence in, 106–107

Poor, receiving of as practice, 158–160

Postmodernism, 17, 25, 28–31, 100–103

Power, ideologies of and truth, 101–103

Practices: and cultivation of environments, 182–188; and hospitality, 154–158; and learning, 160–161; and offices, 151–154; for parallel culture, 147–161; purposes of, 149–151; and receiving the poor, 158–160

A Prairie Home Companion (film), 165–166

Prayer, 137–140, 151, 153–154

Predictability: and Internet, 115, 116; and laws, 64–67; and modernity, 75, 121; and Newtonian mechanics, 79–80; and return to Romanticism, 108–110

Private-public dichotomy, 67–69, 81–82

Private schools, 107

Program-driven church, xiii

Protestant churches, 17, 141. *See also* Churches

Psalm 137, 20–21
Public-private dichotomy, 67–69, 81–82

Q

Quantum mechanics, 28–29

R

Ramo, J. C., 50, 51, 52, 90
Rand, A., 152
Rationalism, 9, 108–110
Reagan, R., 50
Reality, concepts of, 23, 63–64, 67–69
Reasons to Believe: One Man's Journey Among the Evangelicals and the Faith He Left Behind (Marks), 94–95
Relativity, 28–29
Religion and commerce, as separate worlds, 158–159
Religious structures, loss of confidence in, 106–107
Resocializing, of Christians. *See* Parallel culture
Resource usage, and global need, 105–106
Returning to the Center: Living Prayer in a Distracted World (Erdman), 138
The Richard and Judy Show (TV show), ix–x
The Rise of the Creative Class (Florida), 111, 122
The Rise of the Network Society (Castells), 15
Robinson, M., 75, 174–175
Romans 12, 161
Romanticism, return to, 108–110
Rowland, S., 130

S

SARS epidemic, 112, 130–131
School for Christian Living, 161
Scripture: importance of understanding, 36–37; reading of, 151, 153–154. *See also* Biblical narrative
Sea Sick (Mitchell), 42–43
Secular people, description of, 132–133

Seder meal, 7
Seeker-driven program church, xix
Self, autonomous, 9–11, 26–27, 33, 63
September 11, 2001 attacks, 55, 91, 97
Servant Leadership School, 161
Sexuality, conflicts in, 132
Sharia law, 93
The Shock Doctrine (Klein), 107
Simple Way, 146
Sine, L., 146
Sine, T., 146
Sirois, C., 120
The Sky Is Falling: Leaders Lost in Transition (Roxburgh), 25
Skype, 97
Small-group movement, 146–147
Smith, A., 61, 90–91, 158–159
Smith, H., 41
Sobel, D., 47–48
Social life, 13–14, 98–100, 102, 105–106
Sound waves analogy, for Internet, 117–119
Soviet Union, xix–xx, 49, 90
Spirit of God, 76–77, 170, 178–179
Squatter towns, in non-Western world, 104–105
Stage metaphor, for modernity, 26–27
Stories, 27, 139–140, 144–145. *See also* Offstage communication
Stranger, and hospitality, 154–158
Strategic planning: alternatives to, 84–85; assumptions behind, 79–82; clarification of, 74–79; lack of and Internet, 116; as methodology, 65–67; missional model of, 179–182; and nature of planning, 62–64; and objectification, 76–77, 78; stages of, 82–84
Subject-object split, of Descartes, 23
Support groups, 107
Surfing the Edge of Chaos (Pascale, Millemann, and Gioja), 48–49
Survivor (TV series), 34
Swine flu, 112, 130–131

T

Taoism, 96
Tapestry (radio program), 96
Technology, rapid change in, 97–100
Tehran, Iran, 131
Teleology, 68
Third spaces, concept of, 98–100
Thirteen Days (film), xix–xx
Thirty Years' War, 13, 22
*The Tipping Point: How Little
    Things Can Make a Big Difference*
    (Gladwell), 121–122
Tiruppur, India, 129–130
Tithing, 159
Tolkien, J.R.R., 147
Tradition, concept of, 25, 26
Trust, and leadership, 138–139
Truth: concepts of, 9–11; and ideologies
    of power, 101–103; and modernity,
    27, 67–69
Tuchman, B., xx
Twitter, 97, 174

U

United Kingdom, 32, 93
United States, xix–xx
Universal gravitation, law of, 61
Universalizing principle, and
    modernity, 76
Unthinkable, age of, 90
Urban revolution, 129–134
Usage time, on Internet, 116

V

Viral infections, as new
    insecurities, 112
Vision statement, in strategic
    planning, 83
Vogue (magazine), and women of the
    Bible, 174–175

W

Wanderer Above the Sea of Fog
    (Friedrich), 109–110
Watters, E., 134
Webinar, 97
*Welcome to the Urban Revolution:
    How Cities Are Changing the World*
    (Brugmann), 129–131
West Bank, 97
Wheatley, M., 80
Who's Your City? (Florida), 111
Williams, R., 93
Women of the Bible, and *Vogue* fashion
    shoot, 174–175
Work, nature of and computerization,
    99–100
World city system, 129–131
World Trade Center. *See* September 11,
    2001 attacks
World War I, 108

Y

YouTube, 97